Surviving a Stalker

Surviving a Stalker

Stay Safe. Get Help.
Reclaim Your Life.

Linden Gross

Foreword by Gavin de Becker
Author of national bestseller *The Gift of Fear*

Incubation Press
Bend, Oregon

Published by
Incubation Press
Bend, OR

Surviving a Stalker: Stay Safe. Get Help. Reclaim Your Life.
Copyright © 1994, 1998, 2000, 2012 by Linden Gross
Foreword copyright © 1994 by Gavin de Becker

ISBN 978-0-9888262-0-5

Earlier editions of this book were originally published as *To Have or To Harm* by Warner Books in 1994 & as *Surviving a Stalker* by Marlowe & Co. in 2000.

Cover and interior design by Robaire Ream

The Library of Congress has cataloged the Marlowe & Co. edition of *Surviving a Stalker* as follows:
Gross, Linden.
[To have or to harm]
Surviving a stalker: everything you need to know to keep yourself safe / Linden Gross; foreword by Gavin de Becker.
p.cm.
Originally published: To have or to harm. New York: Warner Books, 1994.
ISBN 1-56924-04-1
Stalking—United States—Prevention. 2. Stalking victims—Counseling of—United States. I. Title.

HV6594.2.G76 2000
364.15—dc21   00-056054

Printed in the United States of America

For my Mom,
who showed unparalleled courage
and generosity of spirit
in the face of unthinkable odds.

And for my Dad,
whose unfaltering love
and dedication
gave her both the will
and the strength
to fight so hard.

I love you both.

Contents

Foreword

By Gavin de Becker

AMERICANS IN THE MEDIA AGE have become all too familiar with mentally ill people who stalk, and even harm, public figures. When I began to study stalking nearly 20 years ago, it was easy to observe that the problem was getting worse. It was easy to see that an increasingly intimate media presentation of famous people made them more attractive targets for obsessive pursuers. Many people developed unreasonable expectations of the famous, mostly because public figures appeared more and more accessible.

We were coming to know them more closely than ever, but we had to observe them from farther away. It became routine to pass through a metal detector to see a president's speech, to visit city hall, or to see an actor taping a television show.

I could not have imagined then that stalking would become a problem for the public at large. By the late eighties, however, it was clear that for women—and sometime men—the stakes of resisting romantic attention had risen sharply. And suddenly what we once only read about in the news had come home to hundreds of thousands of regular citizens.

Yet until Linden Gross's striking book, few asked why fear had all too often become an element of courting.

"I was trying to let him down easy." With these words begins a story I hear several times each month. Before meeting me, this intelligent young woman may have told it to friends, a psycholo-

gist, a private detective, a lawyer, a police officer, maybe even a judge, but the problem persisted. The actors and the scenery change each time, but the play remains the same: It is the story of a situation that once seemed innocent, or at least manageable, but is now frightening. It is the story of someone who started as a seemingly normal suitor but became a stalker.

Although it is fashionable for the news media to report on stalkers as if they are some unique type of criminal, those who choose regular citizens (as opposed to famous people) are not. They are not from Mars; they are from Miami and Boston and San Diego and Chicago. They are the man *our* sister dated, the man *our* company hired, the man *our* friend married, the man who lives next to *us*.

Against this background, we must see stalkers as part of ourselves in order to better understand this issue. Giving talks around the country, I sometimes ask the men in the audience, "How many of you ever found out where a girl lived or worked by means other than asking her? How many have driven by a girl's house to see what cars were there, or called just to see who answered the phone, and then hung up?"

The overwhelming show of hands each time has taught me that the acceptability of these behaviors is a matter of degree.

After one speech, a policeman, who asked to talk with me alone, confessed to me that he had relentlessly pursued a female student at the police academy while on staff there. She said *no* to him for 18 months, but she avoided too explicit a rejection because she feared its possible impact on her career. "She gave me no indication that she wanted a relationship with me, but I never let up," he said. "It paid off, though, because we got married."

Yes, I suppose you could say it paid off, but his story reveals just how complicated this issue is. Because for many in my generation, there is one strategy to use above all others: *persistence*. That same strategy lies at the core of every stalker case.

Some invisible line exists between what is all right, and what is going too far—and men and women do not always agree on where to place that line. Victims and their unwanted pursuers never agree; neither do victims and the police, nor victims and the court. Until, of course, a situation escalates into violence.

Men pursuing unlikely relationships with women—and getting them—is a commonly promoted theme in our culture. Consider movies like *Flashdance, Tootsie, An Officer and a Gentleman, Heartbreak Kid, 10, Honeymoon in Las Vegas, Indecent Proposal* and *Against All Odds. The Graduate,* the icon of a generation, teaches that if you stay with it, even if you offend a woman, even if she says she wants nothing to do with you, even if you've treated her like trash (and sometimes *because* you've treated her like trash), even if she's in another relationship, you'll eventually get the girl. Dustin Hoffman's character uses stalking techniques when he tricks people into telling him where a wedding is; he pretends to be a family member and then a minister to get further information. He races to the church and bursts in right after the ceremony. And what happens? The girl leaves her new husband in the church and runs off with him. In other words: He gets the girl.

The stories included in this book teach many lessons. One of the most important is that *persistence only proves persistence—it does not prove love.*

I have found in my years of studying this issue that men and women often speak a different language, and often in just those situations where the stakes are highest. In this timely book, Linden Gross serves as our interpreter. We need one. For hundreds of thousands of fathers (and mothers), older brothers (and sisters), and countless movies and television shows have taught most men that when a woman says NO, that's not what she means.

Surviving a Stalker makes it painfully clear that we as a society have something worse than just a double standard: We have a dangerous standard.

Although there are cases where women are the unwanted pursuers, in situations involving regular citizens, men are the stalkers far, far more often. And as with all forms of criminality, men are more often violent than women.

Most stalking cases don't look alarming when they start. Few of these men introduce themselves as stalkers. That's why the warning signs in every story the author tells are so important. The persistence, denial and the pushiness may be hints. But as soon as a person introduces fear as a strategy, it is time to stop contact and apply the lessons of this book.

IMAGINE A PLACE where women are taught to be nice when rejecting, and men, on the other hand, are taught to be nice when pursuing. Imagine a place where a person can be held hostage by threats that are often unspoken and undefined, but real nonetheless. Imagine a place where the cost of rejecting ranges from unpopularity all the way to fear, intimidation and even death.

That place is where we live, and as this book shows so powerfully, it won't change unless we change it. *Surviving a Stalker* succeeds where the news media and the criminal justice system fail: It places this vital issue into perspective, shows how we got in, and how we can get out.

Linden Gross's work will help all of us understand a dynamic that has been characterized by confusion and misinformation. It will save some lives, and improve many others. It will help those victims who need to know what to do right now, and more importantly, it will help many of you never to become victims at all.

Gavin de Becker—America's leading authority on stalking—is the author of the national bestseller The Gift of Fear: Survival Signals that Protect Us from Violence.

A Note to the Reader

WHILE ALL THE STALKING INCIDENTS described in this book are real, certain names and, in some instances, other identifying characteristics, have been changed. Whenever a name is changed, an asterisk follows the name when it first appears.

Although exhaustive efforts have been made to insure the accuracy and completeness of the information contained in this book, we can assume no responsibility for errors, inaccuracies and incompleteness. Despite the best efforts of the author and publisher, the book may contain mistakes, and the reader should use the book only as a general guide and not as the ultimate source of information about stalking.

This book is not intended to reprint all the information available to the author and publisher on the subject of stalking, but rather to simplify, complement and supplement other available resources. The reader is encouraged to read all available material, and to learn as much as possible about stalking. Further, readers should use their own judgment or consult law enforcement agencies, victim advocacy groups or experts in the stalking arena for specific applications to their individual problems, since each stalking case is unique and should be analyzed by professionals in the field who have all the relevant facts.

Acknowledgments

"**Y**OU KNOW A LOT ABOUT THIS SUBJECT," my friend Gary Berner announced over a glass of wine as we discussed the possibility of creating a television series about stalking. "Why aren't you writing a report or a book?" That question launched me on an endeavor that has been marked by unparalleled generosity.

My overwhelming gratitude goes out to Gavin de Becker, who shared not only his time but also a lifetime of experience, work, study, and thought.

Other contributors who played a central role in making this book a reality include Jane McAllister, John Wilson, Jim Wright, and the Los Angeles Police Department's Threat Management Unit (TMU).

Of course, a project of this size must have its seeds somewhere. My thanks go to Nancy Kalish, my former editor at *Cosmopolitan*, who assigned me two articles about stalking before it had become a hot topic.

Along the way, Rafael Kozadinos, Genevieve Van de Merghel and Elizabeth Crane delivered invaluable editorial and research assistance. During the final deadline crunch, my parents, Jackie and Leonard Gross, dropped everything to provide me with a stellar line edit as well as some sorely needed perspective.

Most of all, I'd like to acknowledge those individuals—be they named or not—who bared their pain and their souls to enhance my understanding of stalking and the devastating impact it leaves in its wake. May the rough seas calm soon and see you all safely back to shore.

1

Are You Being Stalked?

PICTURE BEING PURSUED . . . HUNTED . . . by someone who knows your every move. He calls so often that every time you answer a phone, no matter where you are, you think it's him. Most of the time you're right. You walk out your door, your place of work, your health club, your favorite restaurant, and he's there. You look in your rear-view mirror, and he's there too.

You begin to think you're paranoid, but you take extra precautions anyway. No matter what you do, you can't seem to shake the guy. Then you go away for a holiday. His incessant barrage of letters—some threatening, others declarations of love—finds you although you left no forwarding address. "Hey, somebody is watching you," reads one note. "Somebody is watching you in or out of the office, in or out of bed, in or out of the bathroom. The road ahead for you is a real bitch. It's going to get more and more and more ugly!"

You've no place to run. No place to hide. Literally. Panic sets in. You fear you're going to die. There's nothing you can do.

WELCOME TO ELAINE Applegate's* life. She had been involved with Dan Thornton* for just a few weeks. Initially, the handsome, six-foot-five-inch dentist presented himself as kind, gentle and sensitive, precisely the Alan Alda type she had been looking for. Once they became involved, however, he seemed to

1

metamorphose overnight. First, the alcohol problem he had concealed from her surfaced. Then came his irrational jealousy and possessiveness. When he started trying to restrict what she did and whom she saw, Elaine, an accomplished CPA with an unwaveringly high sense of self-esteem, broke off their involvement. Her decision, however, was not one he would accept.

He phoned her day and night. He followed her wherever she went. He vandalized her property. He threatened to hurt those friends she spent time with. He threatened to hurt her.

Afraid of what he might do, Elaine began to fear for her life. She lost her appetite and her ability to sleep, both symptoms of clinical depression. She lost her ability to concentrate. Her performance at work declined. She began to see a therapist, and to take anti-depressant medication.

"You've got a real problem on your hands," the local police told her. "But there's nothing we can do. We're helpless." They encouraged her to keep a log of his calls and to hand over the recorded messages he had left on her answering machine. In addition they advised her to obtain a restraining order from the courts that would legally restrict him from contacting her in person, on the phone or through the mail.

"You're just trying to set up this paper trail so that if he kills me, you can arrest him," Elaine charged.

"That's right," they responded.

AMERICA HAS BEEN hit with an escalating crisis it doesn't know how to handle. Across the country, several million people have fallen victim to individuals who have obsessively focused on them. Not that long ago, the news spotlighted only celebrity cases. The shooting of John Lennon in 1980 set the tone for an era of unparalleled violence toward public figures. In 1981, John Hinckley, Jr. sought to impress Jodie Foster by attempting to assassinate President Ronald Reagan. The following year, actress Theresa Saldana was repeatedly stabbed by a Scottish drifter named Arthur Richard Jackson, who perceived himself as "the benevolent angel of death." And in 1989, an obsessed fan shot to death 21-year-old Rebecca Schaeffer, co-star of the television series *My Sister Sam.*

In the last 30-plus years, such incidents have snowballed. Tens of thousands of people in the United States are pursuing some kind of unwarranted and inappropriate contact with media figures, spurred on by today's celebrity culture.

But unwanted pursuit is not reserved for the rich and famous. While the prominent cases may attract more media attention, the majority of stalking victims are people like you and me. The U.S. Department of Justice's 2009 special report entitled "Stalking Victimization in the United States" asserts that "during a 12-month period, an estimated 3.4 million persons age 18 or older were victims of stalking."

That's 3.4 million individuals whose lives have been torn apart. "Stalking is an act of terror that builds a prison of fear around its victims," said former Attorney General Janet Reno.

A 2010 Center for Disease Control report estimated that one out of every six of U.S. women (16.2 percent) and one out of every 19 of the nation's men (5.2 percent) are or will become stalking victims. But talk to any number of women, especially those aged 18 to 24 who experience the highest rate of stalking, and even that estimate will sound low. Universities surveyed about unwanted pursuit all had stories to tell. One university attorney spoke of a college-aged admirer whose letters to a fellow classmate went from doting to threatening. Eventually the disturbed student sprayed animal blood on the door of the young woman with whom he was infatuated. "But no harm was done," the attorney concluded.

Gavin de Becker, the author of *The Gift of Fear* and widely regarded as the country's foremost authority on stalking, disagrees. "He meant that there had been no attack," said de Becker, whose work in the assessment and management of thousands of stalking cases has earned him a position on a congressional committee, three presidential appointments, and an award from the FBI. "There was tremendous harm in terms of fear, anxiety and disruption of day-to-day life."

No *physical* injury was suffered in that incident. In fact, millions of pursuit cases do not end in violence. As early as the mid eighties, however, stalkers had started becoming increasingly brutal.

Detroit, Michigan, August 30, 1985

Shortly after Sandra Henes files for divorce, her estranged husband kidnaps her from a parking lot, rapes her repeatedly and threatens her with a .357 magnum in a desperately ill-conceived attempt to save their marriage. "You'll never get rid of me," he raves. "I'll always be in your life. The only way I'll leave you alone is if I'm dead." The assault ends when the Detroit SWAT team breaks down the door 18 hours later.

Chicago, Illinois, August 5, 1989

After violating a protective order three separate times, Sheila Gallo's former husband kills her. Their divorce had been final for just two days.

Richmond, Virginia, February 9, 1989

Regina Butkowski is kidnapped and later shot in the temple by a weight lifter who had become obsessed with her after she befriended him at a health club.

Monroe Beach, Michigan, October 3, 1990

Deborah Frost's old high-school boyfriend kills her while out on bond. The young man, who came from "a nice family" according to the victim's mother, had never gotten over her. Eleven encounters with the law over a ten-month period did nothing to change his intentions or the outcome.

Milwaukee, Wisconsin, March 9, 1992

Shirley Lowery waits in the hall outside a courtroom where she's applied for a restraining order against the man with whom she had once lived. Before she ever makes it inside, Benjamin Franklin stabs her 19 times, fulfilling his promise to make Shirley pay for leaving him.

Boston, Massachusetts, May 30, 1992

Eleven days after Kristin Lardner gets a permanent injunction to keep Michael Cartier away from her, the 22-year-old bouncer walks up to her in the middle of a busy street during daylight hours and shoots her repeatedly in the head. He was on probation at the time for the beating of a previous girlfriend. "If the courts had checked his record or spoken to police when she sought help, he would have been locked up rather than set loose to kill her," Kristin's sister Helen Lardner, a Washington lawyer, testified before the U.S. Senate Judiciary Committee.

THESE DAYS STALKING has gone positively techno. Stalkers, even those who aren't particularly tech savvy, don't even have to leave home to know their victims' every move. Stalkers hack into emails or remotely install spyware on their targets' computers, enabling them to capture screen shots, monitor sites visited and even log all key strokes, giving the stalkers a record of all communication and passwords. There's more. Global positioning systems (GPS) can be installed on cars or remotely in cell phones allowing the stalker to track their victims' every move. And then there's video surveillance. Tiny cameras with microphones are hidden in everyday items such as pens, stuffed animals and picture frames and then monitored remotely through a variety of websites options.

This may sound like a farfetched spy movie, but tactics such as these have become frighteningly routine. According to The National Center for Victims of Crime's Stalking Resource

Center, "one in four victims report that the offender used some form of technology. However, this is likely to be an underestimate of the actual rates since offenders can use many of these technologies against a victim without the victim's knowledge."

STATISTICS ON STALKING remain somewhat limited, principally because the cases wind up being classified as the crime into which they usually escalate, such as assault or homicide. But most authorities agree that the overwhelming number of stalking victims are women. In fact, 90 percent of the 1,500 women killed by their current or former mates each year in this country were stalked before being murdered. That doesn't mean that most stalking victims are killed. But "there's a far greater chance that an ordinary citizen case is going to result in a tragic conclusion than the celebrity," said Lieutenant John Lane, former head of the Los Angeles Police Department's Threat Management Unit (TMU), created especially to deal with stalking cases.

Stalkers don't just prey on their individual targets. In cases involving family units, children frequently wind up as the victims. Take Andrew Taylor*, for example, who made good on a prior threat. After his attempts at reconciliation—and his intimidation campaign—failed, he kidnapped his one-month-old daughter from her mother, a respiratory therapist. Authorities found the bodies of the unemployed actor and the baby, whom he had strangled, by a nearby beach. Eight months later, a South Dakota man shot his estranged wife and their two children just before their divorce was to become final.

OBSESSED PURSUERS WILL frequently harass a third party to whom the actual target is attached in order to gain the intense impact and reaction they seek. "The easiest way to get to me is to get to the people I love," said Sarah Jane Williams*, whose grandmother wound up in a nursing home after being knocked over when a prowler—presumably Sarah Jane's stalker—broke into her home.

How did he know where to find the 98-year-old woman? Or for that matter Sarah Jane, whom he continues to harass by phone even though she changes her number so often it takes her a few seconds to remember her current one?

Today's easy access to information has made us all potential victims. In his book *Privacy for Sale*, Jeffrey Rothfeder explained how the proliferation of billions of computerized records containing information about personal, private lives means that a person with the right skills or contacts can find out virtually everything about us, from our whereabouts to our finances to our purchasing habits and family ties.

Why would one person obsess about another to the point of craving this sort of intimate information?

Anyone who has ever fallen in love or been infatuated knows how close the experience can be to a spiritual or drug-induced high. Suddenly your thoughts are consumed with one single being. Everything you see or do seems to bring him or her to mind. You find yourself doing things you wouldn't do under any other circumstances. Like calling repeatedly only to hang up, or using a fake voice just to see if anyone is home. Or driving by the house or apartment again and again just for a glimpse.

The truth is that, for most of us, we're in love not just with the person, but with our projection of what kind of couple we'll make, the needs that he or she will fulfill, and the idealized notion of love in general. Before we've even gotten to know with whom we're really dealing, we've fallen in love with what that person could represent to our future.

Those individuals whose lives are a void waiting to be filled, however, take those feelings and amplify them. The person with whom they're infatuated becomes their reason to exist. Any contact is better than no contact, any information a way to feel more intimately involved even if no relationship exists. That

emptiness also helps explain the explosion that takes place during the separation or divorces of many couples, when those who
have used their relationships to define their identity simply can't
afford to let go.

In a culture where male violence is highlighted daily in the
press and glorified nightly on television, the inability to accept
rejection can easily mutate into dominance—particularly if it's
the man who has been cast aside. "It has been sanctioned in society for a thousand years that a man has control over his woman,"
said Michael Paymar, co-founder of the Duluth Domestic Abuse
Intervention Project and co-author of the "Domestic Violence
Information Manual."

The social conditioning that most American men receive feeds
this distorted view of relationships as ownership, and love as a
predestined occurrence that can't be denied. Even when they
have targeted a woman who doesn't return their affection, the
socially accepted notion that men choose women, rather than
the other way around, feeds their sense of righteousness. "She's
the only one for me," says the ardent suitor, as if that should be
the determining factor in her decisions.

THE ADVENT OF the media age has contributed to this notion.
A hundred years ago, our models for relationships were limited
to our parents and the people in the community. Television
and movies changed all that. Not only did they bring us into
an oddly intimate relationship with hundreds of screen couples,
they promulgated the notion that persistence wins. Suddenly,
no didn't mean *no*, but rather *not now* or *ask me later*. The guy
always got the girl, no matter how many times or how insistently
she turned him down. And that was how it should be, because
he really did love her.

Unfortunately, that far-fetched message has filtered down
loud and clear into real life. Even when a woman's right to say
no is acknowledged, her message is disbelieved. The tendency

of some women to communicate purely for effect or games-manship has exacerbated the gap between understanding and meaning.

Take the case of Richard Barton*, a city administrator with a law degree, who was determined to take out Anita Brown* even though she had refused him every single time. The more she said *no*, the more tenacious he became. He began sending her flowers and notes, coming by her apartment, and tracking her all over town. Finally, the 32-year-old got a court order to keep him at a distance. When he violated that, she pressed charges.

At the trial, much to his lawyer's dismay, Richard insisted on conducting his own defense. He called Anita to the stand.

"How many times would you say I've asked you out?" he questioned.

"About fifty."

"And how many times did you say no?"

"Fifty."

"And did you really mean *no* all those times you said *no*?"

"Well, of course," responded Anita. "Why would I ever tell you *no* if I didn't mean *no*?"

Richard turned to the judge. "Your Honor, may I ask the people assembled in the courtroom a question?"

The judge allowed the request.

"How many of you women have persistently said *no* to some-body who you really want to go out with?" he asked. Slowly, hands started rising in the courtroom.

WHETHER THE DYNAMICS that led to Richard's acquittal repre-sent the norm or an anomaly, clear communication between the sexes isn't easy under the best of circumstances. Men and women simply do not talk the same language. Women are taught to let people down easy, for example, to be nice when they reject an admirer. They tend to couch their message in a way that leaves plenty of room for misinterpretation. As a result, the man hears what he wants to. And then he continues to act in accordance with his desires.

However, the woman's preference may not matter even when it is made clear, for men have been socialized to believe that they must win at any cost. Their sense of manhood depends on it. "No one is going to tell me what to do," one stalker of female Asian college students said under questioning. "I'm going to do what I want."

Although national in scope, until 1994 the problem of obsessive attention was virtually overlooked by the legal system, as well as by police departments across the country. That year, the passage of the Violence Against Women Act marked a major change in national and community response to crimes like domestic violence and stalking. Even so, as a rule, the patterns of stalkers continue to be dealt with ineffectually. Most other crimes are single shot events: The police are called in after the illegal deed is done; the perpetrator is then sought and arrested. Stalking, however, involves a series of activities that often may seem inconsequential when considered independently. Only once the sequence is uncovered and examined can the nature of the crime and the terror that has been inflicted be understood.

Even when the stalking patterns are identified, most states often don't arrest a suspect who harasses someone else until a "serious" crime has actually been committed. By then it's often too late.

"What does he have to do . . . shoot me?" Tammy Marie Davis asked her local police after her ex-boyfriend beat her and their 21-month-old child. Days later, he did exactly that, killing the 19-year-old waitress.

Unfortunately, in many cases, incarceration doesn't help much. "We imagine that when someone is arrested, the court system is magically going to solve the problem and the problem's going to go away," said former Los Angeles deputy City Attorney John Wilson, who specialized in handling stalking cases for three years. "That's not going to happen with stalkings. Number one, the court system doesn't understand these cases. And number two, it doesn't have the manpower or the resources to deal with them."

Despite the judicial system's somewhat limited ability to contend with the stalking issue, all U.S. states have jumped to pass their own antistalking laws. "There probably hasn't been a legislative experience like this ever," said safety and privacy authority de Becker. "What that tells us is that you've got an extraordinary problem that was waiting to be addressed."

The rush to tackle this pressing problem, however, has led to flawed legislation, sporadic enforcement and confusion among law enforcement, the courts and the mental health agencies about how to deal with stalkers and their victims. Meanwhile, the problem keeps intensifying. "We're seeing more and more stalking cases," a mental health consultant told the Los Angeles arraignment court in 1991. "It's becoming more prevalent among everyday people."

Since then, statistics and news reports have borne her out. And while the majority do stem from a relationship gone sour, sometimes all it takes to set off these individuals is a pretty face or a smile.

Could You Be a Stalking Victim?

Stalking is defined as the willful, malicious and repeated following and harassing of another person. If someone's obsessively persistent attention is making you uncomfortable or fearful, you need to pay careful attention to the lessons contained in the following pages.

2

You Never Know

STALKING DOESN'T JUST HAPPEN TO someone else. It happens to people all around you, people not so different from you. Who is at risk? Your family members, friends, lovers, neighbors, co-workers and employers. Who else is at risk? You are. And if you—or someone you work with—have been targeted by a stalker, you're potentially most vulnerable at your place of work.

Laura Black sat at her desk, engrossed in the material before her. Hearing the door to her office open, the 23-year-old brunette looked up to see Richard Wade Farley, 39, the man who had pursued and harassed her relentlessly since meeting her on the job. In the next instant she realized that the nightmare that had haunted her for the last four years had just spun out of control. Her former co-worker was draped in ammunition belts and armed with guns. He looked more like an overweight Rambo in fatigues than a computer technician. A moment later, Farley raised his shotgun and fired. It was the most telling shot that he would fire during a bloody siege that lasted almost six hours, taking the lives of seven of Laura's co-workers and leaving Laura permanently disfigured and disabled.

THEIR INITIAL MEETING had seemed harmless enough. Laura, an electrical engineer recently graduated from the University of California at Davis, had worked for ESL—a Silicon Valley high

13

tech defense firm—less than a year when she was introduced to Rich by a friend of his with whom she had been working. She and Rich chatted for a few minutes about nothing in particular. Then Laura went back to work and thought no further about it.

From the moment he saw her brilliant smile, however, Rich thought of little else.

Although his job didn't necessitate his being in the area, Rich made several visits that week to the lab where Laura and his friend, Tom Burch, worked. Each time, he stopped to talk with Laura. A week to ten days after their introduction, the native Texan and gun enthusiast asked Laura for a date. "It made me uncomfortable. I don't like to deal with that type of situation at work," Laura remembered. She turned him down.

But her rejection didn't deter Rich or squelch his growing interest. Soon he stopped using the pretext of visiting his friend and began to drop by her office as well as the lab in order to see her. He persisted in asking her out even though she declined day after day. "I tried . . . to explain to him that I wasn't interested in being anything other than a work friend," Laura recalled.

She remained tolerant until, later that month, Rich demanded that she give him her home phone number and address. "I'll be your friend at work," she said to put him off. When he continued to press her, she refused flat out and told him to leave her office. Even then her admirer persisted. "He said he was flabbergasted, and that he had been cleared for several years, and that the government trusted him and ESL trusted him and I should trust him too," Laura recalled.

Rich, a man co-workers described as cheerful but neighbors viewed as suspicious bordering on paranoid, continued to visit Laura frequently over the next few months. Each time he tried to find out more about the object of his attentions, and to share more about himself. He told her about working toward his bachelor's degree at San Jose State University, about his work stint in Australia, and about efforts to fix up the bungalow he owned in San Jose. He neglected to mention more troubling details, like his aloof and occasionally cruel childhood tendencies that included poking his brother with a nail and stomping on younger boys' fingers, or the fact that although he realized that his mother was the only person who had ever loved him, he never thought about her when out of her presence and considered her something "abstract."

Periodically, Rich continued to ask Laura out—on one occasion to a tractor pull. It didn't matter that she refused again and again. "I would try to talk with him and reason with him and tell him where I stood, and that he should acknowledge that," Laura recalled. She could have saved her breath.

He began to leave gifts, a number of them oddly inappropriate. Like the power toy bulldozer called a Digger Dan that she found sitting in the middle of her desk when she got to work early one morning. Unsure of what to do with the toy, she put it on the floor of her office and tried to ignore it. Thereafter, she had her secretary return any further offerings, including the floral arrangement in the plastic duck Rich sent her for Thanksgiving that year and the heart-shaped mirror he bought her for Christmas.

Still Rich hung on, switching only the timing of his visits. He had been dropping by during the day; now he began showing up mostly during evening and weekend hours when she was alone in her office working overtime on a project. That really disturbed her. She became increasingly annoyed and angered by the unwanted attention. Congeniality turned to harshness. "I would not go out with you if you were the last man on earth," she told him at one point.

By then, however, being with Laura Black was the only thing that really mattered in Rich's life. He could not leave her alone.

"I THINK I fell instantly in love with her," Richard Wade Farley told the jury during his murder trial six years after first meeting

Laura. "It was just one of those things, I guess." Despite feeling rejected by Laura's turndowns, that blind love dictated that he do everything he could to get to know her. So, six weeks after first laying eyes on her, Rich went down to the ESL personnel office and asked a friend working there to find out Laura's birth date for him so that he could surprise her. While the woman retrieved the data from Laura's file, Rich leaned over her shoulder and memorized Laura's home address.

He began to send Laura letters that spoke of love. In an attempt to find out more about her, he checked out keys to her office and her file cabinet from the security office at ESL. No verification was requested. All he had to do was sign for them. He used both to learn as much as possible about Laura. He would check her desk calendar, for example, to determine her schedule and whereabouts. His feeling was that information was power—an attitude he attributes to the espionage experience he claims to have acquired during his ten-year career in the Navy. In actuality, he did no spying himself, but rather provided backup technical support to those who did. His security clearance, however, made him feel that he was part of "an elite society" that had the right to spy on others.

He also continued to besiege Laura with requests for dates. Although she always turned him down, sometimes angrily, he took heart in the fact that she would occasionally treat him with civility.

In December, during one of those periods of relative calm, she happened to mention to Rich that she was going to her parents' home over Christmas. Determined not to be out of touch, Rich obtained a key to her desk by saying he had lost his own desk key and then giving security her desk number instead of his. When he went through her locked drawers, he found a copy of her application for security clearance. It listed the names and addresses of her parents and sister. The single-spaced, eight-page letters that reached Laura in Virginia over the holidays sent an even grimmer message than his prior spoken words. Rich would not leave her alone.

"There is no rational reason why Mr. Farley acts as [he does]," Laura would tell the authorities two and a half years later. She was right. The game had nothing to do with logic.

LAURA DROPPED ALL efforts to be cordial and decided not to acknowledge Rich, but his actions made that difficult. He telephoned her office by day and her home late at night. She hung up on him almost every time, but it didn't make a difference. He began to drive by her house. When she wasn't there, he devoted practically every free moment to trying to find her. When he discovered that she participated in the company's aerobics classes, he joined. He attended every corporate softball game Laura played in and then would insist on going along for pizza afterwards. When he would try to talk with Laura, she just turned away. "I'd tried discussing the situation. That didn't work. I tried just being angry, and that wasn't successful either. So I just thought I'd ignore him," Laura explained from the witness stand.

Despite the cold shoulder, Rich still felt entitled to evaluate her attire when he didn't approve, on one occasion enclosing in a letter a crude drawing of a stick figure with tiny pointed breasts. The caption read: "You can tell the girls from the boys by the bumps."

Desperate to deter him, Laura resorted to rudeness. "It was very clear [to friends and colleagues] that there was an unwelcome situation present, and it almost became a bad joke," Laura told the jury.

The dirty looks, taunts, and even the occasional obscene gesture (like flipping him "the bird") didn't dampen Rich's ardor. The letters, which often took him up to nine hours to write, kept coming. Where they were once coaxing, now they were menacing. He wanted to upset her so that she would at least talk to

him. Hearing her yell at him was well worth the contact that
followed. "I had fallen madly in love with her and I had to see
her, even if I had to make her mad to do it," he later explained.

AS TIME WENT on, however, Rich became increasingly frustrated.
"I have backed off as far as I'm going to," he wrote her that
fall. "I see you as much as six times a week, which doesn't give
you much freedom, so I thought it would be nice to call when
I wanted to see you, and the rest of the time is yours. But you
don't seem to appreciate that. Now I'm thinking of changing
the rules."

For Rich, that meant upping the stakes. He started trying to
annoy her with letters that made reference to her body. When
those no longer had their effect, his remarks became more intimidating. "I started telling her what I wanted her to do and this
bothered her," he said at his trial. "I started invading her space."

The latter efforts were not confined to paper. Having familiar-
ized himself with Laura's schedule by talking with her, by sur-
reptitiously checking her desk calendar and company mailbox,
and by ferreting out information from her colleagues, he would
either follow her or head off to her presumed destination. If she
wasn't where he expected her to be, he would drive around in his
gold Suburban until he found her at one of her other hangouts.
"He'd show up everywhere I was late at night, or when I went
out to dinner," Laura recalled. "I just couldn't shake him . . . .
It seemed that no matter where I ended up, I would see him."

Rich's efforts at tracking Laura were so successful that he
actually began to feel guilty. But he couldn't help himself. "I
have an awareness that I shouldn't be doing this," he testified
in his trial, unconsciously lapsing into the present tense. "But I
just can't stop. I feel a need to be where she is at." He would
even find himself driving to her house on occasions when he had
never consciously intended to, sometimes as late as 4:00 A.M. "I

couldn't really explain it to myself," he said. "I would just end up over there."

When a friend of Laura's tried to intervene, Rich warned her to tell him to mind his own business. "It's not in your best interest for him to interfere," Rich wrote. "He doesn't have any idea what he's getting himself into."

FINALLY LAURA APPROACHED ESL's human resources department. Her allegations prompted personnel to call Rich in for conferences about his behavior. When the agreements made during those sessions (like not contacting her) were broken, Rich was asked to attend counseling sessions as a condition of his employment. The week before his decision about participating in the counseling was due, Rich confronted Laura in the parking lot of her apartment building as she returned from work. She was about to open her car door when his face appeared in her window. For the first time, the conversation included the mention of Rich's prowess with guns and his extensive weapons collection. "Do you intend to kill me?" Laura asked. Rich's denials did not reassure her.

That same week, she received a letter that only increased her alarm. "Time to remove the kid gloves," Rich wrote. "I asked you to see me and you refused which is your right. It's my option to make your life miserable, if that's what you really want . . . . You asked me what I could do. Kill you? The answer to that was and still is, no. If I killed you, you won't be able to regret what you did . . . . In between the two extremes of doing nothing and having the police or someone kill me, there's a whole range of options, each getting worse and worse. How strong are you emotionally? I may just decide to test you."

The chilling message that followed did just that. Should Laura try to flee him, he would follow. She could quit, she could run, but she couldn't hide.

The remainder of the letter offered Laura an increasingly frightening insight into the mind of the man who had become obsessed with her. "You could always go to the police with this, then there's no telling what I would have to do. Please don't push me and try to find out," he insisted. "I'm not really insane, but I am calculating and not fully sure myself how far I'm willing to go. Don't make me find out. I just might scare both of us with what I am capable of doing if pushed into it . . . . Let's say you don't back down and I don't back down and pretty soon, I crack under pressure and run amok destroying everything in my path until the police catch me and kill me. Then the newspaper people will hound you. And let's say you stand up under the pressure and don't crack up, you will never again play with men with the same ease you do now, and I will win."

FOR RICH, THE interaction between them had become a game of wills, a contest to be won or lost. "I win if I get to have Laura as a girlfriend, possibly a wife," he explained to jurors, again lapsing into the present tense. "If she gets rid of me permanently, she's won." Laura's feelings made little difference. "At this time I'm so far in love with her that everything she said is irrelevant. Until I stop loving her, no one else exists for me."

He went to the counseling sessions ESL had mandated, but they didn't help. Even though his job was now on the line, and even though he had met and was dating a pretty new girlfriend named Mei Chang—to whom he would later become engaged—his behavior intensified rather than abated. His tactics of psychological terror involved shaking Laura up on every front. One day she left her keys on her office desk. Rich spotted them as he passed by. He obtained a clay mold and stamped an imprint of her house key in order to copy it. But instead of actually using the key he had made, he left it on the windshield of her car, along with a note saying that he was returning it because she had been a good girl. He had simply wanted to show her how easily he could obtain it.

His fantasy about their relationship intensified as well. "We fight like an old married couple," he wrote her, adding that the company should have sent them to a marriage counselor instead of enrolling him in therapy. "That's basically my best description of the relationship that I feel we have," he asserted when questioned about that statement during his trial.

Laura saw it differently. "He fabricated fights in the letters," she insisted to jurors. "I didn't talk to him. I didn't fight with him. I did not have a relationship with him."

One day Rich cornered Laura in a computer room. "I know you love me," he told her. "Don't ever . . . try to separate us." For Laura, that was the last straw.

Almost two years into Rich's campaign to secure Laura's affections, and three months after telling an ESL personnel manager that he had guns and "could take people with [him]," Rich was fired for poor job performance and harassment. ESL offered him a year's worth of free psychiatric counseling.

Company officials advised Laura to leave work early that day. "They told me what time they were going to escort him out to his car and terminate him," she said. "They told me to get out of town, to stay with friends if I could."

If Laura thought that Rich's firing would solve her problem, she was wrong. Several weeks later, he approached the manager of her apartment complex to ask about renting the flat next to hers. Laura found out about his inquiries and, shortly thereafter, moved to a new residence. It was the second time Rich had driven her from her home. The first time she had relocated, it had cost him one dollar and a trip to the post office to obtain her new address. He uncovered this one just as easily.

HIS PURSUIT OF her did not let up once his employment ended. When ESL security forbade him access to the company parking lot, he waited across the street, then followed her to her home. He registered at the university where she took evening classes. He spied on her from a nearby convenience store. He kept track of the men she saw and when she spent the night with them. Each day while Laura was at work, he went by her house and spent a couple of hours systematically running through number codes that would eventually program the electronic door opener he had bought to gain access to her garage.

One evening he actually showed up at her door, convinced that they had a date he had requested by mail simply because Laura had not contacted him to deny it. "Until I can ask you [out] nicely and have you say yes, I'll be around. Promise," Rich wrote her that summer. That same month, Rich introduced a new form of intimidation: "I have enough money for two more months, then I can always decide to come live with you if we aren't friends by then," he wrote Laura. "I get a job or I live with you, there is no alternative." The message frightened her. "I thought he was going to show up at my door with guns."

Feeling increasingly trapped, Laura considered getting a restraining order, but rejected the idea. "I was afraid that a restraining order would not protect me and that it might set him off," she explained to the jury at Rich's trial. She could not have been more accurate in her assessment.

THREE AND A HALF YEARS IN, even Rich was concerned about the direction his fixation was taking. "This is going to escalate and soon," wrote the man whose passion had already cost him his job, two homes (the bank had foreclosed), his credit, and his standing with the IRS (he owed $30,000 in back taxes and penalties). "Oh God, the shit has hit the fan," he wrote Laura. "All because you think I'm a joke and refuse to listen or understand that I'm gravely serious."

Shaken, Laura approached the police. They told her that she needed a restraining order before they could take any action. Once again, her fear of his violent reaction stopped her. "I didn't feel I had any alternative but to do nothing," she said. "I was [still] hoping that he would go away."

Finally, prompted by relatives, friends and co-workers, and feeling that she had no other recourse, Laura changed her mind. "I've been afraid of what this man might do to me if I filed this action," she stated in her court plea. "However, I am now at the end of my rope. I need the court's assistance and the assistance of the appropriate police agencies to keep this man out of my life."

On February 8, Rich was served with a temporary restraining order pending an official hearing on February 17. The legal document prohibited Rich from frequenting any of Laura's regular haunts, decreed that he cease all phone and written communication with her, and mandated that he keep a distance of 300 yards from her.

It took several days for the reaction to set in. Then Rich panicked. The notion that he would not be able to see Laura terrified him. And so his twisted mind concocted a plot. First he dropped off a letter to Laura's attorney's office alleging that he and Laura had an ongoing relationship. Details about dinner dates, a stay in a cabin and the key he had to Laura's townhouse were thrown in to substantiate his claims, every one of them false.

Two days later, although he had essentially run out of money, he purchased a $600 state-of-the-art semi-automatic shotgun and $1,400 worth of ammunition for it, adding to the six other weapons he owned. In order to display his arsenal in a manner that would properly impress Laura, he rented a Coachman motorhome. He was determined to get Laura into the motorhome, either through persuasion or intimidation, so that he could take photographs of their domestic interaction. He figured that if he could establish proof of their relationship, the court would not issue a permanent restraining order. Better yet, he reasoned, if he could convince Laura not to show up in court, the petition would be thrown out by default. If those plans failed, at least he and his fiancée could drive the motorhome to Reno and get married.

ON THE MORNING of Tuesday, February 17, nearly four years after meeting the girl of his obsessive dreams, Richard Wade Farley
awoke, showered, shaved and drove off to Jack in the Box for
breakfast, as he did every day. Early that afternoon, after returning home to leave off the temporary restraining order he had received and a copy of his last will and testament, he fooled around
in the bedroom with his fiancée Mei Chang and then drove the
rented motorhome to ESL where he prepared to wait for Laura
to get off work. Inside the vehicle, he laid out his camera equipment on a table, set up his weapons display by the door, loaded
the guns and filled the ammunition vest he planned to wear with
more than 800 rounds and more than 20 magazines of ammunition. Ten minutes later, he was bored. He put the clip boxes
and knife on his belt and the revolvers in the belt's holsters. He
looked at his watch. He still had two to three hours to wait.

He finished arming himself. He had a Benelli shotgun in front
of him, the .357 magnum revolver on his right side and the .22
magnum revolver behind that. He had tucked his two semi-
automatic pistols into his belt and draped his Ruger M-77 rifle
across his chest. His new semi-automatic 12-gauge Mossberg
shotgun lay cradled in the crook of his arm. He stood back to
admire himself, picked up his leather gloves and earplugs, and
walked out the door.

Larry Kane was on his way home when Rich passed him in
the parking lot. The 46-year-old data processing specialist raised
his arm to his face in a delayed reaction at the sight of the armed
man. Rich wheeled around and used his shotgun to pump him
full of buckshot. The killing rampage—which would take the
lives of seven ESL employees and wound another four—had
begun.

He missed his next target, who had just stepped out of his car.
Then Rich blasted his way through the glass security doors and
entered the building. When he got to the end of the hallway, he
opened the door to room 1261, the office of the man he had

just killed and a 23-year-old technical assistant named Wayne "Buddy" Williams, who had been with the company just six months. Within seconds, Buddy, too, was dead.

Rich shot six other ESL employees—four of them fatally—on his way to Laura's office. When he entered, Laura had just enough time to register his presence, along with screams from the hallway. Rich raised his Benelli shotgun, aimed and pulled the trigger. The first shot missed. Then he fired again. The shell ripped into her shoulder, tearing muscle and shattering bone. She felt a burning sensation, lost consciousness for just five seconds, and came to with her back pressed to the floor, her right shoulder braced against a bookshelf and her feet against the door. "Blood was pouring out of me like a faucet," she said. She saw Rich's boot and gun reappear. "No, Rich, no!" she yelled as she struggled to shut the door with her feet.

After just a few seconds, Rich reconsidered and allowed the door to close. Laura lay in a pool of blood and began to lose consciousness again. "I thought I was going to die," she said. She blacked out for a second time, again only briefly. When she came to, she grabbed her purse and keys. Then she dialed 911. The line was busy. Dazed, she fled her office. She passed her friend Glenda Moritz lying on her stomach and moaning. The 27-year-old would take a while to die from her injuries. She also saw Helen Lamparter, a 49-year-old software engineer, lying face down. Laura didn't stop. She knew that if she didn't get out, she would die.

Uncertain as to Rich's whereabouts, Laura ducked into a nearby office and tried to call ESL security. As she dialed, a piece of bone fell out of her shoulder onto the desk in front of her. She tried to stop the bleeding with her hand. Her entire fist fit inside the gaping hole in her upper arm.

When the line again was busy, she headed to another office, locked the door, and hid. Then she heard a familiar voice in the adjoining office. She tried to press her ear to the wall to listen, but her shoulder injury prevented her. Nevertheless, she had heard enough to be fairly certain that Rich was on the other side of the wall talking on the phone to the police. By then he had killed his last victim and pulverized computer equipment worth a total of $300,000.

The blood Laura had lost had taken its toll. "I was becoming very faint and weak. My breathing was very gurgly, as though there was blood in there and I was very light-headed," she remembered. "I didn't think I had much time left." Still, she managed to dart through the office on the other side and into the hallway. She cut through another room, down the stairs and out of the building.

After a standoff with the local police and SWAT team that lasted five and a half hours, Rich was finally taken into custody. "I'm the guy who's shooting people," he announced before surrendering. "Tell Laura Black this is about her."

LAURA UNDERWENT FOUR reconstructive surgeries during her 19-day hospitalization. Since then, she's had three more. Still, she can only lift her arm 30 degrees to the side and 45 degrees in front of her. She will never regain full mobility or muscle control of her shoulder and arm. The pain remains constant, often keeping her awake at night.

Two and a half years after the shooting, she unbuttoned her teal blouse enough to show the jury the concave scars resulting from the bullet and subsequent surgeries, leaving them to imagine those on her stomach, leg and hip caused by multiple skin-grafts. She refused to look at the man responsible for the injury. When asked by the prosecutor to identify him, her glance passed over him quickly and kept going. "You could tell she was uncomfortable being in the same room with him," said one courtroom observer.

Rich, looking like an overfed salesman in a cheap suit, was unable to take his eyes off her. The man whose most intense reaction during the trial was to push his glasses back up his nose and tug at his right ear, seemed to drink in her words as he scrawled notes based on her testimony.

Rich displayed no further emotion during the trial, even when hostage negotiator Lieutenant Ruben Grijalva testified that during the standoff Rich told him that he had stopped firing because it wasn't "fun anymore," and that he wanted to "gloat for a while" before surrendering. His lack of remorse about the killings did as much to condemn him in the eyes of the jury as the four months of testimony. On October 1, they convicted him of seven counts of murder in the first degree.

DURING THE PENALTY phase of the trial, defense attorney Gregory Paraskou argued that his client's life should be spared. Rich—one of six siblings who had been uprooted frequently because of their father's work as a mechanic in the Air Force—was described by witnesses as a loner. His family's reported inflexibility and lack of open affection did little to help his difficult social adjustment. Still, argued Paraskou, Rich had managed to lead a productive life during his career with the Navy and his tenure with ESL.

Neither argument swayed the jury. On November 1, exactly one month after his conviction and after less than five hours of deliberation, the jurors unanimously agreed that Rich should pay for the shootings with his life. Two and half months later, the judge sentenced Rich to die in San Quentin's gas chamber. As part of California's state law, that death penalty sentence was automatically appealed. Eight years later, the California Supreme Court upheld Rich's death sentence.

While the verdict and potential penalty may appease his victims, it cannot erase the past. For Laura Black—and for the families and friends of the ten others who were killed or injured—the consequences of Richard Wade Farley's obsession will endure a lifetime.

Restrain Yourself

Restraining orders—also known as protective orders—often incite stalkers to violence. Though most police departments advise victims to get a restraining order, you need to carefully consider your situation, as well as other options you'll learn about, before you decide whether to follow this advice.

3

Work It Out

AMAZINGLY, MURDER IS THE LEADING cause of death for American women in the workplace, and the second leading cause of occupational death for both sexes, according to the National Institute for Occupational Safety and Health. Not accidents or environmentally induced illness. Murder.

With workplace violence on the rise and posing a significant public health problem according to officials, we all are at risk. The Center for Disease Control and Prevention reports that every year 1.7 million Americans are victims of violent crime while on the job, with 700 of those winding up as fatalities.

While disgruntled employees account for much of this turbulence, stalking has spilled over into the work arena as well. Why? Often because you're more accessible at your place of employment than anywhere else. Although you can opt for a new unlisted phone number, change your residence, or even switch personal routines, changing jobs can be tougher, especially when jobs are scarce. "So that's the one place a stalker has access," said Jim Wright, Senior Analyst with the Threat Assessment Group, Inc. (TAG), which he joined upon retiring from the FBI's National Center for the Analysis of Violent Crime.

The examples are plentiful. Larry Voss, a Cheyenne substance abuse counselor, tracked down his ex-wife at the toy store she worked in and shot her in front of her co-workers. She died an hour later. In Houston, a 26-year-old secretary named Maria Escobedo was shot and killed at work by her estranged boyfriend. Another 26-year-old secretary and mother of two was gunned down at the Long Island nursing center where she worked by a man who had shadowed—and threatened—her since she had moved out of the apartment they had shared a year earlier.

For an increasing number of workers, stalking has become the latest on-the-job hazard, even when prior relationships aren't involved. Consider Lisa Snyder*, a nurse who provides therapeutic massage to an upscale Albuquerque clientele, and who has been harassed by a former patient. During his first—and only—session with her, the man, a disheveled 30-year-old, dropped his pants and started masturbating. When she refused to treat him again, he besieged her with obscene phone calls every five minutes throughout the day and night.

For seven years, Greta Van Susteren, a former Washington, D.C., criminal defense and civil trial lawyer who now hosts Fox News' *On the Record*, was phoned and followed by Matthew Brookman*, a six-foot-five-inch man who focused on her after local newspapers covered several famous homicide cases she had tried. To help satisfy his obsession with her, Matthew gathered a phenomenal amount of information about the attorney. His extensive research included pulling her early driving record from her home state of Wisconsin, and peppering her parents—as well as their longtime cleaning lady—with questions about where she was and what she was doing.

His fascination with Greta prompted him to shadow her. One day, wearing an ill-fitting suit with the tags still hanging from the sleeves, he followed her into a restaurant she patronized regularly. He stood so close to her table that her lunch partner asked whether he was with her. "No," Greta responded. "Well, sort of. He goes wherever I do."

In court, Matthew would position himself directly behind her and pretend to be her law partner. When Greta successfully petitioned to have him banned from the courtroom, he sued her and the judge for violating his First Amendment rights.

She tried everything she could to get rid of him. She was mean. She was nice. She ignored him. She had him arrested. Nothing worked. "If we agree not to send you to jail, will you stop following her?" asked his defense attorney. "I won't make a promise I can't keep," retorted the compulsively honest stalker.

Greta was not the first woman upon whom Matthew had focused his inappropriate attentions, nor would she be the last. "The irony is that after all those years, my stalker stopped stalking me because he found someone younger and prettier," said Greta. "So I got dumped by a nut."

Greta downplays the intimidating nature of Matthew's activities. But the judge who ordered him barred from the courtroom apparently understood the impact of his behavior, as well as its potential for escalation. That kind of insight is rare, not just among the judiciary but in most workplace settings.

SHANNON MILLS* HAD been hired to coordinate and run a literacy program for parolees when she met with trouble. Years of working with high-risk populations had taught her how to de-escalate even the most volatile situations. But the 40-year-old San Francisco resident felt uncomfortable with the physical set-up of her work environment. Even though she would be dealing with men who had rap sheets listing crimes from rape to murder, the agency left her on her own. Her office and classroom were located in a posh building for professionals, away from the rest of the staff. Floor-to-ceiling glass sliding doors didn't exactly add to her sense of security.

From the very first, one particular student—a semi-literate drug addict known to be a fire-setter—made her feel ill at ease.

Not only did he seem profoundly disturbed, he appeared to have a crush on her. He brought her presents (which she refused to accept), and took pictures of her in class. She set limits each time. But the message didn't get through.

One afternoon, after saying he wanted to talk with Shannon after class, he reached over to kiss her. She eluded his grasp, then told him she could either kick him out of the program or give him a second chance. Either way, she would not talk with him again in a closed setting, because he had behaved inappropriately and she no longer trusted him. "I didn't mince any words. But I never gave it a lot of charge either," she recalled. "People can get a rise out of feeling that they've made you afraid or caused you to react intensely. I didn't want to give him that power."

On the day he was due to graduate, Shannon requested backup from the agency, fearing that his unhealthy attachment would make it hard for him to receive his diploma and leave. They promised to send over a counselor. The counselor never appeared. So when her student arrived, intoxicated, with a large bouquet of flowers in hand and announced that all good gangsters gave flowers to their victims before they killed them, Shannon had few options. A glimpse of the revolver he had tucked under his pant leg made her even more aware of the danger. Deciding to play dumb, she didn't acknowledge the threat. Instead, she calmly told the class that she needed to get supplies from the office. Then she backed out of the classroom in as non-threatening a way as possible, her hands down and her palms open.

The glassed-walled offices didn't provide much protection. She fled to the back of one, crouched down behind a metal filing cabinet and called the police. She could hear the student storming around in search of her. "Where is that bitch?" he screamed. Convinced that he would eventually figure out where she had hidden and blast his way in, she tried to consider which internal organs she needed to protect most. "I knew if he did find his

way in, it would be all over," she recalled. "Just as I was about
to lose it, the police arrived. My student had his hand on the office's glass door. It was pretty close."

WHILE CERTAIN TYPES of jobs may increase the odds of attracting
obsessive individuals, anyone who deals with co-workers or the
public runs the same risks. Since most supervisors know little
about the phenomenon and nothing about the repercussions
of specific responses, the protection and safety of victimized
employees is a hit-or-miss affair. This makes even non-violent
situations seem ominous.

Ginny Winn, a 39-year-old bank supervisor from Los Angeles,
assumed that the cassette tape left anonymously on her desk just
after Christmas was a gift from a customer. So when she and her
husband drove down to Palm Springs the following weekend,
she slipped it into the tape player. The car filled with music from
Phantom Of the Opera. The end of the tape, however, shocked
them both. "My love for you is undying," a man's garbled voice
proclaimed. "I'll wait my whole life for you."

At first the athletic blonde dismissed the message as a previous
recording that someone had recorded over. But that changed
when she received a letter in January, along with a box of garden
roses and a fake diamond ring in a plastic jewelry box. "Although
the diamond isn't real, the sentiment behind it is," she read. The
return address on the envelope revealed that the sender had been
a bank patron for several years.

After calling her husband, Ginny notified the police. "I
thought that if I didn't show up one night, they might check his
house," she said. "If something were to happen, I felt that some
information should be on record."

Once she had identified her correspondent, she made every
effort to avoid him. All the bank tellers were advised to warn her
the moment they saw him. His thick sunglasses, trench coat and
small goatee made him easy to spot. Each time he would walk

into the bank, she took a break in the back room or headed to the Sav-On Drugstore down the street until he had left.

The bank manager offered to write a letter to the client asking him to desist. Ginny declined, not wanting to offend the man or hurt his feelings. One day when she was out on medical leave, her admirer waited for five hours to see her. At that point, the manager stepped in. "She's not here. She won't be here. Why don't you go," he told the man repeatedly. His words never seemed to register.

The personal pilgrimages lasted over a year. Finally Ginny allowed the manager to send the man a dismissive note that read: *"No one in this branch is interested in you. Kindly leave us alone."* Although the message was met with hostility, Ginny never heard from her pursuer again. She got lucky. He could have just as easily erupted.

MOST WORK-RELATED STALKINGS aren't eliminated that cleanly or easily, especially when the problem proves to be an internal one.

Shortly after 24-year-old Junko Tanaka* began to work at a bank in Los Angeles, she was befriended by co-worker Hiroyoski Sakamato*, a 34-year-old single man who had come to the United States from Japan. They lunched together with other colleagues several times, and then by themselves four or five times. The two even joined a group from work for a weekend outing to an amusement park. But their interactions remained innocuous and impersonal, never touching on such subjects as relationships or sex.

In time, Hiroyoski—a Penn State graduate—decided he wanted more. When he asked Junko out, however, she declined. "It was flattering to me for you to ask me, but I have a boyfriend, and I have no intentions of breaking up with him," she told him. Hiroyoski seemed disappointed, but accepting.

Not so.

Despite Junko's explanation that she lived with her boyfriend, Hiroyoski began to bring her gifts, one of them an expensive handbag. Soon he became overly concerned with Junko's welfare. He even met boyfriend Jackson Waterford* for lunch one day to discuss what could be done to help improve Junko's on-the-job performance, which he judged deficient. His motivation became clearer as the conversation progressed. "Hiroyoski began to downgrade Junko, [saying that] he was finding it difficult to help her anymore," Jackson told police. "He then advised me as a friend that I should consider breaking it off with this girl."

Spurned by Junko and unable to sway her boyfriend, Hiroyoski began to harass her by phone. At first he would call her home and try to discuss her situation at the bank. When she asked him not to phone her anymore, he continued to call but remained silent. One night Junko counted over 100 hang-ups between seven and eleven o'clock. That fall she got a new listing, but the calls continued. Even if she changed her phone number, he told her, he would have no trouble tracking it down.

By Hiroyoski's own admission, the phone harassment was "only the pre-kindergarten stage of this nice game!!!" He began to follow her home and watch her movements. In July, threatening letters demanded her resignation and insinuated that her boyfriend could wind up being assaulted. Next, a memo left on Junko's desk chair outlined Hiroyoski's ultimatum. If she did not leave her job by October 25, he would start imposing penalties. Her immediate action was demanded.

Finally, a letter threatened to harm not only her, but the others in her department should she not accede to his demands. The bank, concerned about the safety of its employees, as well as the possibility of sabotage of bank property, called in the police on October 8. Less than three weeks into their investigation, Hiroyoski was arrested. Forty-five days in jail followed by a court-mandated psychiatric program managed to pierce through

Hiroyoski's warped thoughts and reestablish his equilibrium. "You know, I was right at the edge. I could have killed her," he told authorities. "You guys yanked me back."

INTERVENTIONS DIDN'T BRING Veronica Grayton's* stalker back from the brink. Veronica had exchanged greetings with Edward Warren*, a 36-year-old aerospace engineer and divorced father of two, when she had run into him at the copier. But Veronica, an environmental engineer, didn't carry on a conversation with Edward until the morning he was escorted out of the facility, fired for what he thought was absenteeism. He called her from the guard shack and asked her to come down. "I need to talk to you right away," he said. Assuming the discussion would be job-related, she went to meet him in the parking lot.

Instead, she was confronted by a man whose delusions inexplicably revolved around her. "The Lord has told me to surrender myself to you," he announced. He proceeded to tell her that he had sexually assaulted a woman, and that he wanted to discuss his problems with her. She refused to talk with him.

Two weeks later, Edward approached her at the security guard gate and asked to meet with her so that they might continue the discussion. She refused again. He called later that day with the same request. "No," she said curtly, hanging up.

He began to phone her daily, promising not to let up until she agreed to talk with him. She continued to refuse. When he began to augment calls to her home with flower deliveries to her office, she got scared.

The calls continued even after Veronica filed a police report. Messages on her machine chastised her for her "high horse" and "phony baloney" attitude toward him. On August 2, she formally requested a temporary restraining order against Edward.

Although Veronica remained outwardly composed, the unrelenting harassment had begun to take its toll. "I am preoccupied at work, I am unable to sleep at night, and am afraid to stay in my own home for fear that the defendant will find my house and injure me in some way," she wrote in a report submitted to the authorities. "I have become so threatened by the defendant's actions that I have been forced to stay with friends and relatives much of the time since the harassment began."

On August 15, Edward was served with a restraining order mandating that he not "alarm, annoy or harass" Veronica. Any contact with her either in person or by phone would be a violation punishable by a $1,000 fine or six months in jail, or both. That same day, she received the first of dozens of erratic letters. "I have the power of Satan within me. I am to surrender this power to you," Edward wrote. He said he had been injected with these demonic powers after being abducted by space aliens while driving through the Mojave Desert.

The powers, he claimed, were responsible for the murders of several of his closest friends. Although all had apparently died in accidents or from illnesses, Edward claimed that the Lord had told him that they were dead at his hands. The letter concluded with a detailed account of the sexual assault he had mentioned in their first conversation, and of his sexual fantasies involving "black studs" having sex with his ex-wife and with himself.

A slew of disturbing and increasingly hostile letters followed. "Fuck you and your phony bag of shit," read one. She could take her restraining order and shove it, the communiqué concluded. The rest of the letters were equally abusive and equally upsetting. She owed him, he believed, and it was time to pay up. "I'm telling you to stop the bullshit or I will shove you in the ground," he wrote. "That's a promise."

Veronica tried hard to rationalize the situation. But Edward called at all hours. It seemed that he never slept. Not knowing him, Veronica had no idea what to expect. Her employers had responded to the situation by providing a security system for her home, but she still never felt safe.

On October 15, Edward was arrested and charged with felony stalking. At his preliminary hearing two weeks later, he pleaded guilty. His incarceration, however, didn't stem his incessant communication. Despite being advised not to, he continued to call her workplace every day, and wrote her another 16 letters. They showed clearly how little his attitude had been affected by the proceedings. His was on a mission from God, requiring Veronica's complete and unconditional cooperation, he warned. Anything else would draw "the cross-hairs of [his] anger toward [her] direction."

Because Edward had bypassed the need for a trial by pleading guilty, his attorney was allowed to select the judge who would pass sentence. Not surprisingly, he opted for a magistrate known for his leniency. Three factors, however, persuaded the judge to give Edward the maximum prison sentence allowable, despite the fact that the fired engineer had never inflicted actual physical harm on Veronica. The first: Edward's refusal to cease his harassment of Veronica even from behind bars. The second: Edward's use of cocaine and amphetamines over a period of several years, which had twisted his mind. Third: a court-ordered psychiatric evaluation, which concluded that Edward did indeed pose a significant threat to Veronica. "It is true Mr. Warren has not acted out in a violent way," the judge proclaimed during sentencing. "But it is not less serious and no less threatening to the victim to be told some of the things that Mr. Warren wrote in those letters."

Edward Warren was remanded to a California state prison able to provide the psychiatric help and medications the court-ordered evaluation had deemed necessary. Edward's three-year sentence, however, meant that he was eligible for parole just 13 months later.

IRONICALLY, ONE OF the work environments most impacted by stalking is the judicial system. The problem is so serious that the U.S. Marshals Service, which oversees security for all federal judges and courts, developed a threat assessment system. But pursuers who don't signal their approaches with prior communication are harder to detect.

Los Angeles Superior Court Judge David Milton had presided over two high-visibility stalking cases as a municipal court judge, one involving an obsessed fan's pursuit of Michael J. Fox, the other the stalking of a local anchorwoman. But when he took a phone call from a woman purporting to be a journalist, his knowledge of stalking suddenly became much more personal.

During the initial conversation, the woman stunned Judge Milton with her knowledge of the intimate details of his life. "She began to relate my former wife's name, the names of my children, my political party affiliation, the law school I attended, the year I graduated, and much, much more—much more," he recalled during a television interview.

Juanita Sniffled, a self-professed writer with a history of mental illness, didn't stop there. Every day for weeks, she haunted Judge Million's courtroom. She waited for him in the courthouse parking garage and other places. Then she attempted to intrude on his personal life, appearing one evening at the home of the judge's former wife, Ramona, frightening her and their children.

Although Juanita was served with court orders and warned to desist by law enforcement officials, her delusion that she and the judge were meant for each other overrode such concerns. "She indicated that it was signed in blood that she and I were married spiritually and it would be soon that we would become married," the judge explained.

Judge Milton eventually quit the bench and took a job as a prosecutor in another state.

THE MEDIA'S INCREASINGLY sensationalized reports of stalking incidents feed the imaginations of those who have always wanted to indulge in such behavior, but never had the courage to.

"People want to come out with their own brand of craziness," said forensic psychiatrist Kaushal Sharma, MD, assistant medical director at the University of Southern California Institute of Psychiatry, Law, and Behavioral Science. "So when you have cases of stalking that make the headlines, you will have that very small percentage of those on the fringe who will act out because of that influence."

Despite the growing dimensions of the problem, corporate or institutional procedures often facilitate a stalker's access to you on as well as off the job. Registration or sign-in sheets ask for your name and often your address and phone number, making the information available to anyone who sees the sheet. Too many companies are laid out so that individuals can enter without passing through a central reception area. Employee records aren't properly shielded. Copies of keys to offices, desks and file cabinets are handed over to people whose right to them is never verified.

Inadequate screening of prospective employees compounds the problem. One company actually rehired a man after he had shot a co-worker while working for that very company. The employee, who was obviously disturbed, stalked a second co-worker once he was back on the job.

Whether the problem emanates from a former mate, a stranger or an employee, most businesses and institutions simply aren't prepared to deal with this escalating trend. The tragic outcome of Laura Black's case shows what a grave mistake that can be.

Approximately 18 months after Richard Wade Farley had begun his campaign of terroristic attention, Laura Black finally complained to ESL's human resources department. Accordingly, the department's Jean Tuffley confronted Rich and read him the definition of sexual harassment. Together, she and Rich reached an agreement that he would refrain from going into Laura's office, using her computer terminal, writing her letters or leaving notes on her car. Within a month, Rich had violated that compact. During a subsequent meeting, the company slapped him with a disciplinary warning and demanded that he sign an agreement not to harass Laura anymore. When that didn't work, they came to yet a third agreement, which specified that he attend in-house psychological counseling. That didn't curb his pursuit either.

In February, following eight months of threatening correspondence, Tuffley warned Rich that his ongoing contact with Laura would jeopardize his job. "If I lost my job, life wouldn't be worth living. I have guns and know how to use them," Rich responded, according to Tuffley's court testimony. "Are you threatening to kill me?" she asked. "Yes, and I'll kill other people too," he answered.

ESL's interventions didn't defuse the situation. To the contrary, their management of the case seemed to aggravate Rich and increased the odds of his acting out violently. Their mistakes stand out as a textbook on what not to do.

First, they applied intrusive intervention. Rich was repeatedly told to leave Laura alone. The demands did not sway him or change his conduct. Instead, they compromised his dignity and provoked his anger, thereby increasing the likelihood of a vehement response.

Second, instead of firing Rich as soon as the problem became apparent, ESL kept him on. That delay allowed Rich the opportunity to introduce threats, intimidation, manipulation and escalation (referred to as the T.I.M.E. Syndrome by Gavin de Becker) into his dealings with the company and his harassment of Laura.

Third, ESL negotiated instead of drawing the line and then standing firm. By the time the company fired Rich, he had probably grown to expect that his tactics would continue to work. That kind of shock can quickly escalate into anger.

Fourth, despite Farley's growing obsession, ESL's human resources personnel opted to deal with the problem on their own.

They failed to notify the company's security force about the stalker for way too long.

Finally, assuming that they handled his termination the way most companies do, they most likely rehashed their reasons for firing him instead of directing his attention toward the future. "Companies are used to jumping through hoops in the pre-employment process, but not during the post-employment phase," said de Becker, who has consulted with many of the country's top 100 corporations on security issues. De Becker suggests that final discussions be kept future-based. By asking Rich how he wanted the company to deal with his mail or calls, or what he wanted them to tell future employers, they could have focused his attention on life after ESL. Chronicling misdeeds would have only fed his resentment and heightened negative emotions.

The restraining order Laura had initially opposed as provocative, and which friends, family and company officials had advised her to seek, ultimately propelled Rich from threat to action. Four years of other kinds of direct intervention had primed the pump. In the end, seven innocent—and uninvolved—employees of ESL lost their lives.

WORKPLACE VIOLENCE FREQUENTLY claims third-party victims. On a morning in May, Seaman Michael Stokes, a 23-year-old navy cook on a two-day pass, walked into fast-food restaurant in Ansonia, Connecticut, to confront manager Wanda L. Salgado. Seven minutes later, he shot Wanda, age 26, and assistant manager William Abate, age 28, to death. "[Abate] was at the wrong place at the wrong time," concluded a state police spokesman.

The story remains all too common. "The media is replete with examples of people killed who had no connection with the shooter and only worked with the victim," said Jim Wright.

Often, third parties aren't even aware that a problem exists. When a 64-year-old receptionist broke off relations with the

68-year-old man she had been seeing for two years, the senior mounted a vigil outside her home. She found him in her garage the next morning and asked him to leave. That evening, he showed up at her workplace armed with a handgun, a knife, handcuffs, rope, tape, alcohol, and a tape recorder, and took her and her employer hostage. Help arrived only after the boss's wife called to see why he hadn't come home for dinner. Defying the stalker's orders, the employer picked up the ringing phone and pretended that he was talking to a client. The first time his answers didn't jibe with her questions, she hung up. She caught on the second time around. "Is anything wrong?" she asked. "Yes!" her husband affirmed. "Should I call the police?" "Yes!" By 6:45 P.M., the stalker was booked and in custody.

Regardless of the level of awareness about a case, third parties who attempt to insulate a stalker's target often become victims themselves. In the 1970s, a receptionist in the late Senator Ted Kennedy's office was stabbed by a stalker angling for the politician. Some 20 years later, a man trying to get on the Universal Studios lot in Los Angeles in order to see Michael Landon fatally shot the two security guards who barred his entry.

Employer response to this rising tide of workplace violence has ranged from firing the victimized employee (out of safety fears for other workers) to liberal leave policies for victims who must testify in court or seek psychological assistance. Increasingly, however, workplaces are stressing violence prevention, as well as victim protection in the workplace.

In order to better its bleak record, the U.S. Postal Service—which saw 38 employees murdered on the job in just seven years—instituted employee focus groups to temper its authoritarian management style. In addition, the Postal Service made interpersonal skills a priority when hiring managers. Under former U.S. Postmaster General Marvin Runyon, efforts were also made to tighten the screening of job applicants and improve the workplace climate.

Other businesses and institutions have also worked to improve their responsiveness to emerging problems, perhaps motivated in part by concerns that they could potentially be held liable for negligence. Upon discovering that a receptionist's husband had threatened her, one company contacted the police and then moved the woman up from her ground-floor station to the second floor. A few days later, her husband crashed a truck into the building and smashed her former desk.

Protective measures have also included transferring a potential victim to another store or branch, alerting entrance personnel—such as receptionists and security guards—to be on the lookout, distributing photographs of a stalker to all employees, escorting employees to and from their cars, and hiring outside protection or security services when serious problems arise.

Since interpersonal cases are inevitably preceded by indicators, an increasing number of corporations have also established toll-free employee assistance protection numbers that victims of threats can call for counseling or to confide information regarding emerging problems.

In addition, newly formed security committees consisting of members from the company's security, legal, medical, human resources and employee assistance departments routinely review cases reported inside the workplace. These security committees help in two ways. First, they encourage and stimulate reporting of such matters before they spiral out of control. Gavin de Becker considers this an especially important resource for managers and supervisors, most of whom still believe that taking a problem to a superior is a sign of ineptitude. Second, they ensure the kind of inter-departmental dialogue that might have helped prevent the ESL disaster.

So far, however, these efforts have done little to stem the tide. Kim Springer, a 29-year-old mail carrier from Dana Point, California, can vouch for that.

For over a year, Kim had been stalked by Mark Hilbun, a former co-worker she barely knew. Although his harassment of Kim had contributed to the loss of his job, Mark, 38, continued to proclaim his love for her. He followed her on her mail route, harassed her with phone calls, and left a series of notes. His last note in May revealed his intentions with frightening finality. "I love you," he wrote. "I'm going to kill us both and take us both to hell."

The prior fall, Mark, a diagnosed manic-depressive who had been hospitalized twice, had been brought up on charges of harassing her by telephone. But Kim stopped proceedings against him when he opted for psychiatric treatment and agreed to stay away. A charitable but unfortunate reaction, aggravated by the U.S. Postal Service's lackadaisical handling of the situation.

As Mark's threats increased, postal officials warned employees to be on the lookout for Mark, and ordered them to lock all doors and gates not being used. However, they neglected to alert the Postal Service police until what would turn out to be the day of the shooting, seven days after Kim's life had been threatened. During that time, gates were left unlocked and unguarded.

At 9:45 A.M. on the morning of May 6, Mark simply walked into the Dana Point post office. No one even tried to stop him. "Get down on the ground!" he yelled. Then he began to fire. The shots killed one employee and injured a second who tried to rush him. Before making his escape, Mark also shot through the door to the postmaster's office, where Kim crouched hidden.

The killer remained on the loose for two days. By the time he was apprehended, he had wounded five other people, one fatally. "It's a classic case of where the system fired him, but it didn't solve the problem," U.S. Chief Postal Inspector Ken Hunter told the *Los Angeles Times*. A number of those close to the situation would term that an understatement. "All the signs were there," said Kim's boyfriend, Steve Eberhardt, the day after the shooting. "As far as I'm concerned, this never should have happened."

Minimize Workplace Worries

If you're being stalked, one of the places you're most vulnerable is at work, since your stalker knows exactly where and when you'll be there. So don't try to keep your stalking a secret. Alert co-workers, security guards, receptionists and your bosses. Have your calls screened by a receptionist or voicemail. For further protection, you may even want to consider moving to a less exposed work station.

4

Why? Understanding the Incomprehensible

W HAT COMPELS SOME PEOPLE TO become obsessed with others, to hound, threaten, injure and sometimes kill in the name of love?

As with most research into criminal behavior, explanations range from the biological to the environmental. Physiological studies, for example, reveal that sexual attraction and the onset of feelings of love often trigger a surge of natural amphetamine-like substances in our bodies. Some professionals in the field theorize that higher than usual levels of these chemicals may lead to the aberrant behavior of love-obsessed individuals.

That's a tantalizing notion. It would explain the incomprehensible and even offer the possibility of a bio-chemical solution. Other behavioral scientists, however, postulate that some event or series of events during formative years provokes the deviant behavior, especially in view of similarities between repeat stalkers and serial rapists and killers.

The fact is that the stalking phenomenon is still too new and the studies are too few to determine what causes these obsessive behaviors. There aren't enough physical and social scientists exploring the issue. So all they've been able to ascertain for certain are the traits these people share.

Here's what we know:

Stalkers are above average in intelligence. They usually read a lot and will engage in considerable research—as well as expenditures that reach into the thousands of dollars—in pursuit of their objectives. They know just how far they can go without breaking the law. And they refuse to take no for an answer. Two thirds of stalkers pursue their targets at least once a week and often daily. They don't rely on a single method, but usually have several in their arsenal.

Lack of a core identity also ranks high on the list of stalker characteristics. In an effort to make up for this inherent deficiency, love-obsessed individuals psychologically latch onto another person to validate their own worth. "If I could just be with her, I would have accomplished something," reasons the stalker, whose identity almost immediately becomes submerged in the other person's. Perhaps because of this deficiency, almost one out of every three stalkers has stalked before.

Should the obsessed individual fail to make a connection—whether from the outset or after a relationship has been attempted—he or she has no well-developed sense of self upon which to fall back. Without the coveted liaison, they have nothing. Since that emotional void is intolerable, the obsessed person can't afford to accept the rejection, whether overt or implicit. As long as the stalker continues the pursuit, he can convince himself that he hasn't been conclusively rejected.

When rejection can no longer be denied, the emptiness and humiliation cause obsessed individuals to act out in ways that destroy them as well as their victims.

JOSEPH BLACKSTONE*, A 53-year-old lab technician, describes himself as a hereditary obsessive-compulsive, and his 30-year marriage as a business partnership rather than a relationship. For two years he had an affair with a waitress from the local country club. Then she broke it off. "I went insane over it. Literally and irrationally insane over a period of five or six years," he recalled.

"I felt this need to drive by her home in the daytime, and sit outside her house for hours at night. I'm not sure why, even now. I phoned her incessantly. I sent letters saying 'You did me wrong. Why? Why?' For those years, I couldn't eat or sleep. My life was a black hole."

Work had always been sacred to Joseph. He had always held two or three jobs at once. The stalking of his ex-lover put an end to that practice. He didn't have time for both. Gaining power over her took precedence. In the meantime, his work, his relationship with his wife and family, and his physical health all suffered.

His obsession ultimately landed him in a sanitarium, where he underwent extensive therapy. The cloud he had been operating under began to lift. "I thought I wanted her back. In retrospect, I guess I just couldn't let go. In the process, I ruined two lives," he said. "I saw her as my emotional fulfillment. I'd invested all my eggs in that little basket. When she left, my basket was empty. I felt a void within myself."

SOME MENTAL HEALTH authorities hypothesize that the need to possess someone who's unavailable often stems from childhood feelings of rejection and abandonment. The idealized or fantasy relationship is subconsciously perceived as a way to rewrite history, to fill all of life's deficits. "There is that magical quality that feeds the fantasy of the stalker and makes him feel that this person can fulfill his emotional needs . . . and make him feel lovable," asserted the late Bruce Danto, MD, an early pioneer in the field of forensic psychiatry and the psychology of stalking. Denial of the opportunity to make up for the damage suffered during the early years can lead to feelings of desperation and panic, as well as a sense that the imagined connection must be preserved at any cost.

Faulty socialization can also play a significant role. "We're not taught to take responsibility for our behavior, or to accept that we can't always have what we want," said E. Eugene Kunzman, MD, former medical director of the Jail Mental Health Services, Department of Los Angeles County Mental Health. That sense of license is fed by the sort of permissiveness that prompts a school to overlook a ball player's transgressions or the public to accept a rock star's excesses.

Perhaps that explained O.J. Simpson's behavior. No matter what the evidence, only he will ever know for sure whether he murdered his former wife and her friend Ronald Goldman. But there can be no doubt that O.J. abused Nicole Brown Simpson while they were together, and then stalked her after the marriage had ended. Evidence of O.J.'s violent tendencies surfaced as early as 1985, when he shattered the windshield of Nicole's car with a baseball bat. During the course of their stormy marriage, friends periodically noticed red marks on her wrists. Although most around her knew that the relationship obviously had a violent side, little was said about it.

In the wee hours of New Year's Day 1989, however, O.J.'s physical abuse of Nicole became public. "He's going to kill me! He's going to kill me!" she screamed when police showed up following her 911 call for help. She had hidden in the bushes outside their home, clad only in a bra and sweat pants, to await their arrival. Her face had been badly beaten, her lip cut. Her eye and cheek were swollen and bruised. A hand imprint was visible on the left side of her neck. "This is a family matter," O.J. told the officers when questioned about her condition, which required treatment at a hospital. "Why do you want to make a big deal of it?"

The police had previously responded to reports of domestic violence at the Simpson household and had not taken any action. This time, O.J. was arrested and charged. But because of his fame, he was accorded favored treatment. Not only did he not serve any jail time, he was allowed to pick his own psychiatrist and conduct the sessions by phone. The court even let him determine how he would fulfill the 120 community service hours he had been required to perform. "I think the judge was trying to accommodate him, rather than help him understand that this was criminal behavior," said Alana Bowman, head of Los Angeles' City Attorney's domestic violence unit.

Nicole finally left O.J. in 1992; their divorce became final that same year. Yet O.J. refused to let go. He tracked her with the single-minded purpose that had made him a sports champion. In a further attempt to control who she saw and what she did, he phoned her male friends and tried to scare them off.

A multitude of 911 calls, including the two made on October 25, 1993, attest to his ongoing harassment of her after their split, and to her well-founded fear of him. "My ex-husband has just broken into my house and he's ranting and raving outside [in] the front yard," Nicole told the dispatcher. Less than a minute later, she called back. "He's fucking going nuts," she exclaimed sobbing. "I don't want to stay on the line. He's going to beat the shit out of me."

Authorities attest to O.J.'s ongoing terrorization of Nicole, and to the fact that she feared for her life. But aside from the 1989 case, she never brought any charges, perhaps afraid of his reaction or perhaps afraid to challenge the public persona his fans worshipped. "They won't believe me," an anguished Nicole told Cynthia Garvey in December 1993. "He's charming. People just don't know."

The self-centered, self-serving approach to the world in general—and relationships in specific—that O.J. Simpson exhibited encourages a sense of entitlement for the famous and non-famous alike. "I was just going to hang in there until I got what I wanted," Richard Wade Farley testified during his murder trial.

Such thinking is typical among those who consider themselves above the law. "If there is something that the criminal wants, he knocks down every barrier until he gets it," wrote clinical psychologist Stanton E. Samenow, PhD, in his book *Inside the*

Criminal Mind. "There is no need to justify the crime to himself either before or at the time he commits it. In cold-blooded fashion, he does whatever suits him; he is the only one who matters."

The same can be said of the stalker. He manipulates relationships through intimidation, blames his victim(s) for not cooperating with him, and minimizes the impact of his own actions. His goal, however inappropriate, justifies all behavior. And his own sense of inadequacy drives it.

ONCE AN INDIVIDUAL merges his identity with that of his target, escalation of obsessive activity is almost inevitable. In the face of unrequited love, the stalker raises the stakes for attention and, sometimes, for revenge.

Michelle Ward, a petite, dark-haired cashier from Charlotte, Michigan, didn't think twice about a conversation she had with a customer she had never seen before. The man complimented the 22-year-old and handed her beauty pageant entry forms he had ripped out of a women's magazine. "You should be on TV," he told her.

For the next eight months, he came through her checkout line almost every night. He always looked the same—clean-cut, not unattractive, usually dressed in a sweater, dress shirt, and tie. Then, in October, he called her at the store. "I've been watching you," he said after identifying himself. "I want to take you out."

It took Michelle a few minutes to put the voice to the face. Her reaction to his proposal, however, was immediate. She refused, saying she didn't want to date. She thought that would be the end of it. But when she left work that night and walked across the darkened parking lot, she found him standing on the hood of her car. "I really want to go out with you," he said. Michelle declined once more. "I've got to have you," he insisted. Then he tried to grab her. Michelle managed to slip into her car, lock the doors and escape.

The stranger continued to come into the store and to wait for her in the parking lot at the end of the day. Her managers insisted that she treat him like any other customer, but his persistence frayed her nerves. "Stay away from me. Leave me alone," she screamed one evening.

"I'll get you when you least expect it," he whispered. "We'll talk more about it later."

Subsequent statements seemed to substantiate her growing fears that he might try to kidnap or rape her. "I can't wait to take your clothes off, and I'm gonna get your clothes off," he promised at one point.

Frustrated with the lack of support from her employers, Michelle finally quit her job in December. That's when the phone calls started, up to 30 a day. In January, Michelle started noticing footprints in the backyard. By spring, she was finding food wrappings and discarded leftovers outside her house, along with tissues covered with dried semen. One night, Michelle walked out to find her dog's chain wrapped in a 13-loop noose and hung at neck height from the clothesline. The dog had not been harmed, but the implications were clear.

The stalker's attempts to intimidate Michelle and disrupt her life became increasingly bold as the months went by. "Every time I turned around, I didn't know if he'd be standing behind a tree or in the backyard with a ski mask over his face," she recalled. "I was just petrified." In addition, she resented how much of a focus he had become. Keeping a journal provided an outlet for those emotions. But some days the intrusion into her life made her so angry that she couldn't even write about it and would heave her diary across the room.

Years later, she remained haunted by her stalker. "I'm living a never-ending nightmare," she said. "He has tunnel vision, and in that tunnel he sees me and him together. I'm scared to death of him because I don't know what he could or would do."

For a stalker, that's the next best thing to getting the girl. He has succeeded in making himself the focal point of her life.

MOST MEN SHARE the ability to idealize and even deify women, Peter Rutter, MD, stipulated in *Sex In the Forbidden Zone.* "In this way, it can at any moment seem to be the sole object of value worth pursuing in life—regardless of the consequences." It is the attachment, rather than the specific object of desire, that actually matters. Richard Wade Farley, for example, pursued two other ESL co-workers before finding Laura Black. "He was like a magnet waiting to find something to attach to," observed one ESL employee.

Sometimes the stalkers themselves don't appreciate the nature or importance of that bond until it's threatened. Then they're propelled into action to preserve what has become their lifeline.

For a year and a half, Suzanne Hollister* sporadically dated a carpenter. She was one of the few female employees of the Los Angeles general contractor for whom he worked. Although the relationship never became physically abusive, it was less than healthy. Sid Barry* berated Suzanne for her weight, threatened to leave her if she didn't do what he asked, and constantly found her wanting in comparison to his previous girlfriend, with whom he claimed to be still in love. His periodic drug binges just made matters worse. Suzanne, 34, tried to adapt her behavior in order to avoid his emotional explosions, but her actions never seemed to please him. Finally she severed their romantic connection, but continued to see him as a friend.

Six months later, Sid talked her into trying to make the relationship work again. No sooner had they gotten back together than Suzanne realized she had made a mistake. Sid wanted to move in with her and even proposed marriage. When she refused both offers, he quit his job and threatened to live in his car. To appease him, she offered him temporary shelter over the coming Christmas holiday. "As soon as you get a job, you're out of here," she told him. He chose not to believe her. "Let's get married," he countered. Suzanne told him that she would never become his wife. "We'll see," he said.

Once he had moved in, Sid was hard to dislodge. Although Suzanne wanted nothing more to do with him, she had begun to fear his reaction, for as her interest had dissipated, his had taken root. "I've never loved anyone like you," he told her. All she could do was encourage him to continue to look for work, so that he could afford his own accommodations.

Shortly after the holidays, which she spent in Hawaii with her parents, Suzanne decided to fly to San Francisco to visit Mark, a gay male friend. Sid asked to come along. "You're not invited," Suzanne told him. Her response didn't sit well. "If you go up there, I'm going to show up at the airport and I'm going to kill Mark," he announced.

Sid's threat signaled the end of their attempted reconciliation as far as Suzanne was concerned. For Sid, however, the fight to possess Suzanne and dictate her actions had just begun. When she demanded that he leave, he refused. He finally relinquished her house keys, only to hold onto a set he'd had copied. After her father flew in from Hawaii and forced Sid to surrender the duplicates and leave the house, he started to call her nonstop, both at home and at work. "It's over," Suzanne tried to explain. "There's nothing you can do. Move on with your life."

He refused to accede to that request. Soon he started swinging by her office. "Just be my friend," he pleaded. Although the visits petrified her, Suzanne stood her ground. "I don't want to be your friend. You need help," she answered. That's when he began to talk about killing himself in her backyard. "Well, that's too bad," Suzanne told him, trying hard to be strong.

Urged by her mother, Suzanne began to take precautionary measures. After her father returned to Hawaii, Suzanne floated between several friends' homes for a month. When she couldn't bear that any longer, she hired an off-duty police officer for a week and moved back home. She paid the officer $1,000 to meet her after work and then stay in the house for seven nights. Sid lay low during that time. But less than 30 minutes after the off-duty policeman had left on his last day of service, Sid appeared in Suzanne's driveway. A girlfriend's husband—a 230-pound former pro-football player—responded to her frightened call and rescued her. But there would be no reprieve from the overall situation.

Sid began to stake out Suzanne's house from a spot up the street. Around Easter, he called to tell her that he had stolen a gun. His announcement finally convinced Suzanne that she had to obtain a restraining order. Before she could complete the paperwork, however, Sid confronted her at her tennis club. "You're going to be so sorry for what you've done," he told her, tears running down his face. "You're not going to be able to live with this when I commit suicide." Suzanne didn't want Sid to think that he could rattle her. "I'll try," she said, stoically attempting to bridle her fear. "Where's the gun?"

Two months went by. Suzanne had begun dating the man she would eventually marry. Sid, however, had not let up. So she obtained a restraining order, which mandated that he keep a 100-yard distance from her property line, as well as from her place of work and several regular destinations. For a while, Sid observed the restraining order to the letter, but never its intent. Instead of leaving her alone, he opted to camp out in his car exactly 101 yards from her driveway, and even slept there at night. Suzanne warned her neighbors and the police about his presence, but there wasn't much anyone could do.

Finally the police ran a check on Sid's license plate and found that there was an outstanding warrant for his arrest due to an unpaid traffic ticket. Aware of his constant harassment of Suzanne, they took him into custody and impounded his car. Still, they weren't convinced that they could hold him. As soon as she found out, Suzanne drove to the station with a copy of

California's new stalking law. In addition, she brought copies of Sid's eight previous restraining order violations. Finally, she produced a letter he had written her, that read: "Suzanne, don't put me in jail. I don't want to hurt you." Without the information and evidence she provided, the police would have released him the following day.

When Sid's case was finally heard three weeks later, he was sentenced to 30 days in jail and three years of probation contingent on his going to counseling. Since he had already served 20 days for not making bail, he was back on the street just 10 days after his hearing. "That's the best we can do," the city attorney told Suzanne. The distraught victim asked about her options. "People do change their names. You could move elsewhere," he said.

Suzanne and her future husband, Tyler Wright*, actually considered relocating, which one in seven stalking victims do. They found, however, that they could expect little in the way of governmental or legal assistance. Suzanne's career wasn't going to make matters any easier. "There aren't many women in construction. He'll be able to find you," one of the vice presidents at work told her. "You're not going to be able to disappear."

Instead, she and her husband bought a handgun and two cellular phones. They installed a half dozen motion detector lights, including one that would set off an audible alarm inside the house. As soon as Sid's jail term was up, they returned to the locked state of siege they had been able to forget during his short stay in prison. The day that Sid was due to be released, Suzanne couldn't check her tears. "I'm tired of this. I'm scared," she told Tyler as he dropped her off at work.

Three hours after being released, Sid showed up at Suzanne's place of work, in direct violation of the conditions of his probation. Forced to serve out his suspended sentence, he returned to jail. Suzanne and Tyler had made plans to move into a new house during that time, hoping to keep their new location confidential. But Sid was released two months early, before they'd had a chance to relocate.

His time in jail had obviously done little to abate his fixation. Within days of getting out, he had called Suzanne's mother to say that he just couldn't understand what had happened. According to Sid, the only problem was Suzanne's irrational rejection of him.

He kept closing in on Suzanne and her husband. Once, the couple came back from a weekend ski trip to find that all the motion detectors they had set up around the house had been stolen. Under the balcony, they discovered a footprint made from the firefighter-type boots that Sid usually wore. Not long after, Tyler took Suzanne's car to go get the morning paper. A man walked up to the driver's window while he was stopped, his hands in a begging position. Only when he got close did Tyler recognize the stalker, who had obviously assumed that Suzanne was behind the wheel.

Sid began calling again, and would quote the Bible to her. "He found God in jail," Suzanne would later comment sarcastically. And he resumed his stakeout spot down the street. One morning he followed her to work. She raced through downtown at 50 miles per hour, careened into the parking lot and sprinted into the building.

Finally, after sending Suzanne an incoherent manuscript detailing his love for her, he wrote her a letter requesting eight hours of uninterrupted time together in order to understand why she was doing this to him. He would wait for her for three days in the parking lot of a nearby supermarket, he promised. If she didn't show up, he was going to sell his possessions because he had a final present to give her. Suzanne felt sure she knew what he meant. He was going to kill himself and take her with him.

Aware that there was a new warrant out for his arrest, again for restraining order violations, Suzanne and Tyler checked the parking lot. When they saw Sid there on the second day, they called the police. After he had been booked, the female arresting officer cautioned Suzanne that Sid had talked about nothing but her and how deeply he felt about her. "I'll do three years in jail to show her how much I love her," he claimed.

WHILE THE THREAT of incarceration does divert some stalkers from acts of intimidation or outright violence, for others like Sid Barry, it's inflammatory. Occasionally, the resulting rage is turned inward. More often, stalkers lash out, either at the person they perceive as responsible, or at those around them.

After extensive therapy, Bob Falini has begun to come to terms with the reasons behind his own abusive actions. Over a five-year period, he became obsessed with almost every woman he dated. Each time the pattern was the same. He would concentrate so completely on his girlfriend that the emotional charge was like a drug-induced high. The rejection that inevitably followed would so depress him that he was unable to eat, sleep, or work. "You don't even know what to do with your hands," he said in hindsight. He experienced anxiety attacks so intense that he felt like he was dying of a heart attack. Then the anger would come, followed by banging on the doors of his victims in the middle of the night, smashing their windows, badgering them at work, and pounding nails into their car tires.

The wrath an obsessed individual feels is often compounded by his fears that his very identity is at risk. "First I've been rejected. Then the individual won't talk to me," Bob explained. "I'm shut out of what seems like my life, which was actually our life together."

The quest—and in some cases punishment—of the object of the fixation becomes a way to alleviate the torment. "You feel so bad, you'll do any pursuit to get out of the way you feel. Because you've been crushed . . . . The abandonment that you're feeling just makes you feel so horrible you want to die . . . . You just don't want to be you anymore. It's maddening."

BUT HOW DOES a person supposedly so much in love rationalize doing harm to the object of his affections? Some stalkers blame their targets for the failure of the fantasy relationship and for the resulting frustration, pain, and emptiness they suffer. Others believe that the objects of their obsession really do love them but just don't know it. Thus, the stalkers conclude that the power of their love justifies any actions they take.

In a paper titled "Unrequited Love and the Wish to Kill," forensic psychology consultant J. Reid Meloy, PhD, suggested that at some level, a "perceptual fusion" exists between the obsessed individual's sense of self and the identity of the love object. This perceived union of identities may involve projecting onto the victim the character traits the stalker doesn't like in himself. Conversely, a stalker may envy those characteristics he lacks. Either way, as this narcissistic self-absorption—so characteristic of identity disturbances—amplifies, empathic regard for others diminishes, thereby increasing the likelihood of violence.

This kind of egocentrism can also lead to liberal re-interpreting of the facts of a situation. George Martin-Trigona's pursuit of Florida anchorwoman Jane Akre included researching her "to find out what made this woman tick," and contacting her boyfriend's ex-wife in order to discover more about him. Operating by the philosophy that "all is fair in love and war," he remained convinced that he had been a perfect gentleman, even though his unwanted attentions frightened Jane, prompting her to seek and obtain a restraining order against him. Instead of identifying his behavior as harassment, he saw it as the natural order of things. "If men gave up on the first or the second attempt at pursuing a woman, the human species would have died out a million years ago," he reasoned. "I'm not stalking her. I just want her to know that I'm the right guy for her."

Gavin de Becker would call him a "scriptwriter." Not only did George expect Jane to respond to him, he created a complex scenario that justified his conduct. He had already developed unrealizable expectations of how she would respond. In this case, he met her rejection of him with denial. Other scriptwriters try to manipulate situations, and may eventually use fear as a strategy to make the situation accord with their preconceived notions. Their expectations, rather than reality, drive their behavior.

Richard Wade Farley, the man who stalked Laura Black for four years, typifies this trait. The personal movie he had "written" starred himself and Laura as the happy couple settling down for life. That he barely knew her and that she wanted nothing to do with him was beside the point. The attractive brunette with the engaging smile fit the bill, and was therefore expected to play the role.

Once the curtain had risen on Rich's imaginary relationship, Laura's reactions to him—whether positive or negative—simply fed the fantasy. In his mind, she had already bought into his project. She just didn't know it. So he managed to justify her pulling away from him for a time. Once he was no longer able to ignore or rationalize her rejections, however, disappointment crystallized into hostility.

Rich could not accept that Laura wanted nothing to do with him. "For Richard Farley, letting go was tantamount to jumping off an emotional cliff. It was something he could not do," argued his defense attorney during the trial's opening statements. "And in the face of the rejection, he did the only thing that he could do: he followed the only path that in his own mind he could follow, and that was to pursue Laura Black."

In other words, Rich decided that the woman of whom he had become enamored did not have the right to reject him. That's not a particularly new—or unfamiliar—concept among men. In the 1981 *Hite Report*, the two most frequently mentioned qualities used to define what it means to be a man were being in command of a situation and dominance. As a result, their counterparts have historically had little voice and even less power.

THE WOMEN'S MOVEMENT has challenged this patriarchal notion on both the personal and professional fronts. But relinquishing prior dominance doesn't always come easy. In domestic situations, for example, men used to calling the shots feel compelled to react when the woman decides to leave. By refusing to let go when they've been rejected, they're not only asserting male power, they're protecting their own identities, which are bound up in the masculine myth.

"Stalking is a crime of power and control, both of which can be very intoxicating," said Michael Paymar, whose work with men who batter their partners brought him into contact with male stalkers. "The stalker's message is that you, as a woman, cannot make the decision."

Consider O.J. Simpson's relationship with Nicole. "She was right out of high school, this sweet young thing. She didn't even know who he was. He scooped her up . . . brought her into his life, and, dammit, she was *his,*" a close friend of the couple told *People* shortly after her murder.

Accordingly, she was his to abuse—physically and emotionally—during the marriage and after the divorce. Like most stalkers, however, that's not what O.J. sees when considering his history with Nicole. "I loved her, always have and always will," he wrote on June 17 in what many considered a suicide letter, but which experts termed a textbook example of a spouse abuser's denial. "If we had a problem, it's because I loved her so much."

ALTHOUGH FAMOUS, IN many ways O.J. typifies the male stalker. But what about female stalkers? Although their cultural conditioning differs from their counterparts, they share the belief that they have a right to dictate or govern someone else's life.

When Janice Huston*, who stands five feet eight inches tall and is in her early twenties, needed a place to stay, Arnold Washman*, 33, offered to put her up. Two weeks later, he asked her to move out. That didn't jibe with the scenario Janice had conjured for their future. So she tried to force him to change his mind. Her intimidation campaign included sitting outside his home and threatening to kill him, his family, his friends, his dogs. Being arrested for trespassing the day before New Year's Eve didn't discourage her. It inflamed her. Three months later, she broke into Arnold's house and found the revolver she knew he kept. Luckily, Arnold awoke and managed to disarm her. Janice pleaded guilty to stalking and was sentenced to one year in county jail and 24 months of formal probation. The prison sentence was suspended, however, contingent on her seeking counseling. So she served just the 36 days that preceded the trial.

The short time in jail did little to squelch Janice's obsession. Upon her release, she began to stake out Arnold's house and then follow him whenever he left. In addition, she continually harassed him, as well as members of his family, on the phone, eventually threatening the life of Arnold's girlfriend.

Finally, she climbed the steps of Arnold's porch in the middle of the night and started pounding on his front door. Arnold didn't answer. Still she refused to leave. Her anger overflowed into threats. "I'm going to burn down your house," she promised. "I'm going to end your life if you don't let me in!" Then she issued the standard stalker's battle cry: "I have a gun and I'm going to kill you. If I can't have you, no one will."

IRONICALLY, THOSE WHO strive to control relationships in this way often have been denied control over their own lives. "When you have someone who has not had very much power and is looking for something over which to exercise power, the individual becomes a non-entity in the equation," said Threat Assessment Group senior analyst and former FBI supervisory special agent Jim Wright. "For certain personalities, part of the satisfaction they obtain from stalking is the terror they instill. He can leave a note and see you react. He can make a phone call and hear you react. He can see you keeping your drapes closed 24 hours a day. And suddenly, he has a tremendous amount of power over another's life. For every action that he takes, he sees a reaction. It's like pulling the strings of a marionette."

Consider Edward Warren, the aerospace engineer who promised to shove Veronica Grayton, a former co-worker, into the ground. Taken away from his mother after she was deemed an unfit parent and raised by his father, a cold man who provided neither love nor encouragement, Edward never developed a healthy sense of self. Although his teeth were so crooked that he refused to smile, he never considered getting braces until his former wife, Gabriela Warren*, suggested it. "That was something that other people do," she recalled. "He wasn't good enough."

Edward had proven his brilliance when he made the leap from machinist to engineer with a perfect test score. But although that helped his self-esteem, it wasn't enough. Then, at age 31, he discovered cocaine. "He got hooked instantly," said Gabriela. When his cocaine habit became too expensive to support, he switched to speed.

Edward had always had an addictive personality, whether it came to watching the news, smoking, or gambling to the point of maxing out all the family's credit cards. But his excessive drug use seemed to trigger the mental disturbance that set in during his early thirties. Although he remained a devoted father to his two children, his moods swung for no apparent reason. Suddenly his driving became dangerously wild. A drop in his work performance cost him his job. He lost his wife as well.

After his marriage crumbled, he became increasingly paranoid, whether about a stranger at the door or the space aliens he knew abounded. That's when he began to focus on Veronica. It was as if she provided him with a fixed point on which to center a life gone astray. Through his fantasies, he could turn her into whatever he wanted. And through his phone calls and letters, he could manipulate her reactions to him. He was back in control.

That's the key. How stalkers achieve that power over someone else, however, is limited only by their imagination.

Safety Is What Counts

If you've become the victim of obsessive attention, you've probably spent a lot of time and effort trying to get your stalker to stop what he's doing. But let's face it. Stalkers, by definition, are obsessed; they're not about to listen to reason. The only behavior you can change is your own. And that's just what you need to do. By changing your routines—including where you hang out—you may be able to discourage your pursuer. This isn't fair; but when it comes to your safety, it is reality.

5

Courting Disaster

STALKERS KNOW WHOM TO TARGET and just how to get to their victims. That's what makes them so insidious. When you don't respond according to plan, they'll often switch venues or even target whoever they feel is getting in the way.

Deborah Pritt's* stalker, Betty Taylor*, did both. The moment she could no longer elicit satisfying reactions from Deborah's husband, to whom she had developed a fatal attraction, she brought Deborah into the loop. When Deborah and her husband refused to play along, she forced them to. Her final weapon of choice? The very court system that should have protected the couple.

DEBORAH FOUND OUT about her husband's affair with Betty almost three weeks after a woman she had never seen pulled up behind her in a Charleston, South Carolina, fast-food drive-through and walked up to her car window. "You know, two can play that game," the skinny brunette said to her. Deborah had no idea what she was talking about.

The stranger followed the mother of three to the mall where she worked as a receptionist at the customer service desk. Fifteen minutes into the morning staff meeting, the office phone rang. Deborah picked it up. "I'm fucking your husband, I'm fucking your husband. Na, na, na, na, na," said a female voice that

Deborah recognized from her recent encounter. "Pardon me?" Deborah replied. "Na, na, na, na, na," repeated the caller before hanging up.

"Boy, you really ticked this person off," one of her co-workers joked. Everyone laughed. Deborah shrugged it off. "I must have pulled out in front of someone on my way to work," she thought. The matter, however, would not be so easily disposed of.

For the next two weeks, the woman followed her wherever she went. Some mornings she would wave to Deborah as she passed by. On others, she would menace her. She would drive alongside of Deborah and glare at her, take her picture, mouth obscenities or attempt to run her off the road. "This is nuts," thought Deborah. "She doesn't even know who I am."

A second phone call at work—which brought her husband, Dave*, into the picture again—only added to her confusion. "Where, oh where is Davie?" chanted the female voice that Deborah had already grown to recognize.

Finally, she reported the incidents to her boss, who called in the woman's license plate number and, through connections at the DMV, obtained a name and an address. Neither rang a bell with Deborah. He advised her to call the police, which she did. "I'll contact this individual and get back to you," said the officer who took the report. Two days later, her husband confessed his adultery. The woman harassing Deborah had been his lover for a single afternoon.

The hefty electrician had met Betty Taylor while walking the family dog in a county park. She approached him, saying that a black man had accosted her in the woods and would he please walk her to her car. Over a period of three months, she would run into him—at first just on the weekends, then almost daily—and join him for a stroll. Soon he began to receive letters from her, all expounding on the theme that his wife and children were taking advantage of him. "Poor man! Your life is a living hell," she wrote, adding that one day soon his wife and his three kids would leave him. "You're gonna get to be an old shell of a man with absolutely no one."

Dave had never strayed during his 25-year marriage. But the barrage, along with her insistent kisses and caresses during their walks, was beginning to weaken his resolve, although apparently not quickly enough for his admirer. "Look," she finally told him. "Your goose is gonna be cooked, one way or another, 'cause all I have to do is tell your wife that we had an affair. She'll throw you out and you're gonna lose everything. So you might as well go ahead and have some fun while you're at it."

So, on a Thursday afternoon in September, he slept with her. By the following Monday, he had decided to call it off. "I can't do this. It isn't worth it," he told her.

BETTY DIDN'T TAKE the news well. She began to follow him, tracking him down when he walked the dog even though he made a point of rotating his destinations. At night, she would wait for his return from his 12-hour swing shift. When he ran late, she would ring the front doorbell and then take off. She left packages for Dave at work, and gifts (like a figurine that resembled Stoney, the family dog) for him in the Pritts' mailbox. And, over a period of six months, she left letters taped to his steering wheel or the back door, and mailed others to his office. Most referred to Black Monday, her code name for the day he had called a halt to their affair.

At first she focused on the great love she and Dave shared, assuming responsibility for what had happened. She apologized for the pain she had caused. That same letter, however, referred to the inevitable nature of their relationship: "This love of ours is just meant to be."

Soon, extolling their supposedly predestined relationship took a back seat to berating Dave for the nature of his marriage as well as his treatment of her. Her written missives and recorded messages betrayed not only her hurt, but also the desire to lash out in kind at those she blamed for her pain. "I just wanted to die and kill you with me," she wrote. He had deliberately allowed her to be hurt, she indicated. As a result, she prayed that he and his soul rot in perpetual hell.

She threatened to tell Deborah about the affair and speculated about how she could get her revenge. "I might just hit you with a Mack truck," she fantasized in one letter.

In the end, however, she opted for hurting him financially, through attorney and settlement fees resulting from the court cases she levied against him.

BETTY'S HARASSMENT BEGAN to take its toll. Suddenly, Dave's blood pressure shot up uncontrollably. A birthday card from her made him feel as if she were closing in on him even more. Although the sentiment expressed seemed almost like a truce declaration, Dave's pursuer had listed his place of birth. Since he knew that she could not have gotten the information from his driver's license, he had to assume that she had found a way to retrieve the information using his Social Security number. The knowledge that she was investigating him unnerved Dave. Her threats terrified him.

Still, he thought he could keep his indiscretion from his wife. He did take certain precautions, like installing motion detectors outside their home and caller ID to their phone service. Deborah assumed that he was simply being a typical man wanting to ex-periment with new toys. When his wife filed a police report in April, however, he realized that she was going to learn the truth eventually and that he had to come clean.

"It was too much in the beginning to grasp," Deborah re-called. "Some of the story sounded so far-fetched that I couldn't help harboring little pockets of doubt." But the subsequent let-ters that arrived in the mail verified every word Dave had told her. Still, Deborah couldn't squelch her anger, especially since he had brushed off her bewilderment over Betty's harassment of her. Comments like "that's crazy" had made her feel as though she were losing her mind.

It took Deborah a while to come to terms with her resentment toward Dave and her feelings of betrayal. "Eventually, however, I was able to set those aside and see the incident for what it really was: a stupid mistake," she said. "Ultimately, he was the first victim. I couldn't have done anything worse to him than she was already doing. She punished him for me."

THE MORNING AFTER Dave confessed to his wife, the police officer who had taken Deborah's report of harassment returned to her workplace. "I've contacted this individual and she doesn't know anything about it," he told her. "If you have anything further to say, you're to speak with her attorney." A few days later, that attorney notified Deborah's employers that they could expect to be sued for violation of privacy. Shortly thereafter, Deborah and Dave learned that The Fury, as they now referred to her, had filed well over 50 lawsuits against others, most of which had been settled out of court. They would soon have a solid firsthand understanding of just how damaging such harassment can be.

First, however, came more standard stalking patterns. Like the time Dave decided to stop at the mall to see Deborah following a doctor's appointment. As he pulled into the parking lot, he noticed Betty's car behind him. She approached his car and told him she had a recording she wanted him to listen to. "I don't want any contact with you," he responded. When he started to drive off in order to end the conversation, she grabbed his left arm, gouging it with her fingernails as he jerked away.

Dave pressed charges of assault. Three months later, on August 1, Betty got her revenge. At 9:30 P.M., while Deborah was napping on the couch in front of the television, the police knocked on the front door and promptly placed her under arrest. Betty had filed a statement with the police saying that it was Deborah who had been threatening her.

Deborah was charged with disorderly conduct. The case was tried at the beginning of September. She was found not guilty.

Less than two months later, she was once again arrested following a complaint from Betty, this time for reckless driving. According to Betty, Deborah had braked abruptly on the turnpike, almost causing a rear-end collision. Instead of questioning Deborah's accuser about why she was following Deborah's vehicle so closely—or at all—the judge issued a continuance. "If there's no more activity in the next year, then we'll just dismiss all the charges," he said.

To a person like Betty Taylor, who had admitted to putting nails in the driveway of the last married man with whom she had had an affair, that must have sounded like an open invitation. "It was as if the judge just painted a great big bull's-eye on my back and gave her a year to find the dead center of it," said Deborah.

During the next 12 months, Betty filed seven lawsuits against Deborah and four against Dave. In addition, she filed countless complaints against both. She also continued to besiege Dave with convoluted letters that would swing from accusing the Pritts and their attorney of lying about her, to reminiscing about the feelings that, in her mind, she and Dave had shared. "I have never loved anyone the way I love you, just like I know you never loved anyone like you loved me."

Either way, she blamed Deborah for all that had transpired. "God damn Deborah for starting this shit," she wrote in one note. The sentiment would be repeated often, along with her promise to "nail Deborah's ass to the wall" in retribution. "She started this mess, but I *will* end it and I will *never* forget!"

Frequently, she would send three copies of the same letter—mailing one, messengering another, and delivering a third by hand—to the Pritts. Some correspondence actually addressed Deborah directly. But for the most part, Betty preferred harassing her in person. Wearing mirrored sunglasses and a look of fury that seemed to say, "I'm ready to rip your face off," she would circle Deborah's centrally located desk. "There were times when I'd be sitting there and I would feel as if someone had just kicked me in the gut," Deborah recalled. "And I'd look up and there she'd be, glaring at me."

A birthday card left in the cabinet behind Deborah's office chair allowed little doubt about Betty's intentions. On the front, a black hooded figure with red glowing eyes held a birthday cake. Inside the message read, "You can run, but you can't hide."

At first, management was supportive of Deborah's situation. But Betty threatened to sue the company for up to $5,000 for invasion of privacy stemming from the Department of Motor Vehicles inquiry Deborah's boss had made. When the case was settled out of court for $1,500, Deborah's superiors issued what amounted to a gag order. She was to discuss her stalking situation with no one at work. No matter what Betty did, Deborah was to treat her strictly as a mall customer. Their restrictions made Deborah feel like a leper.

Even county police officers who once would routinely stop to chat began to avoid her. They couldn't understand her reluctance to prosecute. Yet her attorney had advised her not to play into Betty's game. Although the activity was clearly illegal, pursuing the issue would have only encouraged The Fury and provoked a lifetime of harassment.

Deborah and Dave weren't the only family members hurt by Betty's obsessiveness. When Deborah told her youngest son that a woman in a white truck persisted in following her to and from work, the child blanched. He had seen the same truck slowly cruise past the house, make a U-turn and return. The incident had spooked him so badly that he had fled inside, closed the door and peeped out through the curtains.

"We wound up apologizing to our kids," Deborah recalled. "They have been exposed to things—like their mother being arrested—that no one should have to see."

Ten months later, Betty renewed her judicial assault on the Pritts by filing four charges of harassment, slander and assault against Deborah and two charges of malicious prosecution and slander against Dave. Acting as her own attorney, she asked the court to assess actual and punitive damages in the amount of $7,000 for each. That summer all six cases were either dropped (at least temporarily) or dismissed.

Despite the positive outcome, the experience haunted Deborah, especially since Betty, acting as her own counsel, had great leeway with questioning during the trial. Peering close into Deborah's face, her eyes heavily lined in black, she verbally eviscerated her witness.

"How did it make you feel to know that your husband had an affair with an older woman?" she asked.

"I don't really know," Deborah replied.

"You don't know? You don't know much, do you?"

Deborah responded to every question. She was challenged each time. "You hate me, don't you? You really hate me?" Betty demanded at one point. "Now don't lie to me. You can't lie in court."

NOT LONG AFTER, Deborah dreamed that she was being operated on while still conscious. In the dream, she looks at her exposed intestines when a surgeon wearing a mask heads toward her. The heavily made-up eyes leave no doubt as to the surgeon's identity. Deborah lies paralyzed, completely exposed. There's nothing she can do to protect herself. "I woke up screaming," she recalled.

Deborah also began to fear for her own safety, especially since Betty seemed to materialize every time she got in her car or went to the store. "In her eyes, I'm the person to get rid of," she said, aware that Betty viewed her as the major barrier between herself and Dave. "I spend my time running from Betty."

Although she now recognizes the wisdom of not filing coun-ter-charges against the woman or obtaining a restraining order (which her attorney had also advised against in her particular situation), at the time the decision made Deborah feel like a sacrificial lamb. "I felt like enough was enough, that somebody needed to do something to save me," she said.

That sense of abandonment was compounded when she com-plained to two police officers after Betty had followed her to work, and later overheard one of them say, "Oh yeah, she's one of those two women that keep accusing each other of following each other." That was the last time she called the police, despite Betty's ongoing harassment, which has cost the Pritts upward of $10,000 (including attorney fees, therapist fees, medications and lost income due to so many court appearances).

Deborah and Dave had made a point to schedule time every evening in which to update each other on any new developments and to share their frustrations. "Oh God, I got another letter today. This one's a beaut!" Dave would tell her. But Deborah's fermenting anger frightened him. "I just don't understand this, none of this makes any sense," she would yell, her arms flailing. Oppressed by his own turmoil and struggling with severe guilt over what he had precipitated, Dave had trouble handling his wife's emotional outbursts. All he could do was apologize.

Deprived of an outlet at home and at work, Deborah began to internalize her stress. Although she had coped well up until then, she slipped into a profound depression. Suddenly she couldn't concentrate. She couldn't sleep. She felt nauseated all the time. Persistent headaches, along with pains in the back of her neck and shoulders, almost incapacitated her. Her blood pressure, which had never been a problem, skyrocketed.

Finally, she went to see a therapist who had worked with other stalking victims. On her first visit, she brought in several of the letters Betty had written. "For over a year, I had been forced to prove my whereabouts and my actions to the police and to the courts," Deborah explained. "Because in the back of people's minds, there's that shadow of a doubt that said, if these charges have been filed against you then something must be wrong."

The psychologist provided critical reassurance and reaffirmation. "You're dealing with a borderline personality disorder," he announced after reading over the stalker's letters. Then he referred Deborah to the staff psychiatrist who could prescribe a low dosage of anti-depressants. He diagnosed her with Post-Traumatic Stress Disorder, commonly known as PTSD or "shell shock," the condition that many Vietnam, Iraq and Afghanistan veterans have experienced.

Although her physical symptoms began to abate within two weeks, Deborah remained on anti-depressants for nearly a year. Her emotional state improved rapidly as the psychologist helped her come to terms with what was happening to her. "He validated my anger and my fears and let me express them," Deborah said. "He told me that it was okay and that there was a reason to be afraid." Her sessions with him proved to be her safety zone— the one place she could share her nightmare and be supported rather than judged.

Betty's activity has subsided, but there's been no concrete resolution to the stalking. Despite the counseling, the experience continues to impact Deborah. "I feel a tremendous loss of self," she said. "It used to be that everyone I met was a potential friend. And I don't feel that way anymore. I'm very guarded now. The other night the Fraternal Order of the Police called me about buying tickets to a fundraiser they were holding. When the officer attempted to verify my mailing address, I freaked out. 'How do I know you're a police officer,' I told him. 'I'm not talking anymore.' After hanging up on him I thought to myself, 'My God, I thought you'd gotten past that.'"

Deflect Weapons of Destruction

How your perpetrator chooses to manipulate or harm you is almost beside the point when it comes to stalking, especially since the way a stalker tries to inflict emotional, financial or physical damage is limited only by his or her imagination. You can limit the impact by how you respond to the situation. When possible, don't play his or her game.

6

Limit the Obsessive
Interaction

STALKING IS LIKE A LONG RAPE. The stalker's objective is to force you into surrender. Victims respond not with a single reaction, but with a progression of emotions akin to Elisabeth Kubler-Ross's five stages of loss: denial, bargaining, guilt, anger and then acceptance. But because you participate, however unwillingly, in the crime, you also experience depression, anxiety and fear.

Put yourself in the place of a stalking victim. Whether you've just split up with a mate who refuses to let you go, or attracted the unwanted attention of a co-worker or stranger, what would your first reaction be? "This can't be happening," you would say to yourself. "Things like this happen to other people. Not to me." Then you would assume that you must be imagining the whole affair. "I'm just over-reacting. I must be paranoid."

By doubting your own reality, you've begun to doubt yourself. In one quick step, you've put yourself at a disadvantage.

When you finally realize or accept the fact that you *are* being victimized, you try to bargain with your stalker. If you can just appease him by giving in to some of his wishes, then maybe he'll leave you alone, you figure. "Okay, fine," you tell him. "I'll meet you for coffee." But the demands escalate. And now that you've established a precedent, the stalker expects you to respond in similar fashion.

Anxiety sets in. Never knowing when or where he's going to turn up or what he's going to do next, you can think of little else. You don't feel safe at home, at work, or anywhere else. The more frightened you become, the more debilitating your anxiety. In trying to cope with the situation and manage your emotions, you basically start to short-circuit. "You're using so much mental energy that you begin to eat up your supply of neural transmitters," explained Dan Coler, a Richmond, Virginia, psychotherapist. "At which point the synapses of your brain start shutting down and large parts of your brain just stop functioning. Suddenly you can't concentrate. You feel like you're an ant struggling to carry a matchstick. Little things that never bothered you before are major catastrophes."

Exhausted, you have no resources left.

That's when the depression hits, so profound that you feel like you're in a deep dark hole that you can never climb out of. Your self-esteem begins to disintegrate. You can't function normally. Recurrent nightmares, sleep and eating disorders, and a growing sense of apprehension about everything afflict you.

You begin to wonder why this has happened to you, what you did to encourage it. Should you have said yes to him? Should you have said no more firmly? If you had just walked the other way, taken another job, or married someone more suitable, none of this would have happened, you reason. Then, as if to cement those notions of culpability, the stalker goes after someone close to you. Maybe the person you're dating. Or your mother. "You can't control what he does," said the therapist you've started to see. It doesn't help.

With time you begin to realize that you're not to blame. As with the rapist, the stalker's act is what counts. You just happened to be there. The more fully you acknowledge how little the situation actually has to do with you, the harder it is to countenance the impact the stalker has had on your life. You get angry—so angry that you're ready to do almost anything to get him out of your life.

Finally, you accept what your life has become. And while you mourn the innocence, trust and insouciance that you've lost, you can finally start to deal with your situation objectively. Which means that you can finally limit your ongoing role in the obsessive interaction.

IF YOU'RE A stalking victim, you certainly can't be blamed for the harassment to which you're subjected. But you may have inadvertently contributed to the problem. Most stalking cases—those that don't involve public figures—aren't lightning strikes or shark attacks. "There is something about who the stalker selects and where he finds his encouragement early on," said Gavin de Becker. "Stalkers, like all predatory criminals, circle around the victim and test her a little bit. With a jab here and a look there, they try to figure out whether their target is going to hurt them, or whether their target is going to play into their scenario."

Once a stalker has selected someone he suspects won't assert herself, he'll most often manipulate his victim through fear. But guilt also serves as a valuable weapon for establishing a power base.

Theresa Esquibel met Ted Miller*, a resident in her college dorm, in the fall of her freshman year in college. The two clicked well and soon started sharing the intimate details of their lives. He talked of the problems he'd had with his parents and of an early attempt at suicide. And he helped boost Theresa's self-esteem, which a serious car accident and long recovery had shattered.

Midway through the fall quarter, Theresa began to realize that her new confidant might want to be more than her friend. A discussion just before the holidays relieved her concerns about his interest. "I love you as a sister, nothing more," he told her. "But that means a lot to me because I'm an only child." Later that night, after they had spent hours talking, he began to hold her. Although the contact wasn't sexual, the physical closeness made her uncomfortable. Even so, she said nothing, hoping she was wrong. The Bible that Ted gave her for Christmas, however, clearly betrayed his true feelings. On the inside cover, in tiny print, he had carefully written the words *I love you* over and over again, line after line, covering a page and a half. "That's so you'll always think of me," he told her.

Theresa returned from the holiday break feeling stronger and more ready to deal with the mental and emotional rigors of fitting in to college life. Of course, investing more energy into her classes and reaching out to new people meant that she had less time for Ted. He took it personally. "You never come by my place. I always have to come find you," he would say. Or, "I left two messages on your machine, and you've been back from class for five minutes."

He began to monitor her arrival in the dorm and to show up at her door immediately upon her return. When she told him that she needed some time alone, he accused her of not being a true friend. The hostility increased when she began to date someone steadily. Theresa tried to maintain their friendship, but that was getting harder and harder. "It was like I was his wife and not treating him fairly."

Unable to contain his jealousy, Ted would pepper Theresa with questions about her relationships with other men. Then he would sit on the dorm landing and chronicle her comings and goings. One night as she and Joe, her boyfriend, left for a dinner date, he heaved a book against the wall just as the elevator doors shut. When Theresa later questioned the violence of his reaction, he told her that he wanted to make a point to them before they went out, in a way that would give them no time to react to him.

Life had begun to close in on Ted. Upset about his father's plans to re-marry, devastated by the news that a close high school friend was fatally ill, he couldn't bear the notion of losing his main source of emotional support. In an effort to hold onto Theresa, he became controlling and domineering. "Don't you ever reveal anything I tell you," he said to the increasingly intimidated young woman. "I'll be able to tell if you have just by looking at your face."

As the weeks passed, Ted's anger grew. He accused Theresa of betrayal, and tried to intimidate her with allusions to the kinds of violence of which he was capable. "I have so much anger, I could kill anyone who wrongs me, and I would if I ever lost control," he told her at one point. Another time, he threatened to kill Joe.

One night he called her room. "Goodbye," he said into the phone in a quivering voice. Afraid of the message's implications, Theresa raced to his room. When he finally agreed to let her in, she found him sitting at his desk, his eyes expressionless, his lips pressed tightly together. Lined up before him were six bottles of prescription medications.

Theresa spent the night trying to dissuade him from killing himself. He responded by trying to get close physically. "You are responsible for my life, I have no one else to count on," he told her while caressing her face. "Don't leave me. You are the only one who can help me."

As the weeks went by, Ted continued to monitor Theresa's activities and to try to control her actions, especially with regard to Joe. "Did you fuck him?" he asked upon the couple's return from an impromptu trip to San Francisco. "I'll find out anyway," he said when she refused to answer. "Word will get out. I'll know."

By the time Ted dropped out of school later that year, he had succeeded in making Theresa feel responsible for his decline. Four years later, she finally began to come to terms with the idea that he was emotionally and mentally unstable. But his face still haunted her dreams.

SOCIETY ENCOURAGES WOMEN to be soft and loving, and to use their sexuality—in the guise of smiles, flattering clothes and gentility—to deal with the world in general and men in particular. To a potential stalker, those traits can be interpreted as receptiveness or malleability. That's usually all the encouragement he needs.

Take Theresa. Ted tested the waters by initiating physical contact more appropriate to lovers than friends. Although she felt uneasy, she said nothing because she didn't want to offend him or damage their friendship. Sign number one. Then he put guilt trips on her, about not calling, about seeing other people. Instead of getting angry or resolutely establishing her position, she equivocated and tried to explain. By the time he threatened to kill himself, he could be fairly certain that Theresa would respond to the script he had written in his mind as precisely as if she had rehearsed the role for months. By not challenging Ted's obvious obsession, Theresa encouraged it.

Differences in conversational styles between men and women contributed to her unintentional support of the situation. Typically, women don't communicate their desires directly. Even as girls, they tend to express preferences as suggestions rather than commands. Uncomfortable situations are discussed or alluded to rather than disputed.

Men usually don't have such compunctions. If they want something or don't want something, they say so. So when a woman doesn't speak her mind, men often assume that their behavior is acceptable—especially if that's what they want to believe.

"Much—even most—meaning in conversation does not reside in the words spoken at all, but is filled in by the person listening," writes Deborah Tannen, PhD, in her best-selling book *You Just Don't Understand*. If misinterpretations occur when people speak plainly, just think of the potential for distortion when objections are couched obliquely or never voiced at all.

While most men don't hesitate to say what they think, they too can fall into the trap of protecting someone's feelings at the expense of a message that the other party can't deny.

WHEN NATE SERENDON* gave Edith Barstow* a place to stay after she had gotten into a fight with the man who had brought her to a local ski resort for the weekend, he thought they might wind up in bed. He didn't expect the buxom brunette to leave her belongings at his condominium. Nor did he expect the relationship that evolved. It was as if their one night together had given her license to stay with him whenever she wanted. "I never really told her differently," Nate admitted. "After a month of casual dating, I tried to give her subtle hints that we weren't getting along, that we were not compatible and that maybe we should go our separate ways. But it started getting worse, because I couldn't say no."

Edith began calling him at his job to yell about his unwillingness to make the relationship work. "All she wanted to do was fight about it, and all I wanted was for her to be out of my life. But she couldn't accept that," Nate recalled. Still, he couldn't bring himself to advise her of the blunt truth.

It took Nate six months to pack up Edith's belongings and finally inform her that she was no longer welcome in his home. Her harassment of him would last two years beyond that. "I was too nice. If I hadn't been so compassionate at certain times, she would maybe have gotten the message sooner," he said. Yet he doesn't believe he compromised his message by not being more direct. "I couldn't have been clearer," he asserted, apparently forgetting those months when he refused to confront her even though he had begun to feel that he would never get her out of his life.

THAT INABILITY OR unwillingness to impose limits and set boundaries for fear of hurting someone sends out a signal as clear as a green light.

Leta Koups*, a 32-year-old wife and mother of a 4-year-old, had worked in the South Bend, Indiana, public library for about a year when a newspaper journalist started to do research there. Before long, Shana Billingsley*, a tall, thin woman in her late thirties, was coming in daily. She would spend three to four hours there, check out up to six books and then be back the following day. Pleased to have such a steady patron, Leta helped Shana with her project as much as she could.

At the end of the first week, the journalist brought her an assortment of fruit. Leta chalked it up to a token of gratitude. But the gifts kept coming, and got bigger. The flowers, candies, and books made Leta uncomfortable, but she didn't protest. Friends dismissed her concerns. "She's just lonely," said one.

That fall, Shana moved to Indianapolis. That's when the letters started, at least two to three a week and at least three pages long. Although the correspondence struck Leta as odd, the two women continued to see each other from time to time. On Leta's birthday, Shana wanted to celebrate. So Leta drove down, and Shana took her to dinner at a seafood restaurant. After dinner, she had Leta select from eight separate desserts that she had picked up at a special bakery in a neighboring town. Then they went to the theater—again Shana's treat. "This is too much," Leta thought. Still, she didn't protest.

The letters, always intense, got darker. "I felt suicidal until you called," read one. So did the phone calls berating Leta for not coming to visit and for not doing as much for her as she did for Leta. It was as if Shana was keeping score. Eventually, she suggested that Leta leave her husband (whom the journalist considered to be an arrogant jerk) and move in with her.

Finally, Leta couldn't take anymore. "I can't be the kind of friend you need," she announced over the phone. "I have a husband and a child. I can't reciprocate in the way you want."

Shana lost all control. After a few minutes, Leta hung up on her screams. "I'm the type of person who never hurts anyone's feelings. I never say no," the librarian said in retrospect. "Maybe I should have."

THERESA, NATE AND Leta were doing what most of us were taught to do. They were being nice. To the obsessive, however, that can easily be misconstrued.

Diane DiMarco, now a nurse, started volunteering at a hospital in Los Angeles when she was 15 years old. At the time, she worked in the rehabilitation department, where every summer a group of older teenagers returned for physical therapy. Among them was Albert Rossner*, who had lost most of the mobility on his left side after being hit by a motorcycle. Two years after the accident, he still walked with a limp, and could not even hold a pen in his left hand.

Albert developed an attachment to the pretty volunteer with the sweet disposition and quick laugh. He followed her while she worked and hung out with her on her breaks. Diane was not entirely pleased with the attention. "But I was young, nice, and didn't want to hurt anyone's feelings," she said. So she let him be her shadow.

Although Diane chose not to judge Albert harshly, his actions aroused concern among her friends. One of the other teenagers in the rehab group stopped her late one night. "I want you to know that I stole his records and he's a really dangerous person," he told her. "You shouldn't be around him."

Diane heard the words but not the message. "You shouldn't have stolen those records. You could get in trouble," she said to the boy. "Don't worry about me. Just think about your own rehab."

"I'm serious," he insisted. "This guy is dangerous."

Diane brushed the warning aside. Within weeks, however, Albert grabbed her when she didn't accede to a request. "Let go, you're hurting me!" Diane demanded. Luckily, another volunteer passing by told Albert to leave Diane alone.

"She's my girlfriend," Albert countered.

He left at the end of the summer, but returned to the facility that Christmas with a ring in hand. "By then, I was at least smart enough to say, 'No, I can't take this,'" recalled Diane. Shortly thereafter, Albert got kicked out of the hospital for having sex with another patient. That's when Diane's problems intensified.

First, Albert secured Diane's address from the hospital register, which she had to sign every time she came to work. Then he began to write her letters. Increasingly, his penmanship, which he had to relearn following his accident, assumed the stylized characteristics of Diane's printing. Then he started to call, usually in the middle of the night.

The intrusions upset Diane's parents. "This is your fault," they told her. "You encouraged him." They refused to allow Diane to take the calls, and finally she stopped answering his letters.

Albert dropped from sight for nine months, only to appear outside Diane's house one afternoon as she was returning from school. Afraid, she drove past her home to the graphic arts studio she now worked at part-time and called home. "He came to say hi," her mom explained. "I told him you weren't there and wouldn't be there."

But Albert had seen Diane head to the studio and followed her. To protect her, the studio personnel lied and said she was nowhere to be found. So Albert asked to use the bathroom, remaining locked inside a long time. The smell that lingered after he left suggested that he had been doing drugs.

A friend of Diane's brother drove her home, even though her parents' house was just five doors away from the art studio. Sure enough, Albert was back at his post. "You stay away or you'll have to deal with me or her brother," the friend said. "And her brother's nuts."

A few months later, Albert wrote Diane from prison where he had been remanded for kidnapping and rape. In the letter, Albert said that he felt it was his duty to apologize to every woman he had ever been around, since he had wronged them all.

Diane panicked. The young man really was dangerous! Although he would obviously be locked away for a number of years, eventually he would get out. Unsure about what to do, Diane consulted her high school counselor. "Phone the prison social worker and say that you don't want to receive any calls from him and that you want to be notified about his release. And notify the hospital about your concerns to help build a case against him should anything happen," she was told.

Diane felt completely alone. She couldn't talk to her parents, since they held her responsible. Her male friends all promised to kick Albert's ass or kill him if he got out and got near. The macho act didn't help, either.

That was 12 years ago. There's been no further contact, except for a single Christmas card that expressed the usual holiday sentiments along with an ominous postscript: "Watch Yourself."

Although Diane has worked hard to forget, Albert's actions did jolt her into the real world. "I was Little Miss Social Worker, there to save the world and make everybody happy," she said. "I thought all these guys were my friends. But when I think about it, they were all a mess."

As DIANE WILL attest, one of the first unwritten rules of courtship (especially for women) is to let an admirer—or even a lover—down easy. "The rejecter usually feels guilty and doesn't know how to say *no* without hurting the pursuer," said Dr. Roy Baumeister, Social Psychology Area Director and Francis Eppes Eminent Scholar at The Florida State University and co-author of *Breaking Hearts: The Two Sides of Unrequited Love*. "So the most common tactic is to lie low, continue to be nice, and wait, hoping the infatuation will fade. It's like a conspiracy of silence, where one person doesn't want to openly speak rejecting words and the other doesn't want to hear them."

That tactic, however, extends the rejection process, allowing the pursuer to become more, rather than less, emotionally involved. "People send mixed messages, saying to the unwanted lover something like, 'You're a nice person, and I'd like to be your friend, but I don't want to get into a relationship just now,'" said Dr. Baumeister. "Even when telling the would-be lover the bad news, the rejecters often sugar-coat the rejection with conciliatory words."

As the would-be lover's sense of involvement grows, so does the likelihood that feelings of betrayal and anger will result when he or she is finally rebuffed.

One stalker killed the fiancé of the woman with whom he was obsessed. Throughout his relentless pursuit, she had maintained contact with him in the hopes of keeping the relationship friendly. Her relatives even got in the act. "She's going to marry someone else, we hope you understand that," they told him. "Now let's leave her alone." Instead of accepting the rejection, however, he responded by removing the obstacle.

Although obsessive individuals often erupt when a relationship fails to meet their expectations, their opening salvos can amount to full-scale seductions. When Gail McNeil met Skip Nelson*, the handsome contractor seemed successful, charming and downright nice. He brought her flowers, took her to dinner, and pampered her with love and attention. Although she was 50 and he only 33, the age difference didn't matter. He adored her. To Gail, whose previous husband had been cold and abusive, Skip seemed like the man she had always been seeking. Even her daughter, Erin, along with the rest of the family, approved of her choice.

Skip's appealing facade in fact hid a virulent cocaine addiction and an obsessive nature that refused to let go of what he had latched onto. Three years later, when Gail, having learned of his habit, demanded that he choose between her and the drugs, he declined.

Instead, when she walked out, he followed the pretty blonde to the city to which she had relocated. And when she wouldn't take him back, he decided to make her life hell. He spied on her. He followed her. He left notes. He called her mother with rambling messages about Gail. He stole her license plates. He pawed through her garbage in the middle of the night. He smeared feces under her car door handles.

"She wasn't buying the image he wanted to project. That's when he lost it," said Gail's daughter, Erin.

ONCE A STALKER has hold, he usually tries to make it increasingly difficult—or costly—for his target to break away. In normal cases of unrequited love, the objects of unwanted pursuit often suffer from feelings ranging from frustration and anger to anxiety and guilt, according to Dr. Baumeister. With stalking, however, the emotions are more analogous to those of a hostage.

Victims usually play right into the situation, especially since their first inclination is to award the benefit of the doubt. They dismiss the behavior with excuses about how the stalker—whom they often know—is probably going through a rough time. When the situation escalates, they try to appease their pursuer by meeting his demands. "Which throws gas on the flames because it endorses the stalker's claim on your life," said psychotherapist Dan Coler, who became involved in the issue when several clients turned out to be stalking victims.

At this point, targets usually become consumed by their own inner conflict. Suddenly they realize that the person they're dealing with is not normal. Bewildered, sometimes terrorized, they're caught between the desire to get away or to call the police, and the desire not to rock the boat.

That ambivalence is accentuated by feelings of being trapped. "That's when the victim starts to disintegrate," said Coler. "Their self-esteem begins to fall apart. They begin to fundamentally doubt their perceptions and judgments." Often they blame themselves for what's happened, a premise that others sometimes support.

Freelance writer Janet Spears* originally met Jack Beardy* in Topeka, Kansas, when she was 33, single and lonely. She liked the bright, happy-go-lucky attorney, even though he still lived with his parents, couldn't hold a job and drank to excess when he became depressed. They became friends and occasional lovers. Jack always managed to be entertaining and romantic, and being with him was highly seductive. He cooked candlelight dinners for her and talked to her more like a close girlfriend than a date. But after working her way through college, Janet was searching for financial security, which she knew Jack could never provide.

Although the relationship had never been exclusive, Jack balked when she started dating men she considered more eligible. Then she met the man she would eventually marry. That made it worse. Jack began to bombard her with gifts—dozens of roses and hundreds of stuffed bears—in an attempt to win her affections. He left notes on her car and long ardent messages on her voicemail. If she stayed out all night, he demanded to know where and with whom she had been. He began to follow her, showing up wherever she and her fiancé happened to be. "At lunch, we'd glance over, and there he'd be," Janet recalled.

Consumed by the belief that he and Janet were soul mates and that Janet just didn't get the picture, Jack started watching her all the time. He called her at work, as well as at home. Long sexual messages were punctuated by crying jags and emotional manipulations. "I know the real you. You're making a mistake," he told her. "No one will ever be as good a lover as I am. No one will ever give you the time and attention that I do." Finally, Janet managed to talk him into seeing a psychologist.

"He's madly in love with you," the therapist reported. "You've giving him mixed messages."

"Maybe that's true," Janet thought. Being bombarded daily with two to three hours of messages about how and why she was making the wrong decision began to tear her up. The stress soon affected her physically and emotionally. "I became very insecure in my relationship with my fiancé," she admitted.

Not even her marriage curbed Jack. Convinced that she could reason with him, Janet met him in the park one afternoon. "I just want to be your friend," he insisted. But when she got pregnant, he began addressing his notes "To the pregnant whore."

Jack finally left town because he couldn't stand living so close to Janet. Yet, despite the two years of grief he inflicted on her, she still feels guilty. "He was one of my best friends," she said.

That remorse, coupled with a sense of culpability, feeds the obsessive interaction beautifully. The victim becomes so vulnerable that the stalker's delusional thinking can actually start sounding reasonable. "If you had seen me as I wanted you to, I wouldn't have done anything to hurt you," asserts the stalker, who is now functioning like a cult leader trying to keep his following of one in line.

"The relationship of victim to stalker is very analogous to the cult dynamic," said Coler. "If you, as a cult follower, want out, the leader will tenaciously hound you and try to twist your sense of reality. In a stalking situation where you've lost control of your life, you cease to trust your sense of reality because your actions cease to have any impact. The more you try to escape, the more entrapped you become."

If the stalker, like the cult leader, succeeds in isolating you from family, friends and co-workers, his task becomes even easier. Without their feedback and support, there's nothing to negate the sense of reality that he strives to instill.

ALTHOUGH ALL KINDS of women have become stalking targets, there are those "professional victims" who have a pattern of attracting this kind of abuse.

Katie Kupowski*, an attractive 50-year-old advertising executive, had a history of unsuccessful relationships with men. After being molested by her father as a child, she wound up marrying the exact same type of man. Her husband molested their daughter, then killed himself. From there, Katie drifted in and out of several marriages and relationships. None succeeded. She had a brief homosexual experience with a friend, but then returned to more traditional relationships. She was involved with a man when Audrey Busman*, a lesbian in her late twenties who had been discharged from the military for homosexual activity, reentered her life.

Katie had worked for Audrey's father in an advertising company in the 1980s and become a family friend. Audrey was a girl at the time. When they ran into each other at a movie theater years later, the women agreed to get together and catch up. Audrey called the following week.

The conversation quickly moved from pleasantries to confidences. "I remember you from when I was a child. You were always very kind," Audrey said. "I've had some real problems, and I'd really like to have someone to talk to."

So they had lunch. Over the next three weeks, an affair evolved. And though Katie found the relationship titillating, the sex was so brutal that it made her feel as if she was being raped. After just three weeks, she tried to back away from the relationship. Audrey, however, had other ideas.

Over the next eight months, the lesbian (whose sister, ironically, had been murdered by a stalker) sent Katie letters and gifts. Frequently she showed up at Katie's house to confront her in person. "When are you going to tell your boyfriend that you're really in love with me?" she demanded. "Why are you doing this to me? I thought you loved me." She even broke in to Katie's house one evening when she was out of town, absconding with her Rolodex and some personal papers.

The intrusions so concerned Katie that she went to the local police department. "There's nothing we can do," she was told. Unwilling to let it go, she called the Los Angeles Police Department's Threat Management Unit (TMU). Specifically created to deal with stalking, the unit took only those cases that meet its strict criteria. After interviewing Katie, they decided to accept hers.

Within days, Audrey had been arrested for burglary and released on bail. The day she got out of jail, she let herself into her father's house and armed herself with the handgun he kept hidden in his closet.

That Sunday, Katie threw a brunch for members of her incest survivor therapy group. She had left her doors and windows open to take advantage of the sun and fresh air. Audrey had no trouble getting in. She confronted Katie in the hallway. "If I can't have a relationship with you, life is not worth living," she announced, pointing the gun at her own head. Katie screamed and bolted over to a neighbor's to call the police. Katie's guests quickly followed suit.

Audrey barricaded herself in the house for the next 10 hours. Occasionally, she would step out on the porch and try to provoke the SWAT team that had moved in. "Shoot me, shoot me," she yelled, waving her gun at various officers. A hostage negotiator tried to reason with her, but it was Katie who finally talked her into laying down the handgun and giving herself up.

A jury convicted Audrey on two felony counts (assault with a deadly weapon and pointing a loaded gun at a police officer). She was sentenced to seven years in jail. Angry and convinced that she is the victim of a conspiracy, she has refused to participate in any therapy. Since being imprisoned, she's sent numerous death threats to her father, and has also threatened the arresting officer, the district attorney, the judge who tried the case and her own attorney. When she's released, she's likely to pose a very real concern to all those she blames for her predicament.

Although Audrey has never menaced Katie Kupowski, the latter could very well head that list. Until then, Katie's air of sweetness and vulnerability will no doubt continue to mark her as a plausible victim to be manipulated. Several summers ago, following the Audrey incident, Katie awoke in her new second story apartment to find a stranger standing over her with a gun.

Regrettably, he had noticed her from his residence across the street and taken an interest. Although he did nothing more than watch her, Katie no longer felt safe. Once again, she had donned the victim's mantle and reengaged in the obsessive interaction.

Defuse Empty Threats

You want to cut off all response to your stalker . . . and even to his or her threats. Your reaction or response is what gives a threat its power—or lack of it—and in large part dictates what happens next. So take precautions and use all the informational and safety resources at your disposal, but don't let him or her know how scared you are.

7

The Toll

STALKINGS THAT RESULT FROM A relationship gone bad are hard enough to fathom. But consider being the target of a man you've never met.

Philip Harris*, now in his late sixties, first picked Jane McAllister, a human resources executive, out of a crowded Richmond, Virginia, community meeting. Philip had disrupted proceedings several times before with disorderly conduct that at one point included unsheathing the hunting knife he wore on his belt and throwing it into the middle of the room. Often the pseudo cowboy launched into tirades against women, denouncing them as sluts and whores. Although aware of his mental instability (his long psychiatric history included involuntary commitments), people tolerated his behavior. "They knew he was crazy, and didn't hold him accountable," said Jane.

That would prove to be a mistake.

Jane—a tall, slender woman with long hands and a cultivated, genteel manner reminiscent of the Quakers—had spoken up at one of the meetings. Shortly thereafter, Philip started calling her. Message after message detailed how much he thought about her and how much he admired her. Then he would ask her out for dinner. The attention disturbed Jane's friends, but she just laughed it off and remained civil toward him.

Jane's upbringing had taught her to accept people others
shunned. When vagrants passed through the middle-class neighborhood where she grew up, Jane's mother always fed them out
on the back steps. "That was a real value we were instilled with:
not to turn people like that away." And so when Philip latched
onto her, she didn't rebuff him even though he was "really
weird, bizarre and most unwelcome."

But Philip interpreted Jane's kindness as a come-on, which
she had never intended. He started sending her love notes, written in lacy calligraphy on flowery stationery. At one point, he
mailed Jane his business card, which listed only his first name,
middle initial and phone number. On it he had scrawled a demand for her to call.

Jane decided to ignore his approaches until the day he cursed
in response to her outgoing message, which promised to return
the call. "Bullshit!" he exclaimed. The abusive response infuri-
ated Jane, so she called his machine. "Don't ever, ever do that
again," she ordered. "It should be quite clear to you that if I
wanted to go out with you, I would have called you."

Amazingly, the calls stopped. The next time she saw him, he
looked like a scolded puppy. If she walked into a meeting he was
attending, he would walk out slowly, his head hung low. Then
he disappeared. Jane was told that he had admitted himself to a
psychiatric hospital in Minnesota.

JANE THOUGHT NOTHING further about the episode until nine
years later. On her way home from a flying lesson, she stopped
in a 7-11 to get a cup of coffee. And there he was, substantially
heavier, his traditional cowboy hat and boots replaced with a
shaved head and an earring the size of an ashtray. "How are
you, Jane?" he asked, his manner cloying, his gaze fixed on her
breasts. As Jane backed out of the store, he talked about himself, embarked on flights of unrelated philosophy that resembled
stream of consciousness more than conversation, and bom-

barded her with questions about herself. What had she been up to? Was she married? Did she live in the area?

Jane finally made her getaway, and called a close friend as soon as she got home. "Forget about it," her friend said, trying to reassure her. But Jane's disquietude was well merited. Although she had moved since his departure, Philip easily found her address and phone number. From then on, he called her at least four times a day to ask her out. Suddenly, he began to appear wherever Jane happened to be. He turned up several times at her place of employment, hanging out in front during lunch. He came to her home looking for her.

"I'd see him everywhere," Jane recalled. "Then I'd go home and there'd be three messages from him." In February, four months after his return, he confessed his feelings to Jane. "I can't control myself," he admitted. "We have to do something about this." Then he asked her to marry him. He told her about the doublewide trailer he had picked out for them. He even described the color of the shag carpet.

Alarmed, Jane approached Philip's therapist, with whom she had previously dealt while working in employee support programs. "I know you're bound by confidentiality, but I need to know if I should be concerned," Jane asked. "Am I in any danger?" The therapist's answer essentially boiled down to two words: "Be careful."

THAT SCARED JANE. "It's an awful feeling when someone you really think is creepy is obsessed with you morning, noon and night." That month, she ran into Philip in the presence of friends, and confronted him. "This has got to stop. And I mean stop. That means the phone calls, the letters, the drive-bys, and following me," she announced. When he started to mimic her, she let him run through his routine. Then, using her professional personnel voice, she repeated what she had said. "I need for you to hear this," she insisted.

Suddenly, his demeanor changed into that of a penitent 10-year-old. "It was like I was dealing with two different people," Jane recalled. She accepted his apology. "Philip, I believe you. I don't think you intended to scare me. But this needs to stop." Philip promised he would never bother her again. "That should take care of things," Jane thought.

She was wrong. Confronting Philip only intensified his obsession.

By May, Jane's stress level had escalated right along with his harassment. She approached the police only to be told that since he had committed no crime, there was nothing they could do. "What did you do to provoke him?" asked one officer.

The constant uncertainty Philip's instability engendered proved too much. Jane began to crack. "What's the matter with you?" asked her flight instructor as Jane was preparing for her final exam to obtain her pilot's license. "You can't remember things you knew last week."

Jane explained. The instructor not only understood, he put her in touch with a police detective with whom the flight school had connections. "Chances are that he's not going to do anything if he hasn't done anything by now," the detective told her. "But call 911 every time you see him in your neighborhood." Jane left feeling that she had finally been heard by the police. "All I have to do is call and I'll be protected," she thought.

Wrong again.

A few days later, while sitting on her back deck eating breakfast, as she did every morning, Jane looked up to see Philip standing in her neighbor's front lawn, six inches from her property line. "I'm going to buy this house," Philip said, nodding toward the For Sale sign. "There's nothing you can do to stop me."

When Jane dialed 911, the dispatcher notified her that the police could take no action until her neighbor called, since Philip was trespassing on the neighbor's property, not hers. Mere intimidation was not a crime.

PHILIP CONTINUED TO crash through every boundary Jane tried to set up. He haunted her at public gatherings. "I'll wait until Jane is dead. Then I'll dig her up and have her," he once announced. When she was called on to speak, he made digging motions.

Having joined the Y Jane belonged to, he would stand in the Nautilus room in jeans and cowboy boots while she worked out. Although she complained, the management refused to pull his membership. "Not only could I invoke no legal sanctions, but his rights were always upheld above mine," Jane said.

When he discovered that she volunteered at a rehabilitation hospital, he started cruising the parking lot. He even showed up at the tiny airport where she took flight lessons. "To this day, I don't know how he knew about either," Jane said.

In an attempt to get him to cease and desist, Jane hired an attorney. Her interaction with police was constant. "I had two [police] cruisers in the driveway every other week. The neighbors probably figured that I had a crack house going." When she approached them to explain the situation, she discovered that her stalker had beaten her to every house in an effort to find out more about her. In at least one instance, he implied that he was a therapist who was terribly concerned about Jane's mental health because she ran into her house every time she saw him.

The police did everything in their power, but they were as frustrated as Jane. "They told me the classic line: 'Until he does something more, like assault you, there's nothing we can do.'" At one point they even advised Jane to provoke him. If she set up a sting, then they would have a violation they could act on. Jane declined.

A full 10 years into the renewed stalking, Philip moved up another rung on the ladder of violence. Jane had asked a friend to walk her to her car following a visit to the rehabilitation hospital. The two noticed Philip in the parking lot. He seemed particularly unhinged, screaming about killing people and shacking up with women. "Women are just whores anyway!" he yelled.

His departure relieved Jane. Almost immediately, however, she realized that he had headed for his vehicle. Then she heard the tires screeching around the corner. "He's going to run us down," she thought. She shoved her friend between two parked cars and quickly crouched behind her as Philip's truck sped past.

Jane approached the head of hospital security about denying Philip access to the property for the one hour a week that she spent there. Since she was neither a patient nor an employee, her request was refused. "If he hurts me on your property, don't think you're not liable, knowing what you know," she exploded.

She tried to avoid her stalker. But he would find her at various community functions. He would always sit next to her, even if he had to reposition furniture to do so. If she moved to another seat, he would rise and repeat the process.

At one meeting, he tried to take her hand. "I really love you and I want to make amends," he told her. Jane put her hands in front of her. "Stay away from me, stay out of my neighborhood and leave me alone," she responded. "You can't keep me out of your neighborhood, bitch," he answered.

Another time he confronted her with an announcement. "I have something for you, and the police are not going to be there when I decide to give it to you," he said. He couldn't have been more explicit as far as Jane was concerned. He was going to rape her.

When Jane complained to the various group leaders, however, they didn't want to take sides. Philip, they stipulated, had as much right to attend the functions as anyone else. To avoid him, Jane's only option was to cut herself off from that part of her life.

APRIL MARKED A year and a half that Jane had lived with her constant preoccupation and stress. Exhausted, she had few emotional resources left to draw upon. "I felt like I was doing everything in my power to protect myself and help my situation, but nothing was working. I wouldn't see him for two weeks, think it was over and then he'd return with a vengeance."

Increasingly, her escalating anger and sense of futility would get the better of her. As she was jogging near her home one day, a small dog belonging to one of the neighborhood youngsters suddenly chased after her, snarling. Jane turned on the dog. "I was really out of control. I was screaming," she recalled. "If I had caught that dog, I would have killed it."

Her reaction horrified the dog's young owner. Although the incident lasted only a minute, the memories of the child screaming for his mother and trying to get his pet under control while keeping Jane away still bring tears to her eyes. "I came away from that really in touch with how I'd lost my humanity," she said, her voice quivering. "My capacity to create that much distress in another human being was very disturbing to me. Because that is so against what I'm about fundamentally. It really jarred me."

That night she confided in a close friend: "If there's just some way I can keep my grasp on my humanity, I'll survive this thing."

Fear began to color her life like a camera filter. Her interactions with other people became guarded, cynical, angry. "I feel like my mind has been stained with what's happening. I can't get away from it or past it. It's part of my every waking moment," she tried to explain. But under such tremendous and unrelenting strain, many long-standing friendships began to erode. "I'm going to lose everything," she thought.

Jane had considered buying a gun, but she had been raised to abhor violence, and she wasn't sure she could use one. As the months dragged on, however, her rage began to diminish that compunction. "One night I put a crowbar in my car and went out looking for him all over the city," she said. "I'm not proud of this. But I was so frustrated with the inability of the system to deal with this situation, I thought, 'Fuck it, I've got nothing to lose.'"

Something had to give. "I knew I couldn't continue on this downward spiral. If something didn't change, I was either going to kill him or myself." Instead, she decided to form a support group for stalking victims like herself.

The original group consisted of six women. They gathered in Jane's living room, while a police car cruised the block. At first they reviewed the particulars of one another's stories and shared the resulting emotional trauma they had undergone. Later, they focused on—and tried to troubleshoot—whichever case seemed the worst that week. The forum not only gave the women an outlet, it allowed them to trust again.

Eventually, the group evolved from support to activism. Members started to accompany each other to court appearances. They wrote letters on each other's behalf. They made phone calls to other advocacy groups involved with similar social issues, and then met with them. "We really wanted to learn how to take on the stalkers, as well as the establishment. We didn't want to blunder into something unwittingly, or further endanger ourselves," said Jane. Realizing that the problem extended beyond themselves, they contacted the media. "We have a trail of dead women to prove this is a problem," Jane told reporters. Finally, the group pushed for antistalking legislation. One objective was to help the Virginia legislature rewrite the state antistalking law so that it satisfied concerns of constitutionality as well as the needs of stalking victims.

Their foray into the political arena helped them reclaim the sense of personal strength and autonomy that their stalkers had stripped from them. "For me, starting up the group and being outspoken and aggressive about this problem was about taking things into my hands and taking my power back," Jane said. "But there was a price tag. You become a pariah of sorts. Many people close to me were either threatened by what I was going through or simply thought I'd gone off the deep end."

Some friends couldn't deal with it at all, and distanced themselves. That still hurts Jane deeply. "This problem steals things. That's why I'm still grieving over it."

JANE'S CASE DIDN'T end there. After Virginia passed a law against stalking, she didn't hear from her stalker for a year. Antipsychotic medication seemed to account for the reprieve. But on a summer afternoon, she drove past him on her way to the store. Actually, she didn't really worry about the chance encounter because she didn't think he had recognized her, since she was wearing sunglasses and driving a new car. Besides, he was traveling in the opposite direction on a four-lane road.

However, Philip had spotted her. He made a U-turn and followed her into the parking lot and then into the store. Jane approached one of the employees she knew, explained the situation, and requested assistance. Philip was asked to leave.

When Jane called the police to report the incident, however, the sergeant told her that they didn't want to get involved. The commonwealth attorney's office said much the same. Constitutional challenges to the stalking law made them leery of pressing charges on that front. "What you need to do is confront your stalker, provoke an attack and we'll consider doing something," Jane was told.

PHILIP WAS BACK on the prowl. He would drive around town until he found her car, stay just long enough to make eye contact with her, and then leave. "That's the cat-and-mouse game," said Jane. His behavior continued to escalate. At a community meeting, he mouthed off about suing those people who had accused him of stalking. When a friend of Jane's asked him to be quiet, Philip threw a cup of hot coffee in his face. And when his membership at the athletic club they both belonged to was finally revoked because of his harassment of Jane, he threatened to kill one of the executives. "He's certainly capable of violence," Jane said at the time. "We just don't know what direction it will take."

Despite the renewed hostilities, she managed to stage her own emotional comeback. Not long after Philip again began his stalking activities, she engaged in casual conversation with a man in the street. He was getting out of his car with a small child. "I was lucky to find a meter with an hour on it," he said to her in

passing. "Yeah, that's really a lucky sign," Jane answered. About
20 feet down the street, she realized how long it had been since
she hadn't felt threatened by a casual remark from a stranger.

Surviving High Anxiety

Be aware of how your heightened levels of stress will
affect the rest of your life. Stalking victims experience
much higher levels of anxiety, depression, insomnia and
social dysfunction than the general population. Because
of your diminished tolerance, it may take very little to
send you into orbit. Expect and try to plan for these
over-reactions.

8

Nipping Fixation
In the Bud

B Y DEFINITION, OBSESSIONS THAT DON'T stem from personal ties or connections occur at random. Which is exactly what makes them so terrifying. You can do little to guard against a stranger reacting in a disproportionate manner to your smile or demeanor. And you can do even less once the obsession takes hold and seeps, like a stain, into your life.

Lee Gilman*, a 25-year-old art director, attracted the attention of her West Los Angeles neighbor. The two-dozen white Chrysanthemums left at her door while she was away one day were accompanied by a message that read, "I've been admiring you. You're beautiful." Signed "Stanley," the note had a happy face at the bottom.

Over the next month, her faceless admirer wrote her rambling letters, several of which contained pages of incoherent poetry. She would walk down the street to the market, be gone just 20 minutes and return to a new missive. Each contained the same line: "If you want to meet me, leave a note under the left rear tire of your MG."

The underlying message couldn't have been more clear to Lee. Somebody was watching her every move. At night she would sit in her tiny house with the lights off and look up at the four-story apartment complexes that rose high above her on either side to see if she could spot the silhouette of someone looking down. "I was totally paranoid by this point," she said.

She called the police who told her they could do nothing until the author of the notes actually did something to her. Not a comforting notion. Afraid, she called an ex-boyfriend who drove up on his motorcycle and stayed with her late into the night. "I didn't count on your motorcycle friend," read the letter she received the following day. This time, a sad face replaced the happy one at the bottom of the page. Finally, Stanley stopped writing. "I guess you're not going to respond," read his final note, his signature happy face cut through with a dotted line.

Lee heard nothing more and never saw a trace of him. A month later, however, her cat disappeared. That day, when she opened her mailbox, she found her cat's collar, so mangled that it looked like it had been put into a Cuisinart. Since the collar tags listed only the cat's name and Lee's phone number, whoever had put it there had to have been familiar enough with her to know the cat was hers.

Convinced that Stanley was responsible and unsure about what he would do next, she moved, thereby removing herself as a possible victim. "I couldn't stay there anymore. I felt totally unsafe," she said.

Lee never discovered her stalker's identity. But as luck—in this case bad luck—would have it, he targeted her anyway, perhaps because his vantage point allowed him to peer into her life, or perhaps because she appealed to him.

Either way, Stanley implemented a campaign to initiate a relationship whether Lee wanted one or not. Like most stalkers, he got his wish. Although it may not have provided the gratifying results he had envisioned, a connection, however negative, did develop.

THE KEY IS to sever that connection before it's cemented in the stalker's mind. Just as the wrong response can hurt, the right response can help.

When the attractive man behind Anne Shaw* smiled at her and said hello while she was writing a check for her groceries, the lithe office manager returned the greeting. A week later, she received a lengthy letter from him, even though she hadn't supplied her Malibu, California address—or even her name, for that matter. She figured he must have leaned over her shoulder and gotten the information from her check. The letter told her more about his life than she wanted to know. But it seemed straightforward, even sweet. "You'll kick yourself if you don't follow this up," the author concluded.

Anne didn't kick herself. Nor did she respond. The stranger's second letter revealed how wise that was. "I've been driving by your house," he wrote. "I really wish you would contact me. I know we're perfect for each other."

The episode still perplexes her. "All I did was say hi to the guy," she exclaimed. "He was very good looking, and his attention was flattering at first. But his notion that we were perfect for each other scared me. It was completely irrational."

LISA ERINDON'S* STALKER not only fixated on her after seeing the attractive blue-eyed brunette in the market, he convinced himself that she was actually in love with him. This delusion, called "erotomania," usually involves the stalking of (and obsession over) a person of higher social or economic standing, like a celebrity. Diane Schaefer, for example, was arrested an eighth time in 1990 for stalking Dr. Murray Brennan, the renowned head of surgery at New York's Memorial Sloan-Kettering Hospital. During her eight-year obsession with Dr. Brennan, the 41-year-old aspiring medical writer followed him to professional conferences around the world, besieged his office with calls, became so familiar with the intimacies of his life that her startlingly accurate letters managed to disrupt his marriage. She even stalked his wife, who began to fear for her life and the lives of their children. Diane not only believed that the object of her desire loved her, she testified about conversations they had had during their supposed affair. The conversations were imaginary.

In Lisa's case, however, Sheldon Kelford* simply spotted her as she ran into the store to pick up a couple of items. Certain that the 32-year-old masseuse and part-time actress had fallen for him, he turned her into his personal research project. He obtained her parents' address and phone number by calling the DMV, giving them the license plate number of the car she had driven away in, and convincing the operator that the owner of the car had dropped a very expensive gold bracelet that he wished to return personally. Then he went by her parents' house—the address the DMV had on file—and used the same story to convince her mother to supply Lisa's phone number.

In an effort to find out all he could about her, Sheldon also approached a number of her parents' neighbors. "I'm a high-school friend," he would tell them. "I was trying to get in touch with her, but her parents aren't home." Then he would try to draw them out in conversation to glean whatever information he could.

He found out which high school she had gone to, got a copy of the yearbook, and then prodded her former classmates for more personal information. He called the area's churches until he found which one she had attended while growing up, and contacted other churchgoers.

Once he had obtained as much data about her as possible, he called Lisa to try and persuade her to meet with him. She refused. When he became persistent, she told him to go away. Still he called, three and four times a day. "I'll kill myself, because no one loves you like I do," he told her.

He stopped phoning for a nine-month period, then one day he appeared at her job site and convinced her colleague that he just wanted a chance to get to know her. Figuring that Lisa should at least hear what he had to say, the colleague set up a meeting between the two. "You looked at me in the grocery store," Sheldon told her. "You're the one who likes me. If people would not keep me from contacting you, you'd come to me."

EVEN WHEN stalking doesn't disrupt or destroy your life, it makes you keenly aware of how vulnerable you are. An aggravated stalking can leave you feeling so out of control that you sense you have no life at all. "I'm a very strong woman," said one victim. "But it decimates you and your family. There's no recouping."

Suzanne Jurva still hasn't managed to expunge from her memory the stalking that haunted her through her college years in Michigan. A couple of months into her freshman year, the television producer began to receive bouquets of carnations every Friday. Years spent training to be a competitive figure skater had essentially precluded boyfriends. Having a secret admirer felt wonderful—until he started including notes with the flowers that berated her about the various men with whom he had seen her. Over Thanksgiving weekend, he sent a letter to her parents. "Your daughter sleeps around. She's a whore. Do you know what she's doing around campus?" it read.

The culprit turned out to be a doctoral student from Iran. The discovery of his identity did little to deter Reza Faiznah*. Extravagant presents (like a huge sapphire necklace) alternated with notes that read: "I just bought an orange fish and it died. In my culture, this is a symbol of death to someone who is important to you. Just writing to tell you that you are going to die."

He quit his own classes so that he could wait outside each of Suzanne's classes in order to take her photograph as she appeared. Whether she was skating or participating in a dance-a-thon, he was there to point his telephoto lens at her. A warning from university authorities to stay away or be deported had little impact. "It made me sick," Suzanne recalled. "I started to ditch school because I was afraid that I'd run into him."

The activity continued during her sophomore year. "You're a pretty girl. This is going to happen to you a lot. I think you

should just get used to it," a college official told her. That
didn't sound right to Suzanne, then 19. But none of the
adults she talked to seemed willing to help her. Meanwhile, her
sense of safety was being increasingly compromised by notes
that warned of impending car crashes in which she would be
decapitated.

The end of Suzanne's sophomore year and the first semester
of the next one coincided with the Iranian hostage crisis, in
which militants held 52 Americans hostage for 444 days at the
American embassy in Tehran. "That cooled him a little bit," she
recalled. Every once in a while she received a note saying that he
still thought she would marry him, that he was waiting for her
and that he couldn't believe the horrible men she was dating.
Compared to the previous two years, this seemed like a substantial improvement.

She spent the summer house-sitting for friends in Los Angeles,
2,000 miles away from her tormentor. She didn't hear a word
from him while she was away. Neither did her parents. At last,
she felt like she could breathe.

On her final day in town, a car pulled up to where she stood
waiting for a bus. An Iranian got out, presented her with his
business card, and announced that he had followed her all summer at Reza's request.

"He couldn't have done worse damage to me," said Suzanne.
"'I will never get free of him,' I thought. 'This man has ways of
getting to me. There isn't a place on the face of the earth where
he won't find me.'"

She felt like a hostage. His hostage. She thought about suicide.
In a moment of despair, she even contemplated succumbing to
him. "I'm so fucked, why not just marry him?" she reasoned.
Perhaps that way she would find a sliver of the freedom she had
lost. Maybe if he got what he wanted, he would let her regain
a portion of the life he seemed so determined to possess. "That
was the deepest, darkest feeling of gloom I've ever had."

Reza's attentions ceased as abruptly as they began. She hasn't seen or heard from him in years. "But he got me," she said. "To this day, I have this feeling in my heart that he's still out there watching me."

So she watches herself. When an opportunity to get into television sportscasting arose, for example, she turned it down even though that had been her lifelong dream. "I thought, 'I can't do anything so public!'" she said.

Nor has marriage blunted the mark that Reza left on her. When she got pregnant, she prayed for a boy. "I don't want a little girl. I don't want her to go through anything like that," she explained. "I can't save her."

FOR JESSICA WEISS*, the answer to that sense of vulnerability was to take matters into her own hands after an intruder entered her Long Beach, California, apartment and stole all her underwear, as well as photographs of the green-eyed blonde in high-school and with her 4-year-old-son. Just three days before, her car had been rifled and her cell phone stolen. An X left on her car made her feel that she had been marked for something. The officer who responded to the second call warned her that she was probably being stalked. "Keep a baseball bat by your bed," he advised. "Don't be alone."

The crimes were traced to Jeff Calin*, the apartment manager's brother-in-law, who had been hanging out in one of the complex's garages. That's where Jessica's intimate apparel—along with a collection of other women's undergarments—were found. The crotches of some of the panties had been cut out. Others were smeared with semen. Also found was a collage of the photos Jeff had taken from Jessica's apartment. He had cut her out of one of the pictures, and sliced her arms off.

Booked for residential burglary, Jeff was bailed out almost as quickly as he was arrested. Afraid that he would retaliate, Jessica bought a can of pepper spray. She refused to let her son out of her sight. She dreamed that someone was going to come in and murder them. "This guy is going to hurt me," she later explained to the judge. "This guy did not break into my house because he wanted underwear. He was there to terrorize me."

Finding out that the key to her apartment was missing only heightened her anxiety. The next day she decided to move.

The police seemed not to share Jessica's concerns. She hadn't been sexually assaulted, nor had she been threatened. So her case was treated as low priority. That's when Jessica decided to get personally involved. "I wasn't seeing the results I wanted," she said. So she took on the role of investigator herself. Her goal was to uncover enough past history to convince a judge to revoke Jeff's bail and award him the maximum sentence possible.

Her search into Jeff Calin's background uncovered three prior convictions for phone harassment, four other phone harassment victims who had not pressed charges, two parole violations (which the police were aware of), and a probable rape victim. Yet none of that information came up during the initial hearing, which resulted in Jeff being released on his own recognizance. "I hit the roof!" Jessica exclaimed. Then she discovered that Jeff had been stalking another mother from her son's preschool.

Two months after his initial arrest, Jeff Calin was re-arrested and held on $500,000 bail. On June 8, he was sentenced to six years in prison, the maximum sentence for residential burglary. "Women do not deserve to be terrorized in their own homes. They should not be made to feel unsafe," Jessica stated in court. "Their children should not be put in jeopardy, ever."

WHETHER STALKING LASTS for days, weeks or years, being the target of someone's inappropriate and undesired attention changes your life no matter what your role or the outcome of the situation.

Sometimes the adaptations required are short-lived. One Darmouth senior attracted the attention of her landlady's son.

Long letters to which she never responded were followed by more personal and increasingly tenacious approaches. If overly intimate correspondence had made her leery of him, his presence made her downright apprehensive. In an effort to avoid having any contact with him, she ceased to answer the phone, came and went as carefully as possible, and even hid in the closet one day when he dropped by the house. When that didn't discourage him, she fabricated a story that she was involved in a lesbian affair with one of her four roommates. Finally, she moved to another house; he didn't follow.

In more protracted situations, the adaptations—as well as the repercussions—can seem inescapable.

ARTHUR NAVARRO THOUGHT he had left his problem behind when he moved to Washington, D.C., to assume the position of White House liaison to the Commerce Department under newly elected President Clinton. In 1988 he had met Russian student Aliana Petrov* and they discussed the possibility of her tutoring him in Russian and exchanged phone numbers.

The weekly lessons began the following Saturday. After their third session, she asked Arthur to attend a jazz concert with her. He declined. Aliana refused to take no for an answer. Unnerved by her reaction, Arthur put an end to the tutoring. "That's when the nightmare began," he said.

The following week, Arthur's roommate saw her sitting outside his town house with a stack of books by her side. A neighbor spotted her peering into his window late at night. Driven by the belief that he really did love her, Aliana followed his every move, whether he was jogging, at work or out socially. She camped outside his house for hours on end. She tried to break in to his house. And the phone calls—which would reportedly total 2,000 over the course of four years—started. Hang-ups were interspersed with extended messages left both at home and at work. She detailed how much she loved Arthur and how she planned to continue harassing him. She asked him out on dates. She talked about his family. She tied up his lines with musical interludes.

In an attempt to discourage her, Arthur called Aliana to say that he had a girlfriend to whom he was happily engaged, and that she should leave him alone. It was a lie, but it wouldn't have made any difference even if it had been the truth.

She inundated him with love letters, scores of which she addressed to him and hand delivered to his parents' house. On several occasions, she stood outside and snapped photographs of their home. "What the hell is going on? Who is this lady?" Arthur's father demanded. After nine months, Arthur's parents obtained a restraining order and she stopped using their home as a mailbox. However, she continued to target Arthur.

To elude her, he moved, had his mail redirected to a private post office box, and obtained a new, unlisted phone number. Yet she managed to leave an increasingly frightening mark on his life anyway, through messages that bespoke her anger, her capacity for violence, and her mental instability. The more Arthur tried to protect himself, the more vindictive she became. "Please tell him that I have grandiose plans to shoot him and that the bullet is coming his way any moment now," read one fax sent to a neighbor. It was signed, "Your most true and long and unfailing love Aliana."

Arthur began to fear for his life, especially when the FBI called him to say that the director of personnel at his former job had notified the agency that Aliana was coming over to kill him. She had apparently told his onetime office partner that Arthur could expect a bullet. Other messages were equally terrifying. One announced that she couldn't "wait to total him just like Rebecca Schaeffer," the 21-year-old actress shot by a deranged fan. Aliana was just waiting to get to him with her gun, she admitted.

She served him notice again and again. "You tell him I'm going to kill him no matter what."

The constant harassment, to say nothing of the fear, affected everything from Arthur's work performance to his relationships. Aliana faxed satanic literature to his neighbors, along with intimations that she would burn them all out. A specific threat against the life of Arthur's next-door neighbor caused the woman to flee to a hotel. "She was trying to intimidate them, and thereby make my life as uncomfortable as possible," said Arthur.

It worked.

Aliana Petrov was not the kind of woman a man like Arthur Navarro would be attracted to. But that was the notion that she set forth through three recordings that Arthur maintains the technologically savvy Aliana fabricated. Others agree, believing she may have spliced them together using the sophisticated recording equipment police found at her residence.

Aliana was charged with one count of stalking and four counts of terrorist threats. Bail was set at $2 million. Although Aliana argued that Arthur had goaded her along, she never denied her actions. Convicted of stalking, she was sentenced to 250 days in jail and three years of probation during which she would receive psychiatric care. The prison time was subsequently shortened.

Aliana's stalking of Arthur tore his life apart. Distance offered him a temporary reprieve when he hit the campaign trail with Bill Clinton. The schedule was hectic, but for the first time he could stop worrying about where or when Aliana might turn up next.

The job offer that materialized after the election seemed like the perfect permanent solution. When asked whether anything in his background might jeopardize his clearance, he answered no. "I paid my taxes. I've never been arrested," he figured. He never mentioned the stalking. It was nothing he had done. He had been the victim. The less said about it, the better.

The government's Office of Personnel Management thought differently. When the stalking episode came to light during his security clearance check, investigators pulled the court records, which included the transcript of Aliana's suspect tapes. "You read these transcripts, you've got to think, 'My God, this guy is a liability,'" said Arthur. To make matters worse, they interviewed Aliana, but didn't follow up with Arthur or any of the law enforcement or judicial officials involved. Suddenly, he became "a security issue." Soon after, he was let go because of alleged presidential cutbacks. "But I was the only one cut," he said.

Ultimately, after intruding on almost every other aspect of his life, Arthur believes that his chance encounter with Aliana cost him the most important job he ever had. "I only met this person four frikkin' times," he said. "This problem is like a virus that's immune to treatment. It lies dormant for a while, then resurfaces."

Trust Yourself

Your intuition may be providing you guidance that you've ignored. Start paying attention to those life-saving messages. If your internal radar signals that you're not comfortable with a certain person or situation, don't make excuses. Get out!

9

Know Your 'Net Worth

T HESE DAYS THE INVASION OF privacy has taken on a frighteningly technological dimension. Stalkers, just like millions of
other people worldwide, have found their way onto the Internet,
only to exploit the technology to their own end.

Nicole Balzac*, a precocious college freshman, found this out
when she decided to sign up for a new Instant Message account
so that she and her high school friends could stay in touch. "I
didn't realize that someone had overheard me give my name and
had written down my online identifier," she said.

That someone was James White*, a reclusive, antisocial computer science major who had been attracted to the young, tech-
nically literate young woman. He introduced himself in IM that
very same day. Nicole didn't reply at first, but when James sent
an electronic apology about his forwardness a few hours later,
she let down her guard and responded.

During the next few weeks, it became obvious that James
knew many private details about her social life. Somehow, he
had to be accessing and reading the messages her friends were
sending her, she realized. When she confronted him, however,
he angrily denied any wrongdoing. Finally she told him she
didn't want to communicate with him anymore. Her decision
fueled his electronic harassment. For the next two years, he

continued to email her, text her, message her, spy on her online activities, and follow her on campus. "I never found out who he was exactly, but I never felt like I had any privacy, either in real life or in cyberspace," said Nicole. "It was creepy." In part to escape James, Nicole finally transferred to another university and stopped much of her online activity. Luckily, she has not heard from him since.

NICOLE IS FAR from alone. As the Internet grows exponentially—with tens of thousands of new users signing on each month—more and more of us become victims of electronic stalkers. "The same traditional crimes are being committed in a new environment where the criminals are allowed anonymity," said Frank Clark, an investigator with the Pierce County, Washington, prosecutor's office. That anonymity, coupled with the lack of regulation and precedents, makes the Internet just about as lawless as any new frontier ever was. And that frontier is growing.

The 2009 Bureau of Justice Statistics special report on stalking revealed that cyberstalking was involved in 25 percent of stalking incidents. But that can vary regionally. While Wayne Maxey, commander at San Diego District Attorney's Office, estimated that cyberstalking accounted for 20 percent of the area's stalking cases, the New York Police Department's Computer Investigation and Technology Unit estimated that a full 40 percent of their caseload involved cyberstalking.

Cyberstalking is defined by the National Center for Victims of Crime as "threatening behavior or un-wanted advances directed at another using the Internet and other forms of online and computer communications."

No one actually knows how many people have become cyberstalking victims. In 2000, Parry Aftab, author of *The Parent's Guide to Protecting Your Children in Cyberspace*, said, "If the [same stalking] ratio were reflected on the Internet [as in real life], then out of the estimated population of 79 million users worldwide, we would find 63,000 Internet stalkers cruising the information highway, stalking an estimated 474,000 targets." Indeed, a 1999 U.S. Department of Justice report seemed to corroborate those numbers. Since then, however, the number of people online has grown to more than 30 percent of the world's population. That's more than 2 billion users. If the math holds, that translates to some 12 million current cyberstalking targets around the globe.

WHILE THE INTERNET'S design makes much of our online activity (like shopping) and communication (like Facebook or Twitter) alarmingly public, the sense of anonymity it provides seems to facilitate—and even depersonalize—harassment. For close to a year, Duwayne Comfort terrorized five students (four female and one male) at the University of San Diego and University of California at San Diego with emails that threatened sexual assault, violence and death. His reason? Because of a physical condition called Marfan Syndrome that had caused elongated bones and long, spidery limbs, he thought they were laughing at him.

"As it turns out, though two students had shared a class with him, three others had never even met him," said Dave Hendron, the San Diego Police Department's award-winning detective who cracked the case. "And in talking to them afterwards, no one even implied that he was funny looking. Most of them hadn't given him a second look."

But that wasn't how the recent college graduate saw it.

After nine months, campus security managed to trace the emails to a computer lab on campus. When they found themselves unable to make further headway in the case, they called in the San Diego police department. Hendron charted all the emails to try to establish a pattern, including which computers were most frequently used, on which days and at which times. Once he had identified the two most likely bets, he set up a surveillance camera on 24-hour record, which snapped a picture of the side-by-side computers every second.

Meanwhile, Hendron also decided to try and smoke out the perpetrator. Using an ISP account from a prior undercover operation, he sent an anonymous email that simply said: *I know who you are.* Comfort's cyberstalking activity instantly intensified—exactly as Hendron had anticipated it would. "That gave us a better chance to catch him," said Hendron.

Indeed, Hendron's message rattled the cyberstalker so much that instead of going to the campus computer lab and using one of his anonymous accounts, he shot back a response from home. The moment Hendron saw that the emails were coming from a different location, he served the Internet Service Provider with a search warrant, and the company quickly identified the house from which the emails were being sent. It was Comfort's.

Finally, a team of police officers moved in. Comfort wasn't home, so they waited. As it turns out, at that very moment Comfort was in the campus computer lab at his favorite machine and this round of email threats was caught on camera. Talk about an airtight case!

Comfort pled guilty to stalking, and was sentenced to some time in local custody before being placed on probation for several years. In addition, he was mandated to attend counseling sessions. An initial order prohibiting him from using a computer was later amended to allow his computer use in the course of employment.

During a probation search, police found no violations and there have been no further complaints. Comfort, however, remains angry, feeling that he's the one who has been victimized by all this.

ALTHOUGH CYBERSTALKING MAY sound somewhat benign since it doesn't necessarily involve actual contact, the preponderance of information about your personal and professional life that's available online makes it downright ominous.

During his ten-month-long cyberstalking spree, Comfort purchased information about his victims from an online company, using a credit card number he had stolen from a professor on campus. The comments he was then able to make about everything from property liens to civil judgments served as incredibly effective terror tactics. Suddenly it seemed as though he knew everything about his targets. He seemed omnipotent. "It scared the hell out of them," said Hendron.

A week before his arrest, Comfort used the stolen credit card to buy a stun gun. That scared them even more and concerned the police greatly. "I feared that he was either going to make a kidnapping attempt or a sexual assault attempt on the victims," said the detective. "So we began doing counter-surveillance on the victims to make sure he wasn't following them."

COMFORT WAS STOPPED before he had moved from cyberspace to real space. Amy Boyer wasn't so lucky.

Liam Youens's crush on Amy had held strong from the time they were in junior high school together. On the four Web pages he put up, he publicly debated about what to do about it. One option was to kill the 20-year-old New Hampshire dental assistant. "Plan B was to kill a kid who was in the wrong place at the wrong time, as he was thinking about Amy," said Tim Remsburg, Amy's stepfather. "Plan C was a school massacre."

Even though more than a decade had passed, Youens knew how to find the dental assistant at work with the help of online information brokers that charged him hundreds of dollars. "It's actually obscene what you can find out about people on the Internet," he wrote on his Web page. Shortly thereafter, he peppered Amy with bullets, and then killed himself as well.

AS AMY BOYER'S death reveals all too painfully, the invasion of privacy has hit frighteningly sophisticated heights. Online companies called information brokers actually make a healthy profit marketing information about you, ranging from your address to your employment history.

Even if you've worked hard to maintain your privacy, a single credit header can undo all your efforts. Credit headers, which top credit reports, include your name, residential address and unlisted phone number, social security number and employer, data that's routinely culled from any bank or car loan application, mortgage or credit card. And though the credit report itself is held to be legally confidential, the header is not. So the personal information you supplied in good faith gets sold by the country's top three credit reporting agencies to online information brokers. They, in turn, sell it to anyone who wants it.

As WITH REGULAR stalking, cyberstalking often begins when you attempt to break off a relationship. The posting of naked pictures taken during a relationship when things were good has become an increasingly popular method of revenge by jilted lovers. The phenomenon is not reserved for the young and restless, according to Maxey. "Never let yourself be photographed in the nude," he recommended simply. "These days such pictures can end up being made public way too easily."

Online vendettas can also stem from downright impersonal contact. The beliefs you express online can make you a target if someone disagrees with you. Even the *way* you express them— especially if you're new to the online rules of the road—can inadvertently offend or humiliate someone.

An obvious lack of online knowledge and experience can also make you a cyberstalking target. Just as in real-life stalking, cyber predators prey on the easy mark. "A newbie [inexperienced user online] will display a lack of confidence in online communication, will lack basic skills in cyberspace avoidance and escape skills, will be unable to block hostile attacks, and will probably not know the Internet complaint and reporting procedures," said Aftab.

To AVOID BEING targeted, Aftab recommends learning netiquette (etiquette for using the Internet), cyber street smarts (which include realizing that a user is not necessarily who he says he is), and gaining technical mastery of the Internet technology.

Following the simple tips below will help you begin to safeguard yourself online:

- Opt for free email services where you don't have to provide your name or address, since most Internet Service Providers make membership directories publicly available. If you're having a problem, change your email address.
- Since women are especially vulnerable to online harassment, select a genderless screen or ID name. Don't use your real name or nickname.
- Choose a complicated password that combines letters, numbers and symbols, and change it often.
- Don't respond to online provocation.
- Don't flirt online.
- Immediately get out of any hostile online communication by logging off or finding another site.
- Guard your privacy jealously. Social media is making that harder and harder to do. Bucking the trend to share every detail about your life on Facebook, MySpace and other social networking sites, however, will keep you a lot safer. In addition, don't post your birthday, age or where you were born since those can be used by someone to identify your social security number. Also keep your address to yourself.
- The default settings on most social networks do not keep any of your information private. Make sure you change that. Regulate who can read your profile, see your posts and photos. Make sure you limit the information your friends can share about you. And find out what information the social network is sharing about you with other websites and businesses.

- People online aren't necessarily who they say they are. Sometimes a stalker will try to get to your directly. Other times a stalker will find out information that his or her target has gone to great lengths to protect by posting questions on social networks like Facebook or MySpace that the target's unsuspecting friends answer. So guard your friends' privacy as carefully as you do your own.
- In discussion groups or chat rooms, never divulge your real name, where you live, and what you do for a living. Remember that these virtual conversations are archived, and can be accessed by anyone.
- On the commercial front, don't fill out forms (including product registration forms) online, or participate in on-line or offline contests, sweepstakes or surveys.
- If you're a university student, refrain from providing biographical information for the free university email service. Better yet, sign up for your own private email account.

FOR MORE INFORMATION about safeguarding yourself and your privacy online, log onto the National Center for Victims of Crime. Other websites that can help include the Electronic Privacy Information Center, the Stalking Resource Center, and the Stalking Victims Sanctuary.

CHILDREN have also become prime targets for cyberstalkers. The FBI labels the sexual molestation of children one of the nation's most significant problems. For the pedophile, of course, the Internet is a playground replete with possibilities. "Parents have the misconception that if their children are in their living room, they're perfectly safe," Deputy Jamie Watson, an online under-cover detective from Bedford County, Virginia, told *48 Hours*. "What they don't understand is their child is in their living room on their computer, [potentially] giving out their home address

[or] talking to somebody who has every intention of taking the child away from Mom and Dad."

If you have children online, make use of available software that can block their access to inappropriate chat rooms and websites. Teach them that they have the power to put a stop to any and all disturbing online contact simply by logging off or finding another site. Direct them never to respond to unsuitable communications (not even in fun). And go online with your kids to see where they tend to surf.

You may have to become something of a sleuth. Teen Research Unlimited reports that more than one quarter of all teens use code words on a daily basis to prevent their parents from knowing what they're talking about online. An equal number of teens say they've had an online conversation about sex with someone they've never met. And, according to Pew Internet and American Life Project, two thirds of teens admit to doing things online that they wouldn't want their parents to know about.

Really knowing the ins and outs of navigating the Internet is especially critical if you're the parent of a young Internet user. So you may also want to consult Aftab's website, located at www.cyberangels.org, which provides terrific advice for users and their parents. In addition to a Cyber 911 help line, the site hosts a volunteer CyberMoms group that monitors Internet chat-rooms, online services and popular websites, and helps kids improve their online judgment. You'll find another great kid-related online safety resource at www.getnetwise.org.

IN SOME CASES, however, all the Web savvy in the world won't help you sidestep a cyberstalking. Amazingly, you don't even have to own a computer to be subjected to Internet-related harassment.

When a 28-year-old office worker scorned Gary Dellapenta's affections, the former Los Angeles security guard posted personal ads in her name that made it sound as though she wanted to have her fantasies about being raped—and even gang-banged—fulfilled. Not content to sign her name to the fake solicitations, he included her address and phone number as well. The result? Dozens of lewd messages and six actual visits.

The victim, who didn't have a computer of her own, had no idea why all this was happening. When she finally figured it out, she put a note on her front door explaining that the whole thing was a set-up. Dellapenta simply amended his postings to say that this, too, was part of her fantasy, and that the men should force their way into her home. (Cyberstalkers have also signed others' names to inflammatory messages they've posted on virtual bulletin boards and chat rooms, triggering threatening responses toward the victim who has been impersonated electronically.)

CYBERSTALKING HAS COME on so quickly that it has caught much of law enforcement unawares. As of 1999, less than one-third of the states had anti-stalking laws that specifically include language dealing with online harassment. Which explains in part why victims are often still not taken seriously, at least until the activity has escalated into the real world.

A lack of state and federal funding for Internet resources is also responsible for a dearth of online familiarity and experience among law enforcement professionals. One couple complained to their local police station about an Internet posting, which claimed their 9-year-old daughter was available for sex. They were advised to change their phone number. Not until the couple contacted the FBI did any action get taken.

As it turned out, the police department had no computer expert and the investigating officer had never been online. (If your police department lacks Internet savvy, you might direct them to the National Cybercrime Training Partnership, led by the Department of Justice with support from the Office of Justice Programs and the National White Collar Crime Center.

Information can be found at http://www.nw3c.org/press-room/docs/archive/2001/nctp_offers_advanced_level_computer_crime_course.pdf)

The responsibility to protect yourself and your children electronically starts and ends with you. Unfortunately, due to the Internet's lack of regulation, even following every possible precaution may not be enough to protect you completely.

So user, go carefully into that dark 'Net. And when Congress considers legislation that would mandate content monitoring systems or prohibit Internet companies from selling our personal information, put your wholehearted support behind it and make sure your voice is heard.

Don't Cozy Up to Virtual Strangers

With the escalation of electronic harassment, it's imperative to remember the first rule of the road when it comes to the Information Superhighway. People are *not* always who they say they are. So play your cards close to the vest when it comes to disclosing your real name or any other personal information, including where you live or work.

10

Even Your Kids
Are At Risk

VICTIMS OF EXTREME STALKINGS WILL often do whatever it takes to get out from under the daily terror. "As a victim, you want to be right. I had the wisdom to know that it was better to be alive than to be right," said one woman who decided to relocate, sell her business and even switch careers to protect herself from her stalker. "Preserving the life of my child and myself was more important than preserving a house, a roof over my head, or a career."

Such repercussions can last a lifetime among even the strongest adults. But imagine the emotional and psychological scars when a stalking becomes a key element in your child's life. Assuming your child survives.

Caty Thayer, a pre-teen from Vermont, was stalked for 19 months. Caty understood all too well the danger she ran. When her mother, Rosealyce, found her organizing her dolls one afternoon, Caty explained that she was deciding which dolls would go to which friends after the stalker had killed her. Yet, authorities took no action. "Despite Rosealyce Thayer's efforts to protect her daughter when the police would not, little Caty was kidnapped and later found dead," reported then U.S. Senator William S. Cohen. She had been raped and repeatedly stabbed.

Strangers aren't the only threat. Some years ago, a 14-year-old Michigan boy was sexually assaulted by a local deputy sheriff who had made a point of driving past and waving whenever the teenager was out in the yard, working on the roof, or catching tadpoles at the local creek. "If you ever tell, I'll come back and I'll kill you. It's as simple as that. I can do it in a heartbeat," he warned. Accordingly, the young victim didn't tell a soul for some 25 years. Not even a counselor. He still fantasizes about "going into the sheriff's office and shooting everyone in there."

WHETHER OR NOT child and teenage stalkings involve molestation, the frightening ordeal leaves a turbulent psychological wake. Erin Tavegia is a Connecticut teenager who was stalked for several months when she was 15. The man who followed her to and from school and parked outside the family house during all hours never broke any laws. He never overtly threatened to harm Erin. But his actions terrified the gregarious teenager. During high school football games, she would search the crowd looking for him. Two years later, his actions continued to haunt her. "I'm afraid of the dark, and I still can't walk around that much," she said. "I carry a blaster with me. And I look all the time. I'm always looking at all the cars."

Eight-year-old Crystal Peterson from Independence, Oregon, also had the misfortune of attracting unwanted attention. For three years, a neighbor—24-year-old Robert Coker—watched the youngster. He left her posters of unicorns, rings, and other tokens of his affection. And he wrote love letters, which in time became increasingly graphic.

Frightened for their daughter's safety, Chris and Debbie Peterson began to limit her accessibility by limiting her life. "I had to be taken into school, brought back home from school," Crystal said. "I only had a little piece of playground I could play on."

Upon approaching the police, however, Crystal's parents were told that there was nothing that could be done from a legal standpoint. Only when Robert broke into the Petersons' home was he finally arrested. Sentenced to 16 months on a burglary charge, Robert swore to return and find Crystal upon his release. "I don't think I'm a stalker. I don't have nothing wrong intended," Robert claimed when interviewed by phone on *The Maury Povich Show*. "I just had a case of feelings for her and that's why I was writing the letters to them. To make them understand."

What Crystal's parents understand all too well is that Robert deprived their young daughter of her innocence and upended their lives. Afraid of what he might do upon his release, the Petersons fled their home. Work, however, hasn't been easy to find. So the hardships have multiplied.

Laurisa Anello, now 19, began receiving gifts of roses, T-shirts, dolls and pizzas five years ago. Drive-bys at all hours of the night, along with physical pursuit worthy of the most dedicated detective, followed. Wherever the Florida teenager went, Bruce Raines—a 24-year-old umpire in the softball league Laurisa had joined—shadowed her. He called the house, as well as her parents' offices, incessantly. When Laurisa started dating, he accosted the first young man who took her out. That's when the notes he had been inserting in the family's daily newspaper turned menacing. "I'm out there. No telling what I might do," warned one. "I'll be watching so I can catch you," read another.

Even after several arrests, Bruce continued to stalk Laurisa. Her mother, Linda, began to secretly tail her daughter. "Just in case he was around," she said. "I just know if he goes over the edge, he's capable of doing anything. That's the horror of it."

Laurisa now attends college. To protect both anonymity and safety, she won't reveal where. "This is the way I have to live," she said. "It's what I've had to do to survive."

SURVIVAL COSTS. THE price, for young victims, is a normal child-hood or adolescence.

Even into her adulthood, Sarah Jane Williams didn't know who had been stalking her since she was a young teen. She had never seen the man and didn't know his name. The only thing she knew for certain is that his harassment deprived her of her freedom growing up and turned a shy bookworm increasingly inward.

"I pick up strays. I've always been like that," said Sarah Jane. "Even when I was in kindergarten, I brought home the neighborhood kids that were the shaggiest creatures and played with them instead of the other kids. That's just the way I was."

Does that explain why Sarah Jane was stalked for so many years?

Who knows?

Fourteen-year-old Sarah Jane was thrilled when she landed her first job as the Saturday receptionist for a computer store. Six months into the job, a caller asked her to respond to a marketing survey he was conducting. The precocious teenager assumed that answering his questions was just part of the job, even if the proposed product—in this case an assortment of different sized tampons packaged in a single box—had nothing to do with electronics.

Within minutes, however, the increasingly personal nature of the questioning had begun to disturb her. When the caller asked whether she bathed or took showers when she had her period, she realized she had received an obscene phone call. Still calm, she put the caller on hold and handed the receiver to a male clerk. "I want to speak to Sarah Jane again," the fake pollster said. That's when the teenager realized that the call hadn't been random. The caller knew her name; he had specifically targeted her.

The elder of two children in a Southern Baptist family, Sarah Jane had led a sheltered life until then. The prurient nature of the call shocked her, as well as her parents. But they assumed it was a onetime occurrence and thought little more about it.

The next call came two weeks later. Sarah Jane had been preparing to go out of town with her parents. "You're getting ready to go on vacation to the beach," the voice said. How had he gotten that information? Either this man was watching her, or he knew someone she knew. Either way, he was a lot closer than anyone had figured.

Sarah Jane didn't hear from him during the week she was away. Upon her return she attended a Friday night party. She was back at the computer store the next day. He called. "Did you have a good time at the party?" he asked, describing the boy she had been out with. Her parents hadn't even known about her date or the previous night's festivities. How had he?

The calls continued sporadically over the next year. When a trap was placed on the store phone at the request of Sarah Jane's parents, the stalker started phoning her at home. The pattern was always the same. He would hang up if one of her parents or her brother answered the phone. If she picked up, he would say, "Hi, Sarah Jane," and then hang up. But whenever she was alone in the house with her little brother, he would call up to 15 times in a half an hour. He knew exactly when her parents were out.

Things cooled down for a few months. Then Sarah Jane turned 15. His birthday call reinforced the belief that she had become an obsession to be scrutinized and analyzed. He would tell her where she had been during the week, like the after-school movie she had attended. He reviewed the outfits she had worn to school. He discussed her braces.

"At this point, I'd gotten more annoyed than scared," said Sarah Jane. "I was a teenager, just starting to go out with guys and friends. But the more the calls came, the more Mom and Dad started to clamp down so no harm would come to me."

Her life became increasingly restricted. "I couldn't go out with anyone my parents didn't know. If I didn't know where I would be every second, I couldn't go. Sometimes I couldn't go anyway."

Not surprisingly, Sarah Jane thought her parents were overreacting. But Sarah Jane's stalker had begun to move in closer. The morning Sarah Jane brought her dog's bowl inside, he called to ask what she had done with it. The message was clear: He had been around the house.

Once his phone calls no longer elicited the reaction he sought, the stalker decided to play for impact in new ways. For example, copper roofing nails periodically punctured the family car's tires. And on one of the few evenings that Sarah Jane had been allowed out of the house alone, he followed her car as she drove home from a girlfriend's house and tried to run her off the road. His calls claiming responsibility for the deeds eliminated any possibility of a coincidence.

By the time Sarah Jane had turned 16, he had begun to target others close to her as well. He would call her best friend, Sherry, demanding to know if the two girls were lesbians and asking about their presumed activities in explicit detail. And while Sherry and her mother didn't own a car, anyone else associated with Sarah Jane could expect to have their tires pierced with copper nails.

Unable to affix blame on one individual, Sarah Jane began to fear and hate men in general. She decided that she wasn't going to date anyone. How could she be sure that the man she chose wouldn't end up being the one responsible for all this?

At 17, Sarah Jane entered college. She never considered going out of town. For three years, she had relied on her parents to pick her up after school functions, follow her to and from work, and accompany her during social occasions. That total dependence would not be easily broken.

In ordinary circumstances, the pretty, longhaired blond would probably have graduated from bookworm to cheerleader during her high school or college years. But her three-year ordeal, which she shared with almost no one, set her apart. "I was an oddball in school," she said. As the months passed, she became increasingly reclusive.

The clues pointed to a computer-savvy loner who had first asked her out when she was 18. That her stalker might well be a member of the church she had grown up in just added to her sense of alienation. Suddenly she didn't feel comfortable in the one place she should have felt secure. Fellow churchgoers, who didn't understand why she wouldn't list her number and address in the church directory, rebuffed her.

That July, on the family's annual seaside holiday, Sarah Jane met Zack and fell in love. On her return, her romantic haze was shattered. "I'm going to slit your throat . . . from ear to ear," the mystery caller said. As he began describing the razor blade he intended to use, Sarah Jane hung up. After consulting her father, she called the police.

A homicide detective chronicled the events that had occurred since she was 14 and suggested a sting operation. On the assumption that the caller wanted to date Sarah Jane even though he had never indicated as much, she would go out with him and the police would be there to apprehend him. After discussing the possibility, however, Sarah Jane's parents decided against it. Laying their daughter out as bait seemed too great a risk.

Still, they believed that the police would come up with a plan to help them catch the man who had fixated on their daughter. Instead, they found that the officers themselves were eager to get up close and personal with Sarah Jane. When she reported a harassing call at work, they hung out and talked to her. One asked her out on a date despite knowing about Zack, to whom she was now engaged. Another told her that she should model for *Playboy*. "All this hit and I was just like a deer in a spotlight," said Sarah Jane. "I was such an easy target."

One evening, Sarah Jane and Zack were saying good night on the front porch when a prowler crouched in the bushes not two feet away and scratched on the window screen. The couple froze, too scared to move. Then they turned and walked into the house as slowly as possible, pretending that nothing was wrong. The police arrived with sirens blaring, giving the prowler plenty of warning and time to escape. After hearing Sarah Jane's story, one officer turned to her father and said: "You've got a really attractive daughter here, and you're just going to have to get used to this sort of thing."

Having a prowler around the house became such a regular occurrence that Sarah Jane's younger brother began keeping a knife under his bed. He was determined to protect his sister if someone got inside. But the prowler never did try to break in. Instead, he would creep up to Sarah Jane's window—located in the front of the ranch-style home—and scratch or tap at the glass. Although police staked out the house several nights, they never saw anything. Sarah Jane assumes that her stalker had a police scanner, which would enable him to pick up radio frequencies and identify the unmarked cars.

Somehow, he always seemed to be a step ahead of whatever measures Sarah Jane and her family took. When they changed their phone number to an unlisted one, he called it within days. To get away from him, her family moved from the house they've lived in for 14 years to a different neighborhood, forcing Sarah Jane's little brother to switch schools. Even so, within two weeks the stalker had managed to ferret out a listing so secret that the number wasn't even posted on their phone bill. Where Sarah Jane had been, what she had done, her plans—nothing escaped him. Convinced that he had to be eavesdropping to know so much, her parents had their house swept for electronic listening devices. Nothing was found.

SIX YEARS INTO the ordeal, Sarah Jane's stalker realized that the most effective way to get to her was to threaten her loved ones. Twice he called her at work to say that he was going to kill Zack, whom Sarah Jane had married some months before. One March morning, he announced that Zack was dead. Sarah Jane dropped the phone, the color drained from her face. The salespeople in the department store where she now worked thought she was going to pass out. She managed to pull herself together and phone home. Zack answered the phone, having just awakened. She reminded him to make sure the windows and doors were locked and warned him to be extra careful. Then she went to the bathroom and threw up.

The harassment continued. The stalker would call her at the department store, pretending to be a customer, and then masturbate during the conversation. He broke into both her and Zack's cars. He reported Sarah Jane's credit card as stolen so that her purchases were declined when she tried to use it. He placed a dead shrew outside Sarah Jane and Zack's back door, which disappeared and reappeared over the course of a couple of days.

When a colleague from the department store became friendly with Sarah Jane and Zack, the stalker added him to his hit list. "He threatened all kinds of awful things," recalled Sarah Jane. "Basically body parts he was going to cut off." Then he rattled off the friend's address to reinforce the fact that he knew exactly how and where to get to him.

Police speculated that some sort of sweeping computer access made him privy to confidential electronic files. All Sarah Jane knew was that no matter how many times she changed her unlisted phone number or how few people knew it, he still called.

The following month, the phone awakened Sarah Jane on her day off. Zack was at work. She picked up. "I bet it would be really difficult for you to get out of the house now," the caller said. She flung herself out of bed to check. Sure enough, he had wedged the trashcans under the doorknobs at the front and back of the house. She managed to call Zack before the phone rang again. During the next 45 minutes, the stalker called some 30 times. Each time he let the phone ring once, then hung up. Sarah Jane couldn't even make a call.

Although fear compelled her to tell Zack about that episode, she often tried to shield him from other occurrences. "I was trying to handle it myself, trying not to worry other people." Zack began to feel distanced from his new wife.

She didn't share much of what was happening to her with her parents, either. The self-inflicted lack of support that resulted, coupled with the pressures of taking a full course load at school and holding down a full-time job, began to show. "I had a hard time functioning at work," she recalled. "I'd burst into tears over the stupidest little problems." Her stomach would cramp at the least sign of adversity, including but not limited to any stalker contact. Unable to keep food down, she dropped 20 pounds and had to go on a banana, applesauce, and rice diet.

She tried hard to ignore the problem and focus on her academics and her job. "The more he called, the more I threw myself into finishing college and doing my job well." She graduated. A promotion to assistant human resource director and store manager followed the year after.

But ignoring the problem didn't make it go away. In November, Sarah Jane was heading home after giving a male co-worker a ride home. She had just turned down a side street by her house when a car pulled up behind her and tapped her bumper. She ran the red light in order to get away. He followed. Careening through the neighborhood at 50 miles per hour, Sarah Jane tried to negotiate the turn to her street. She didn't make it and landed in a ditch. Her pursuer drove on. Luckily, neither she nor the car sustained any damage.

Over the next two months, abusive phone calls, scare tactics and minor property damage attested to the man's escalating obsession. Afraid that people would assume she was making up a story, for she had little tangible proof, Sarah Jane spoke less and less about her predicament. She didn't even want her husband to tell the neighbors, although he finally persuaded her that they should know.

She clammed up around those familiar with the story as well. "Great! Peachy! Everything's fine," she would reply when asked how things were going. "You don't tell anybody because listening to you becomes a burden," she explained. "I guess it's hard because there's nothing they can do."

Friends began to distance themselves, some unable to cope with the little Sarah Jane did share about the stalking, others put off by how she had changed or how she chose to deal with the problem. Cody, a big floppy puppy from the ASPCA, helped blunt some of the loneliness that even a loving, supportive husband couldn't dispel. But the stalker didn't even allow that element of her life to go unmarked.

One day, Sarah Jane had dressed for work and was putting on her makeup when she let Cody in from the back yard. The six-month-old puppy shot through the door and jumped up on her. Bloody paw prints trailed across the floor and covered the front of her dress. Soon there was blood everywhere.

When she finally quieted him down, she turned his paws over to find that they had been slashed. Shaken, Sarah Jane rushed Cody to the vet. When she finally got to work, her beeper went off the minute she walked through the door. She headed to a phone on the sales floor and asked the operator to transfer the call. "Did you think that I couldn't get to your dog, babe?" the all-too familiar voice asked.

From then on, he drew nearer and nearer. She was run off the road three times in the space of two months. Her stalker would leave evidence in her neighbor's back yard attesting to his presence. But even the private detective Sarah Jane's parents hired wasn't able to nail him. This despite the camera equipment pointed out back from the guest bathroom's shower. "The game seems to be how close can he get to where I can't see him," said Sarah Jane.

The investigator decided to try and flush him out during the department store's grand reopening following a merger with another chain. He would stick by Sarah Jane's side to make sure that nothing happened to her, while at the same time forcing the stalker to make a move.

Figuring that she should be up-front, Sarah Jane told her supervisor—who had previously been so supportive—about the plan. The floor manager was preoccupied with arrangements for the big event, and didn't want any possible disturbances. "Isn't

the CEO supposed to be there that day? That could be a problem," she replied. The danger facing her employee apparently
didn't cross her mind. Shocked, Sarah Jane responded with typical sarcasm: "Well, if the stalker shows up and shoots, I promise
to lure him by the competition."

SARAH JANE'S stalker continued to terrorize her with calls that
swung between love and hate, regardless of what she did or
how she reacted. Well over a decade after that initial phone call,
Sarah Jane's past—and her future—has been compromised by
a man whose identity remained a mystery. "Put yourself in my
position," she said. "I'm 24, and I'd like to think about having
children. But am I going to give him that kind of leverage if this
isn't taken care of before then? Can you imagine? Getting that
call at work that said he's got my child? I can see it without it
even happening."

Whether or not Sarah Jane's stalker denies her the experience
of motherhood, he's already cost her the fun-filled adolescence
that most people enjoy. And despite tremendous self-awareness
and self-possession, the effects linger. Although she decided—
against her parents' and husband's wishes—to break away from
their unremitting protectiveness and do things on her own for
the first time ever, she couldn't shake the mistrust that so many
years of anonymous intimidation had instilled. Every day she
would look at the men passing by and think, "That could be
him."

Heads Up! Age Is No Guarantee

Unfortunately, your children's youth doesn't spare them
from the possibility of falling victim to obsessive attention and correspondingly obsessive behavior. So pay
close attention to what they tell you about the adults in
their lives, and to how those individuals conduct themselves with your kids.

11

Sidestep the Long Arm of Abuse

WHILE MANY OBSESSIVE REACTIONS develop out of the blue, most are triggered when one partner can't accept the end of a relationship. "If you leave me, I'll kill you stone-dead," Elizabeth (Betsy) McCandless Murray's abusive husband told her when she filed for divorce less than a year after they had married. "Marriage is for life and the only way out is death."

Betsy tried hard to escape that prophesy. She filed criminal charges against her husband, who had started beating her just ten days into their marriage. She obtained a protective order that he violated 13 times. She took a self-defense class. She left her job as a systems engineer at a Boston artificial-intelligence firm and went into hiding. She kept her new address secret, even after police told her that Sean J. Murray had fled to Ireland to evade arrest and probably wasn't going to return. Neither friends nor the detectives on her case knew where to locate her. In the end, however, her estranged husband kept the promise he had made. Six months after she walked away from her job, he shot her to death at their condominium when she stopped to collect mail a neighbor had been holding. Then he turned the gun on himself.

IN THE BURGEONING history of stalkers and their victims, the extensive measures Betsy took to protect herself sets her tragic story apart. The abuse that drove her to such measures, however, is all too commonplace. The appalling fact is that an estimated three million to four million American women are injured or killed each year as a consequence of domestic violence. According to a study published by the Center for Disease Control, domestic abuse may be responsible for more injuries to women than minor automobile accidents, rapes and muggings *combined.*

Stalking figures prominently in this national disgrace. National Institute of Justice figures reveal that 75 percent of all reported domestic assaults are committed after the couple has separated. Although most stalkings don't end in death, more than 1,000 women a year *are* killed by their estranged mates.

Cassy Baldwin*, a 50-year-old case manager for a Pennsylvania insurance company, is fighting those odds. After several threats against her life, Cassy served her estranged second husband with a restraining order. Rather than keeping Harry* away, the document seemed to provoke him. He vandalized the water pump by the shed behind her house. He slashed her tires. He cut the wires to her television and to the phone. He disconnected her electricity. He spied on her, first from the tops of the tall pine trees bordering the property, and then from a crawl space under the house. "You'll be sorry," he told her. "I'm going to get you."

She knew he had the means to do more than scare her. Before their separation, he had retrieved the 9mm handgun he kept hidden and threatened to commit suicide. "I want you to watch this," he told her. "I just want you to see what it looks like."

Two months later, he turned the gun on her after striking her in the face during an argument. "Are you afraid to die, Cassy?" he demanded. "I'm going to pull the trigger. You afraid to die?"

The incident marked the end of their relationship and the beginning of a series of death threats too numerous to count and too frightening to dwell on. Even though she has moved to another town, he continues to confront her. "I told you before. I won't go down in another divorce," he tells her again and again. "I will end this. And nobody else will have you."

Every once in a while, he reminds her that he can get as close as he wishes. Last February before driving home from work, for example, Cassy donned the coat she had left in her car. Then she noticed something in the right-hand pocket. She reached in and drew out three hollow-point bullets. She called her attorney, shaking with fear and barely able to breathe because she was crying so hard. "He's leaving his calling card," her lawyer said.

Despite the clearly illegal nature of Harry's activity, her attempts to seek legal redress proved fruitless. She was the outsider in a very small town populated by his very large family. He was related to the sheriff in his home county. He was even related to three deputy sheriffs in the county where she relocated.

Cassy's friends downplayed Harry's threats. "He would never do anything like that," they told her. Even her three adult sons—all of whom experienced his capacity for violence—said that she had to be exaggerating. But she knew he wouldn't hesitate to act. Over the course of her brief marriage, Cassy had learned disturbing facts about her husband's past.

Early on in their marriage, Harry admitted that his first wife called him a "mean, hateful bastard," and fled the home they shared with nothing but what she could fit into her minivan. She never returned to claim the rest of her belongings. But that didn't protect her from Harry's violent wrath. Twice he used deadly chemicals to destroy both her lawn and the paint on her new car. At the time, Cassy refused to believe his story. Throughout four years of courtship, he had been nothing but gentle, kind and soft-spoken. But his reaction to Cassy's leaving convinced her that he was capable of much worse.

"I take him dead serious," she said. After the threats started, she bought—and learned to use—her own handgun. She slept with it by her side and carried it wherever she went. "If I have to go out to the trash, I take my gun with me."

Still, he persisted. "I hope your psychic powers are good. That way you'll know when I'm coming for you," he announced over the phone one day.

"What do you intend to do?" she asked.

"Let's just put it this way," he replied. "I'm standing at the edge of a bridge. And I'm going over. And I'm not going alone."

WE ALL HAVE problems with rejection, especially if we're emotionally invested in a relationship. For the majority of us, however, rejection doesn't imply devastation. Even through the pain, however excruciating, our identities remain intact, our sense of self-worth bruised, perhaps, but still operational. That's not the case for most love-obsessed stalkers.

When Karen Winn broke off her extra-marital relationship with John A. Collins—a mild-mannered patrolman from Milton, Massachusetts—he refused to accept her decision. First he tried to intimidate her by threatening to kill her and her new boyfriend and then commit suicide. Next he launched a harassment campaign that included leaving mangled carcasses of chickens, opossums and a skunk on the door of the restaurant owned by Karen's new boyfriend and smearing it with excrement. The night she filed charges, John stormed over to Karen's house with an engagement ring in hand and promised to divorce his wife. Her refusal to accept his proposal sparked another round of abuse. "The victim now fears for her life," said then Assistant District Attorney Heidi Handler.

While "I'll-kill-myself-if-you-leave-me" histrionics may sound like overstated fare, they've become frighteningly real and frighteningly frequent, even among the under-21 set.

In Los Angeles, 18-year-old Matt Walker critically wounded his 16-year-old ex-girlfriend and killed her mother and sister after she took up with another student. The following day, cornered by police, he shot and killed himself. "He was totally obsessive," said a former classmate. "He just had to have her."

After Jennifer Kibbe severed her relationship, her former boyfriend repeatedly called her, followed her, kicked the side of her car from his motorcycle, and threatened suicide. A year later, just days before Jennifer was due to graduate from high school, he came to see her at the retirement home where she worked, armed with a rifle. At Jennifer's request, her boss called the police. When they arrived, the ex-beau jammed a clip into the gun and grabbed Jennifer by the neck. An officer jumped him, and she managed to escape.

"This is the scariest thing that has ever happened in my life," said a teenager whose former boyfriend was arrested on stalking charges. "When you meet a guy that you like and who likes you, you don't expect to end up like this. You figure if you break up and it's a really bad break, [you'll] just hate each other or something. You don't expect him to go nuts over it."

MANY OF THESE stalking cases share another characteristic. The original relationships are often dominated by inflexible, dominating men who are frequently physically and/or emotionally abusive. "The key word is control," said Threat Assessment Group senior analyst Jim Wright. "In domestic relationships, these people have to be the controller all the time. And when they lose control, they've been challenged to the point that they've got to react."

Consider Betsy Murray's marriage. After a passionate and charmed three-month courtship, her husband not only began to beat her regularly, he dictated every aspect of her life. He picked her up after work and forbade her to go on business trips or even out to lunch with her co-workers. He refused to let her visit her mother, and he actually threw away her address book in an attempt to proscribe all her outside contact.

In short, he tried to assume complete control of his wife's existence through a combination of intimidation and the brutal destruction of her sense of self.

Eventually, a woman who maintains a shred of identity will try to escape such treatment. But our society doesn't make it easy for a woman to get away. "No matter how affluent the couple, credit cards can be canceled immediately," said Karen Ahrens, who for two and a half years was the victim assistance coordinator for Olympia, Washington. "I don't know how many I've counseled who went into the bank only to find that their joint account had been emptied." In addition, since most abusers try to isolate their mates from their friends and family in order to solidify their own power and control, the victim often finds herself separated from any other financial or emotional resources.

GETTING OUT, HOWEVER, doesn't necessarily mean getting away, even for those who find the money, a place to stay and the wherewithal to go.

Some individuals retaliate by bludgeoning the woman who left them with an unending stream of expensive, time-consuming litigation regarding divorce or child custody issues. For the last 13 years, Alex Dillard*, a divorced mother of two who works as a nursing supervisor in San Diego, California, has been hauled into court—sometimes as often as 15 times in as many weeks—by the man to whom she was married for just over a year. Though he has yet to attend the psychological counseling mandated by the court or comply with a variety of other court orders, he is allowed to file motion after motion against Alex. And because they share custody of their children, she has no option but to respond.

Others try to control their former mates in a more violent fashion. Cathy Reilly* doesn't regret leaving her husband, who she said physically and verbally abused her on a daily basis. But these days life is even scarier than it used to be. "Then I knew how much he'd drunk and with whom," she said. "Now I have no idea. So I have no idea what to expect, ever. It's like Russian Roulette."

They met in the Missouri furlough house to which Daniel Reilly* had been transferred following a six year stint in prison. Cathy, then a 19-year-old college junior working toward a B.A. in criminal justice, was researching a paper about prison inmates' perspective of the penal system. A friend of hers knew Daniel, a handsome redhead, and thought he would talk.

Cathy was aware that Daniel had been convicted of felonious assault and aggravated robbery—he had plea-bargained it down from the original attempted murder charge—for stabbing a shop owner after getting caught stealing chips and dip in a market. But the gentle, sensitive, caring manner he showed her seemed to indicate that he had changed. "He convinced me that he wanted a new life, that he'd made a mistake and paid for it."

Daniel lost his temper twice during their courtship. During one argument, he locked the car doors and grabbed her by the hair. Afterward, he apologized and said he hadn't meant to hurt her. Cathy believed him. Convinced that he really did want to change his life, she moved in with him. That's when Daniel's heavy drinking—along with the physical abuse that would mark their marriage—established itself as a pattern. Still, she thought she could reform him. Her strict religious upbringing had taught her little about such behavior. And her low self-esteem convinced her that she didn't deserve better. They wed a year and a half later. Cathy was 21. "I had a lot of doubts, but I thought if we got married the abuse would stop," Cathy said.

She cried on the way to the reception. "Are those happy tears or sad tears?" her new husband asked her. "Happy tears," she answered. "No. Those are sad tears," he retorted. "Because you just realized that you've made the biggest mistake of your life."

His words scared her. "I suddenly had this dreadful feeling that things were going to get really bad," she recalled.

Cathy became pregnant within a year. But Daniel's physical and verbal abuse escalated nonetheless. When their daughter was born with colic, he reacted to her continuous crying by drinking constantly. "Shut her the fuck up," he would yell. At one point, he pulled his knife out and repeatedly stabbed the back of the recliner in which Cathy sat rocking her daughter. Alarmed that he might very well harm her baby, Cathy realized she had to get out.

She left when the baby was six weeks old and hid out at a women's shelter. She returned three times, only to leave again. Finally, four months later, she made a permanent break.

"That's when the shit hit the fan," she said. Daniel went through all the emotional phases the counselors at the women's shelter had warned her about. First he got angry. Then he claimed he was sorry. "I can't live without you," he pleaded. When that didn't work, he began to call her constantly. He tried to control her behavior by instilling fear about what would happen to her family if she didn't accede to his demands. "If you date someone else, I'll put your brother in a body bag," he promised. At one point he asked if she had talked to her father lately. "I got the old man this morning on his way to work. He's history." And he threatened her in graphic detail: "I'll kill you and get away with it. And if I don't, I'll be out in 17 years and I'll tell our daughter that I had to kill you because you were a crazy bitch."

Although she changed her number twice, people she had assumed were her friends gave Daniel her new unlisted phone number both times. In response, she cut herself off from all but a tiny fraction of those around her. The risk that people might not be on her side was simply too great.

Still, he managed to see her. Even after a protective order was issued, he took a factory job around the corner from Cathy's new apartment, which gave him an excuse to be in the neighborhood every day. That—along with his ongoing harassment—destroyed any sense of security she might have had. Every time he ran across her in his car, he would drive right up against her bumper, or whip around in front and then slam on his brakes. Since he always seemed to have a new vehicle, identifying him in time to avoid him was almost impossible.

Some evenings he stood outside her apartment at 3 A.M. and cried. Other evenings, he yelled. To protect herself at night from the possibility of his forcing his way into the apartment and harming her or the baby, Cathy dragged heavy furniture in front of the door and strung bells on the door's lock and across the one window that opened. Then she slept on the living room couch. "I figured I could slow him down before he got to my daughter," she said.

She kept telling herself that it couldn't get any worse. It did. Threats to harm her finally materialized during a court-ordered supervised visit with his 2-year-old daughter. When Cathy arrived to collect her daughter, he punched her hard enough to send her to the emergency room. Although five people witnessed the attack, he received only a 60-day sentence, with 57 days suspended, and a $500 fine, $450 of which was suspended. Three days and $50. He even managed to call her from jail—through a third party who transferred his collect call—to advise her that he would be out the following day and expected to see his child.

His attempts to intimidate her continued. His greatest weapon, aside from his ongoing abuse, was the illusion of omnipotence he created. Like most stalkers, he gave the impression that he was everywhere and knew everything. As a result, Cathy developed an ulcer—and a case of insomnia—that defied cure. Like most targets, she ran scared every moment of every day.

"Once a woman denies herself to someone as a victim when she has been his victim before, there will inevitably be an escalation as he tries to force her back into that situation," said Gavin de Becker. "Since control over the relationship becomes the most important goal in the stalker's life, any and all behavior becomes excusable."

SARAH MILLER*, AN attractive Illinois mother in her late twenties, knows what that can cost. Her former husband's past violence—including physical attacks on her and an attempted kidnapping of their 4-year-old son—made her all too aware of what he was capable of doing. When she finally left him after ten years of marriage and brutal battering, he could not accept the notion of life alone. So he tried to control her in the only ways remaining to him. He spied on her, followed her, called her and threatened her. Hunted like an animal, she became haunted by the feeling that every day might be her last. "I'm a normal person who made one mistake, and now I'm paying for it with everything I do," she said. "He's trying to destroy my life."

Once caught in marital abuse, victims come to believe they'll never break free. But that's just the beginning. Stalkers will go to extraordinary lengths to keep tabs on the person they want to hold onto. One young man took a private investigator course to better track his ex-girlfriend. A Detroit bouncer sold everything he owned in order to follow a woman to Los Angeles after she had taken a job with Delta Airlines and then posed as a Delta supervisor in order to learn of her whereabouts from her co-workers.

A STALKER CONSUMED by that kind of obsession winds up blotting out everything not directly associated with the target or the pursuit. He seeks to spark a reaction, any reaction, that confirms the impact he still has on his victim. Nothing else matters—even when the cost is prestige built on a lifetime of achievement.

Judge Sol Wachtler had everything a reasonable man might ever want: a wife of 41 years with whom he was in love, four grown children who remained devoted to him, and a well-paid position as chief judge of the New York State Court of Appeals, which many believe could have propelled him to the governor's mansion or the Supreme Court. But none of this seemed to matter when his former lover—wealthy Park Avenue socialite Joy Silverman—took up with another man. He reacted like a jealous teenager. Then he slipped into a major depression. Instead of acceding to his wife's plea that he see a psychiatrist, he opted to self-medicate with a variety of drugs obtained from several physicians. Finally, he decided that he had to get Joy back, no matter what, and no matter how she felt about it.

The plan started out a simple one. He would call her and hang up, enough so that she would be annoyed and want the intrusion to end. When she turned to him for help, he would stop calling and the problem would be solved. "And then I would again emerge as she once characterized me, as someone who walked on water," Sol told Barbara Walters during a *20/20* interview.

Joy never told him about the phone calls. "Yet, I still harbored this delusion that I could make her need me more," Sol said. So he escalated from phone calls to letters, and from annoyance to intimidation. The correspondence—signed by two characters he invented—grew increasingly obscene and threatening. "I'm going to fuck you over," read the back of one greeting card. He even sent a condom to Joy's 14-year-old daughter, along with a note advising her "the enclosed should be used by your boyfriend before you do it." Luckily, her mother intercepted the letter.

Ultimately, Sol resorted to extortion (from phone booths near his Long Island home, he demanded $20,000 in exchange for photos of Joy) and kidnapping threats. That's when the FBI nailed him. Unbeknownst to Sol, his former lover had, months before, called her friend William Sessions, then head of the Bureau, for help.

Sol, who until the time of his arrest oversaw 5,000 judges, pleaded guilty to one count of sending harassing letters through the mail. During the trial, Sol and his psychiatrist contended that the judge's subsequent behavior was caused by side effects resulting from combining amphetamines (Tenuate) with an antidepressant (Pamelor), along with a powerful sleep aid (Halcion) and codeine for his persistent headaches. The prosecutors and the judge who sentenced him to 15 months in jail, however, thought otherwise. Acts of anger and intimidation carried out by a man in full control of his actions is how they labeled it.

During the Walters interview, Sol spoke of the punishment that has come from the loss of the privilege to ever again sit as a judge and of the disgrace he's brought to "myself, my family, my court and those who believed in me." He did not mention the terror that he introduced into the lives of Joy Silverman and her 14-year-old daughter.

ONE WOULD THINK that the violence often associated with domestic stalking cases would be more preventable than other crimes of passion executed in the heat of the moment. But most police departments treat these situations as isolated incidents of domestic violence. All too often, the result is a tragedy that might have been averted.

When Maria Navarro called 911 to say that her estranged husband, who had threatened to kill her, was en route to her house, she naturally expected help from the authorities. Yet despite Raymond Navarro's prior arrests for battery, and despite a temporary restraining order issued against him because of the obsessive vigil he had kept on her since their separation a year prior, the Los Angeles County Sheriff's Department did not send a unit to investigate. Fifteen minutes after the call, 27-year-old Maria, two aunts and a family friend lay dead.

Six months later, Anna Alfaro's former boyfriend—a North Hollywood gang member named Ruben Dario Garcia—menaced her with a knife. This followed four months of threats and physical assaults. Two days later he abducted her at gunpoint and raped and killed her. Ruben wasn't apprehended until almost five years later.

During the ten months that followed Connie Chaney's split with her husband, Wayne, the 26-year-old mother from Des Plaines, Illinois, filed four 30-day orders of protection. During that time, Wayne tried to run her over in a parking lot and raped her at gunpoint. Two months after being arrested for the latter, a judge lowered Wayne's bail from $300,000 to $100,000 and he walked out of jail. Connie became increasingly frightened, to the point of screaming whenever someone walked up behind her. "He's gonna kill me, he's gonna kill me," Connie kept saying in response to his ongoing threats.

She was finally granted a two-year restraining order prohibiting her former husband from having any contact with her at all. It didn't help. Three months later, on St. Patrick's Day, Connie was proven right. "I couldn't live with myself thinking or knowing she won, or she got me. No! This is war," Wayne wrote in his diary shortly before gunning her down. Ten days later, police killed her murderer in a shoot-out.

As in so many stalking cases, it was a case of too little judicial support, too late. "[She] did what the victim [is] supposed to do. She came forward and reported the crime to police and kept police and the state's attorney's office informed," said Bruce Paynter, a supervisor in the state attorney's office. "What more could [she] have done?"

Good question. "The detective . . . said he [was] busy, he had more important cases to deal with," Debra Burkhart told reporters about bringing her former boyfriend up on charges of aggravated stalking. "I told him, 'Well, will I get first priority when it's written up for murder?'"

But all too often, neither persistence nor an aggressive stance gets results. "I called so many times they finally told me to stop. They said, 'We're getting tired of you calling us,'" said Carol Allen, a Tampa, Florida, resident whose abusive ex-husband started to stalk her after serving a prison sentence. The very next day, the man to whom she had once been married stabbed her in the chest. If she hadn't been wearing a leather jacket, he probably would have killed her. "They listened then," said the 37-year-old.

The reasons for law enforcement's lackadaisical response run from lack of awareness about the problem to, in some cases, a legal inability to do much about the activity. But even the most prompt police action doesn't always solve the problem, since apprehension and conviction provide only temporary safety guarantees.

The day he was released after serving 21 months in prison for trying to kill his ex-wife and two children with his car, Jose Luis Enriquez called the East Los Angeles house to say that he was coming over to finish the job.

In Chicago, Dawn Wilson's ex-husband was arrested nine times in the twelve months following their divorce, on charges of battery, violation of protective orders and forcible entry. That didn't deter him. He continued to trail, threaten, and attack her. Not even a three-year jail term gave her much relief, since he continued to threaten her by phone and by mail from behind bars.

LIKE MANY MEN, Dawn's husband seems to believe that his wife belongs to him and therefore does not have the right to leave him. Even if the relationship doesn't escalate into serious violence, these kinds of men tend to snap when their mates decide to end a relationship. "Which means that not only the former mate, but anyone who is trying to facilitate the separation is at extreme risk," said Karen Ahrens, former victim assistance coordinator for Olympia, Washington. "Especially friends who are harboring the victim."

One Washington couple chose to shelter a 40-year-old woman friend whose ex-husband had assaulted her during their marriage and frightened her badly once she had left him. As a result, they became his stalking victims as well. He shadowed them, emptied a box of nails in their driveway, and ultimately tried to run them over as they walked on the sidewalk. Yet, since the violations spanned two counties, it wasn't even considered a stalking case until Ahrens assembled some 30 reports from various jurisdictions. Her diligence led to his arrest and conviction.

Upon getting out of jail, he promptly violated every term of his probation. His prison term apparently did nothing to alleviate his obsession with his former wife. In the months that followed, reports that he was keeping her under surveillance and that he was going to hire a hit man to kill her continued to filter back to her.

"THE DAY HIS sentence ends, mine begins," said one victim about a similar plight. "I have no doubt he'll be right back on my doorstep."

Don't Go There

If the man you're dating starts showing signs of possessiveness and control, telling you what to do, what to wear, and who you can socialize with, you need to reconsider your relationship very carefully. A guy who wants to control you will often enforce that impulse through violence during the relationship, and stalking once you finally try to break free. Leaving early, before he's had time to become invested emotionally, may save you a lot of pain down the line.

12

Watch for the Signs

UNRELENTING HARASSMENT CONSUMES your life. Knowing you were once intimate with the person responsible for your misery makes it worse. You ask yourself the same question again and again: How could I have married such a monster?

No matter what you do, the threats and the abuse escalate. "They tell me [these obsessions] usually end in death for one or both parties," said one victim in rural Tazewell County, Virginia. "I don't like that solution. I think there should be another one."

That notion of death has become all too real for Rebecca Watson*. On Columbus Day, the 31-year-old divorcee called her boyfriend and colleague—an ex-cop named Andrew Hill*—to confirm plans to go into work that afternoon after meeting for lunch and a video at her place. By 2 P.M., the idea of relaxing for the rest of the rainy afternoon sounded more appealing than catching up on paperwork. So she dropped Andrew off at his car, which, as usual, he had parked in the nearby country club lot in order to avoid antagonizing Rebecca's jealous ex-husband. She watched him jump into his green 1979 Chrysler and turn over the ignition. Suddenly, a ball of flame exploded from under his seat, swept over his head with a deafening roar and blew out the rear window of his car. Andrew dove out the door. "That son of a bitch tried to blow me up!" he yelled.

REBECCA, A FORMER Boise, Idaho, probation and parole officer who still works in the criminal justice field, met Damian Crowell* ten years before. The local boxing announcer left a definite impression on Rebecca that day. She thought he was obnoxious. "You will go out with me," he told her after she declined his initial overtures. In the end, he was right.

Born overseas to Southern Baptist missionary parents, Rebecca had spent her first 13 years in Asia. By the time she returned to the United States, the overweight adolescent felt like an outcast. "I was a big nerd in high school. I knew four people, maybe." The low self-esteem that resulted hung on long after the baby fat had dropped and her popularity had grown. Even at 22, attention from an attractive older man—who could be quite charming once he put his ego aside—was hard to resist.

Within two days Rebecca had capitulated. Within six months the couple was discussing the possibility of marriage. Although Rebecca didn't admit it to herself at the time, she had been primed to rebel against—and escape—her strict religious upbringing. Damian offered her a way out.

Eight months after their first meeting, she married him. But the relationship didn't provide the companionship she had hoped for. She worked during the day and then came home to domestic duties. Damian made little effort to include her in his work or to help her. "I was the little woman, and I sat at home feeling very much alone," said Rebecca.

She tried to talk to him, but he didn't want to hear that she was unhappy. "You're the one who's fucked up," he told her when she suggested they try marriage counseling. "You get help."

Feeling abandoned and miserable, with only her golden retriever to turn to at home, Rebecca fell into an affair. Suspicious, her husband borrowed her keys on the pretext of changing the oil in her car, entered her office in the state building, and found letters from Timothy Scott*, her lover.

Returning home, he confronted his wife, and then called Timothy and demanded that he come to their home to discuss Rebecca's involvement with him. "Don't come over! He has a gun! He wants to kill you!" Rebecca screamed in the background.

Timothy came anyway. Damian greeted him at the door and then moved to stand by Rebecca. "Take this person," he told him. "I don't want her anymore." He then accused Rebecca of sleeping around with colleagues in the probation and parole department. Timothy left after 20 minutes. Rebecca left after Damian belted her across the jaw.

She stayed away for several days, returning only when her husband agreed to go into counseling. Therapy didn't help. Although he didn't hit her again, Rebecca knew he wouldn't hesitate. Meanwhile, he kept an eye on her 24 hours a day. He would call the office and grill Rebecca's secretary if she wasn't there. With whom had she left? When was she coming back? He followed up with other parole officers if the answers didn't satisfy him. His inquisitions raised questions and eyebrows at work.

In a turnabout, the former recluse now refused to leave her alone. If his work required him to leave town, he would force her to accompany him. He cut her down constantly. Whenever she complained about his actions, he flung her affair back in her face. In his eyes, her indiscretion had expunged his responsibility for the failure of the relationship. It was all her fault.

Evidence of her one affair proved that she obviously had had—and was currently having—others, according to Damian. During one of his rages, he accused her of having gotten pregnant by someone and aborting the fetus. When she denied the charge, he forced her to call her gynecologist while he listened on the other line. Their lack of intimacy was her fault too, he railed. It seemed that no humiliation he could heap on her would suffice.

Rebecca had been unhappy and lonely before. Now she was miserable and too scared to leave. Damian had a temper, and he had a gun collection. "I didn't know what he would do. And I was so insecure, I didn't know if I could survive on my own. I was terrified that I wouldn't know how to handle myself." So she stayed, even though the relationship had deteriorated to the point where she hated coming home and being in the house with him.

When Damian lost his job, she supported both of them. That same year, he underwent three major surgeries. She had been tempted to leave before, but she couldn't justify abandoning him when he was critically ill. "Every time I got close to leaving, something would come up," she recalled.

For the next five years, Damian made sure that Rebecca's life revolved around him. Part of the strategy included isolating her from her friends and family. The latter wasn't hard to do, since Rebecca was too embarrassed to admit to her close-knit family that her marriage hadn't worked out. He made certain that she was totally dependent on him, and increasingly unable to function alone.

Finally, after he had called during her lunch hour with his by now routine questions concerning her whereabouts, Rebecca decided that she wasn't going to put up with this anymore. After work, in the company of another woman parole officer with whom she had become friends, she returned home, packed two suitcases, grabbed her golden retriever and left. Her colleague let her stay rent-free in her apartment.

Taken by surprise, Damian reacted calmly. "We'll talk soon," he said. "I want to go to counseling and work this out." But Rebecca knew she would never return.

Not that he didn't try to force her to come back. The relentless campaign continued even once he had started living with another woman three and a half months into the separation. Despite a barrage of flowers, cards and letters, obscene phone calls, and the charge in federal court that she was responsible for a burglary of his house, she held firm. In the meantime, Rebecca's friendship with Andrew Hill had turned to romance.

That October, she moved from the parole officer's apartment to a house owned by some other friends. On moving day, the phone rang at 9:45 P.M., but the caller hung up as soon as she answered. "Bet you your bottom dollar it's Damian," she told Andrew. Fifteen minutes later, someone stood pounding on the front door. Rebecca tried to look through the peephole, but it was covered with a thumb.

"Who's there?" she asked.

"Police! There's been a report of trouble at this address that we're here to check out."

Rebecca recognized Damian's voice. "You're not the police," she countered. "I want you to leave."

"I just want to give you an insurance check from the burglary," Damian said.

Rebecca knew that she was still due her share of the insurance settlement. So when he refused to slip it through the mail slot, she agreed to open the door leaving the security chain attached. In a flash, Damian kicked the door in, knocking Rebecca up against the wall. He pulled a small automatic as he forced his way through the door and pointed it in the air.

"Where is he?" Damian demanded.

"Give me the gun, Damian," she said loudly enough to alert Andrew that her estranged husband was armed. She tried to wrest the weapon from him, but he pushed her against the wall and ran into the bedroom, looking for Andrew. Instead, he found the bed neatly made. He returned to the living room and knocked Rebecca to the ground. Andrew had just come out of the kitchen. Damian pointed the gun at his chest.

"Get out of my house!" Rebecca demanded. "This is *my* house. Get out!"

Amazingly, he did. But he didn't go quietly. He screamed accusations from the porch. "How can you do this to me? We're still married. You're not supposed to be seeing anybody." In an effort to calm him down, Rebecca offered to discuss the situation with him in the house as long as he was unarmed. Damian released the chamber and a bullet fell out. Then he handed Rebecca the gun and walked inside.

They talked for ten minutes. When Rebecca reasserted that she wasn't coming back and announced that it was time for him to go, he left. On the way out, she returned his gun to him. "I didn't want him to come back," she said.

Unwilling to let Damian get away with what he had done, Rebecca filed a warrant against him for breaking and entering and for assault. Andrew filed a warrant for assault and brandishing a gun. Then, afraid that Damian would come after her once the warrants were served, Rebecca packed some clothes, put her dog in the car, and abandoned her new home in favor of a friend's house.

The police didn't take matters as seriously as Rebecca had. Because they had worked with Rebecca and Andrew, and because they knew that Andrew was an ex-cop, they found the incident hilarious. One detective, realizing that Rebecca really felt threatened, offered to have Damian "taken care of" for $100. She refused.

In December, Damian attacked in a new way. Rebecca had been living in her new home for approximately three weeks when recordings of conversations she'd had on the phone were circulated to various men she was dating. While the wording of the attached notes varied, the theme remained the same: "So you think you're the only one."

Rebecca called the telephone company. An investigation revealed that a tape recorder had been spliced into her phone lines under the house. The phone company advised her that wiretapping was a federal violation and recommended that she take action.

When she contacted the police about the wiretapping, they referred her to the FBI. The FBI, however, didn't want anything to do with the case. "It's a domestic," they said, rolling their eyes. Apparently, that rendered it unworthy of attention.

That same month, Damian went to court on the breaking and entering charges, as well as the assault charges. The judge gave him six months for one, twelve for the other, and suspended the sentence. As long as Damian didn't contact Rebecca or go near her, he would do no time.

But Damian couldn't—or wouldn't—stop. He traced obscene messages like LUV269 in the dust on her car's rear windshield. The deluge of letters, cards, hang-ups and obscene phone calls to her unlisted phone number recommenced. She saw his car pass by her house at least twice a night. "He's out there. He's watching me," she realized.

TERRIFIED OF WHAT his next move might be, Rebecca learned to look in her rear view mirror ten times a minute as she drove. Every time she walked out her door, she looked over her shoulder. She never knew what to expect when she checked the mail or answered the phone. Fear made functioning normally at work and at home increasingly difficult. Yet no one, including the police, seemed concerned for her. Instead, people seemed to consider her a tramp.

The court had forbidden Damian to contact Rebecca. But shortly before their divorce became final, he called her. "Well, would you like to go out to dinner to celebrate our anniversary, or would you like to go out to dinner to celebrate the divorce?" he asked. To a bystander, the words would have sounded downright friendly. But they—along with his tone of voice—chilled Rebecca more than his threats had. "It was like he was saying, 'I'm letting you know that I'm aware that this is our anniversary, and I'm also aware that the divorce is almost final, *bitch*!'" Rebecca recalled.

She packed her bags, and that night got out of the house she had lived in less than four months. "You can identify a threat from the intonation as well as what's said," Rebecca asserted.

"It doesn't need to be *I'm gonna kill you* or *I'm gonna hurt you* to be scary."

Two months later, another recording device materialized under her house. She had gone out to pick up a prescription she had phoned in. "A guy called to ask if it was ready," the pharmacist told her. "Not again!" she thought as she raced back home. The only way anyone could have known that she had ordered a refill was if he had listened in on her conversation with the pharmacy. The tape recorder was right back where she expected it to be, just inside the crawl space beneath the house.

No fingerprints were found in the crawl space or on the tape recorder, wires or the fence, so police couldn't tie Damian to the wiretap. But they could nail him for violating the terms of his suspended sentence. Instead of being sent to jail, however, Damian was put on 12 months probation, and told to report to the office where Rebecca and her boyfriend worked as probation and parole officers. "Stay away from her and get on with your life," the judge told him.

Damian, however, had decided to go on the judicial offensive. He sued Rebecca for not paying the mortgage on the house they shared. The judge dismissed the suit when she explained that she no longer lived there. Damian also tried unsuccessfully to sue Andrew for making harassing phone calls.

The summer brought anonymous flowers, clipped articles about female sexual problems ranging from frigidity to nymphomania, letters slipped under the door delineating what an awful person Rebecca was, and a cassette recording of the song "Private Eyes Are Watching You" taped to the door. Unbeknownst to Rebecca, Damian had hired a private investigator to spy on her.

In addition, he began to harass those close to Rebecca, including the men she dated and even her deeply religious 71-year-old mother. She began to fear not for herself but for the lives of everyone who cared about her. "That's how he'll get to me," she told herself. The guilt she felt—and the migraines that resulted—almost incapacitated her.

She already blamed herself for her own misery. Her self-esteem had plummeted. But this was too much. "I'm fair game because I was stupid enough to marry you. So come after me," Rebecca wanted to say. "My mother didn't marry you. The guys I'm dating didn't marry you. None of these people had anything to do with you. Leave them alone."

Rebecca developed new daily routines. Most evenings when she came home from work, she checked under the house to see if another tape recorder had been planted. She watched everything she said on the phone and in her house.

One day, Andrew needed to make a confidential call from her home in reference to a pre-sentence report he had to file for work. As a procedural precaution, he double-checked the crawl space under the house before picking up the phone. There was yet another recording device. "Look what's here," he announced to Rebecca, who had walked outside with him.

They checked the tape that evening, in the presence of a lieutenant from the police department. A conversation they had shared about the case the night before had been recorded. Although police dusted for fingerprints, both tape and machine came up clean.

Damian continued to send correspondence to a number of Rebecca's friends and occasionally to their mates. He tampered with her car, affixing obscene fake tags to her license plate. But the number of episodes diminished.

If Rebecca took any comfort in the five weeks of relative calm, the events of October 13—Columbus Day—shattered that forever. She watched the fireball that Damian's bomb triggered with a sense of disbelief. "I felt like I was watching 'Miami Vice,'" she said. Even after all the months of telling herself that she was just paranoid and then having her suspicions confirmed, she still couldn't believe what had happened. If she had followed through with her original plan, she would have been in the car too.

The blast—which resulted in a permanent hearing loss for Andrew—brought the police and the FBI to the scene. That's when Rebecca found out that a second bomb filled with gunpowder, BBs, shot, finishing nails and tacks had failed to detonate because it had been wired to a painted surface. The lack of a ground, a prerequisite for current to flow, had prevented the bomb from exploding.

The mistake saved Andrew's life.

DURING THE INVESTIGATION, Damian argued that Rebecca and Andrew had rigged the bomb themselves in order to set him up. Within two weeks, however, the list of suspects had narrowed to one. A year after Damian had broken into her house, law enforcement had finally begun to take Rebecca seriously. The problem now was to put together a case that would stick.

At least that's how law enforcement saw it. Things weren't that clear cut for Rebecca. She had lived in fear of Damian, but she hadn't reckoned with a premeditative killer. She also hadn't reckoned with the sudden notoriety the firebombing brought her. The reactions of those around her just made matters worse. "If I sit here will the seat blow up?" one prominent attorney joked. "If we're lucky, it will," she snapped.

After the bombing, Rebecca stayed with friends. Eventually, she returned to her place. Whenever the police thought they were ready to arrest Damian, they would call to warn her, and she would move out. Then they would reconsider, wanting to gather more evidence before indicting him. And she would return home, only to be uprooted the next time. Finally, after months of jumping back and forth, Rebecca just got tired. "I'm taking my house back. I'm taking my life back," she announced. "If he's going to get me, he's going to get me no matter where I am." So she moved back to her house, prepared to stay.

Despite her resolve, the bombing incident devastated her. Coping with the everyday occurrences of her life became increasingly impossible. Anxious, profoundly depressed and feeling thoroughly guilty about the bruises and permanent hearing loss that Andrew had sustained, she tortured herself with questions about what Damian would do next, and with the knowledge that pure dumb luck had saved her and Andrew. She couldn't escape the realization that she had married the man who had tried to kill them. If she had made such a radical mistake, how could she trust herself to make a reasonable decision about anything else?

People didn't understand the depth of her pain. She couldn't explain. Instead, she erected a wall to protect herself and withdrew even more. Finally, she began seeing a therapist. A psychological test rated her anxiety level at 100 percent.

Revealing the intimate details of her married life—and her affair—to the police and prosecutors made her feel like the city tramp. Anticipating the exposure of her private life that Damian's trial would bring added to her agony. She dreaded facing Damian in court.

Her therapist understood. He helped her turn the guilt she harbored into anger, and reminded her that the disclosures would strip away Damian's power to blackmail her. "He doesn't expect you to go through with this because he thinks you don't have the courage," the therapist said. As she walked out, he added a final note of encouragement. "Go in there and nail the son of a bitch!"

Damian's prosecution taught Rebecca about her personal strength in a way that nothing else could have. "I knew when I walked into that courtroom, he was going to stare me down. That was part of the power he had over me. And I determined that no matter how hard it was, I was going to establish eye contact first thing, get it over with. And I was going to make him look away first. That was one of the hardest things I've ever done in my life. But I did it. And it worked."

In an effort to discredit her, Damian's lawyer brought up her affair at every turn, even though the prosecutor objected and the judge denied its relevance each time. Damian had illegally taped a conversation in which Rebecca and Andrew joked about enticing her former husband to violate his probation so they could have him arrested. That was used against her. "You tried to set him up, didn't you?" railed the defense attorney. "Just like you set up the bomb. You did that yourself."

Press accounts labeling Rebecca as Damian's wife (instead of former wife) and Andrew as her lover added to the horror. Rebecca chose not to dignify the insinuations with a response. But she suffered not just for herself but also for her missionary parents and the reactions of their friends.

In the end, the prosecution prevailed. Damian was found guilty on nine counts, including the manufacturing and possession of a bomb and several counts of wiretapping. He was sentenced to 15 years in a federal penitentiary, with another 15 years suspended. He has since been released. Rebecca's one hope is that the threat of going back to jail to serve out the suspended sentence will deter him from further antagonism against her. Deterrents, however, have never worked with him in the past.

Although Damian remarried while in jail, he has not forgotten. Notes to Rebecca's sister, brother-in-law and mother—the last after Rebecca's brother died of a heart attack—are his way of saying that he has continued to track her family.

The reminders are superfluous. "People say, 'Why worry? He's married now,'" said Rebecca. "But it's not love. It's obsession. It's: *How dare you walk away from me. If you walk away from me, I'm going to ruin you, get you to the lowest point of your life so that no one else will want you.*"

He came close. Two years after Damian was taken off the streets, Rebecca still couldn't concentrate enough to read a book, watch a television show or carry on an extended conversation. She would sit and stare at the walls, even on the job. No matter how hard she tried, she couldn't do her work. Finally, unable to function, she quit.

The insurance money she received upon her brother's death allowed her to take an eight-month vacation. The time off helped. When she eventually interviewed for a new position in the criminal justice system, her prospective employers insisted on speaking with Rebecca's therapist to make sure she would put the incidents behind her.

The assurances must have convinced them; Rebecca got the investigator job. But the emotional scars remain. She still checks over her shoulder and screens all her calls before picking up. She still can't believe that all this ever happened to her.

Thankfully, she's coming around ever so slowly. When strangers ask about her ex-husband, she tells them about what happened. "I'm past the shame of it," she said. "It's not my fault."

Just Say No to Power & Control

No matter what anyone else tells you, you're not to blame when it comes to being a stalking victim. You're simply the target of someone who won't allow you to exclude him or her from your life. His or her actions are designed to control your behavior. Remember: You're not a puppet. Just because he or she pulls your strings, doesn't mean you have to react in the manner he or she intended.

13

You're Right: This Can't Be Love

I F YOU'RE INCLINED TO ROMANTICIZE, you might be tempted to view stalkers as lovelorn individuals ruled by their passion for one person. But that doesn't explain the countless numbers for whom stalking has become a chronic pattern of behavior.

Although such patterns usually only come to light when law enforcement gets involved, they're more common than most of us would like to think. Visit college campuses across the country and you'll find any number of students exhibiting such behavior. They'll date a girl, and eventually insist on dropping her off at class, picking her up from class, and knowing where she is at every moment, according to former FBI behavioral scientist Jim Wright, now senior analyst with the Threat Assessment Group. When the girl finally feels smothered and wants to end the relationship, the chronic stalker often becomes abusive. He tends to repeat this scenario with each new attraction.

THE DYNAMIC DOESN'T change just because the couple happens to be married. In fact, the only real difference is the physical abuse and intimidation the budding stalker inflicts on his spouse before she finally abandons the relationship.

When the fear of staying surpassed the fear of leaving, Karen Zydow*—a volunteer for the Council Against Domestic Violence in Lansing, Michigan—walked away from 23 years of physical abuse and marriage. During the next four years, her ex-husband, Nick*, stalked her at home and at work. He beat her (shattering her eardrums in the process), burned her clothing, broke windows, destroyed the interior of her car with acid, shot at her house and held her at gunpoint for three hours. When the law wouldn't—or couldn't—help her for long, she donned a bulletproof vest and then ran from the situation. Finally, Nick stopped stalking her. But he continued his pattern of harassment. "Since then he has married twice and done this to three other victims," she said.

Nick Zydow is a serial stalker. He's not the exception. Dig deep enough into a stalker's past, and you'll usually find similar abuses.

Mark David Bleakley, a former carwash manager, blatantly advertised his proclivity by ordering two personalized California license plates that read ISTLKU and ISTLKU2. Perhaps if he had gotten them earlier, his 26-year-old victim, Leslie Wein, might have been forewarned and stayed away. Instead, she got involved.

Shortly after she broke off their two-year relationship, Mark began to terrorize her. He slashed her tires, poured acid on her car, physically assaulted her, kidnapped her German Shepherd and threatened to kidnap her. On May 24, 1991, Mark was arrested. The first person to be charged under a felony stalking law, he was sentenced to one year, with an additional five years probation. Instead of being sent to jail, however, he was remanded to a lock-down drug and mental health rehabilitation clinic to serve his time.

The very first chance he got, Mark violated the terms of his probation, which ordered him to keep away from Leslie. Allowed a brief leave from the psychiatric facility in order to pick up his car, he tried to track her down at the health club to which they had both belonged. Not a big surprise considering his past, for although Leslie Wein was the first to prosecute him, she was hardly his first victim. According to a detective involved in the case, Mark stalked a total of five women from 1979 to 1992. Two of his previous targets moved out of state to escape him, one out of the country.

ALTHOUGH THE STALKER caught up in the throes of his pursuit might disagree, his motivation doesn't stem from the reaction to a particular individual. Rather, it's the act of stalking that's important. For the obsessed, the object is to find an individual who fits his fantasy and will unwittingly play into his scenario.

Jorge Marquez*—a capable artist whose lack of success at holding down a job is probably due to his allegedly heavy abuse of drugs such as methamphetamine—began to threaten and harass his wife, Teri*, when she filed for divorce after just nine months of marriage. He followed her. He surveilled her. He ran her old white station wagon off the road twice. After cutting her off another time, he jumped out of his car and menaced her with a baseball bat. Bashing a parked car next to hers, he moved toward her, the bat raised over his head. "You're fuckin' dead!" he proclaimed.

"You better cover your fat ass, 'cause you don't have long to live," he threatened soon after. When Teri hung up, he called back. "I'm not kidding," he insisted. He renewed the threat a week later. "I'm gonna get you," he yelled while driving by her residence and honking his horn.

He scared Teri badly, just as he had probably scared former girlfriends Patricia Johnson* and Carole Brown*. Jorge had been on probation for violating a restraining order Patricia had placed on him when he met Teri. Carole, a 28-year-old bartender who responded to Jorge's physical abuse by slapping him back, had also complained to police about being followed and harassed by Jorge after their break-up. Shortly thereafter, she disappeared. Although police have never found a body, several confidential informers told the investigating detective that Jorge had confessed—and at times boasted—of killing her and burying her in the desert. He forbade Teri to mention Carole's name, but he alluded to the killing. "I have a tendency to go out to the desert," he told her. "Lye does a real good job at dissolving body parts."

Jorge denies killing Carole Brown. "I lie a lot," he told the detective who confronted him with what he had heard from informants and from Teri. Jorge doesn't refute the stalking charges. When asked why he persists, he replies, "I can't stand it when they leave me."

WHEN A TARGET proves too difficult to get near or no longer provides the stalker with the emotional charge he feeds on, he frequently transfers his obsession elsewhere. Sometimes it's just a question of proximity. Occasionally, his actions will lead to arrest. But, as so many cases illustrate, even successful prosecution provides only a temporary reprieve. Unless the stalker is taught to reevaluate his behavior and redirect his thinking, additional victims are almost a certainty.

At the age of 21, James Otis Sims met Kaye Campbell, an auburn-haired, green-eyed 16-year-old, at her summer waitressing job in Tuscaloosa, Alabama. He quickly tapped her affections. Nice, courteous and attentive, the tall handsome stranger provided her with a reprieve from a life suddenly made hellish by her parents' ugly separation. They talked when he visited her at the coffee shop during her shifts. He requested permission to ask her out, even though he only intended to drive her up to a fishing shack in order to leave off a ladder. "It was all very innocent, very genteel, very up-front," recalled Kaye, a devout Christian.

However, as the relationship intensified, James became increasingly domineering. He would literally force her to stay out past her curfew. Her protests angered him.

Not surprisingly, the late nights got her in trouble with her parents. "I was not a willful child or a bad kid," said Kaye.

"He was just more trouble than I knew how to deal with." So she tried to break up with James. In response, James began to hound her by phone. He would call in the middle of the night. He drummed up support from Kaye's friends and had them act as go-betweens. And he tracked her. "He'd show up wherever I was. I didn't know enough to be worried. I was just bewildered."

So she just kept on seeing him. The week prior to her 17th birthday, after watching a ballgame at her father's house, they headed to the park where they would often go to talk and sit on the swings. When James became strident about how they had to work out their relationship, Kaye asked to go home.

Instead, he drove her to a different park. There, as if transformed by the midnight hour, James grew less and less rational. "You're perfect because you know God," he told Kaye. "You're going to have my baby and then I'll kill myself."

"It was like I was the Virgin Mary and he was going to leave his legacy," said Kaye. Suddenly afraid that he had lost his mind, she announced that she would walk home. In response, James hurled a heavy set of keys onto her foot, then rushed to comfort her and dispel her pain and fright.

Kaye allowed herself to be consoled and got in the car with him. "I'll take you home," he promised. Instead, he floored the accelerator and sped in the opposite direction of her house, running every traffic signal and stop sign. He kept a hand clamped on Kaye to prevent her from trying to get out of the car.

He finally stopped at the fishing shack he had taken her to on their first date. Over the next two days, he took advantage of her sexually. Police arrested him when he drove Kaye back into town for food supplies. Formal charges, however, were never brought against him.

During subsequent months, James broke into Kaye's house with a knife, forced her to return to the fishing shack at gunpoint, and stalked her. Finally, he disappeared as abruptly as he had surfaced, leaving the teenager to cope with a sense of guilt and the feeling that someone she had cared for had betrayed her trust.

She wouldn't hear from James again for 14 years. During that time, James latched onto others. Parasitical relationships with a variety of elderly people whom he alternately charmed, manipulated, terrorized and stalked provided him with food, lodging and finances. His romantic liaisons replicated the time he had spent with Kaye in terms of both his possessiveness and his controlling nature. Arson and new demonstrations of physical abuse—including locking one woman in a closet for days—were added to his repertoire. The majority of his victims were too scared to fight back, legally or otherwise.

FOUR YEARS LATER, he met 19-year-old Sandy Waite, an Orange County, California, college student and part-time waitress who bore an uncanny resemblance to Kaye. They dated just five months. Almost 20 years later, James still believes that they will live a happily married life raising kids on a farm. Sandy's marriage has done little to squelch his fantasy.

As usual, he initially seduced Sandy with his charm, politeness and attentions. However, his relationship with her deteriorated quickly. James tried to control what she wore, where she went, whom she spoke with and the friends with whom she associated. He chose the movies they saw. Sandy was never consulted. They would go to dinner at his favorite restaurants, even though these tended to serve seafood, which she hated. Eventually, he grew to resent anything—like family or school—that took Sandy away from him. According to James, Sandy was to focus on no one and nothing but him.

That didn't go over well. Independent even then, she had been feeling increasingly constricted by James' expectations and demands. So she broke up with him. Three days later, he tracked her down on campus, grabbed her arm so roughly that her books went flying, and punched her.

During their time together, James had hinted at his potential for violence only once, when he refused to let her out of the car after driving her to a family gathering. His reaction terrified her. "You're in a relationship with somebody you thought was calm and polite enough never to raise a hand to somebody," Sandy explained. "And all of a sudden, you're walking around with a shiner. I just bawled. I couldn't believe it."

She filed a police report that day. Although the police dismissed the incident as a lover's quarrel, James retaliated.

Night after night, he repeatedly circled the cul de sac in front of the Waites' house.

One afternoon, he accosted her in the parking lot after she had left her waitressing shift. Although she tried to roll up her window, he got a hand in. His beating broke her nose, fractured her brow bone and shot her contact lens to the back of her eye socket. He finally stopped and ran when her constant honking drew a crowd from the restaurant.

He punctured Sandy's automobile tires and those of her family with such frequency that their total outlay for new tires extended into the thousands. Eventually, Sandy bought a Nissan to replace her old sports car. The decision hinged on the fact that new tires for the Nissan would only cost $60 each as opposed to $140.

IN ADDITION TO inflicting recurring property and bodily damage, James continued to follow Sandy wherever she went. Once she had parked at her destination, he would await her return and then stand at the driver's side and prevent her from reentering her vehicle.

He would call 20 to 30 times a night, and then harass her during the day. He lost his job, since all his time and efforts were focused on harassing Sandy. He risked having his car repossessed at any moment. Still he persisted. Sandy, he figured, was to blame for his misfortunes, and he wanted financial compensation.

He threatened to get back at her. He threatened her life again and again. He would kill her with a gun, he announced. He let her know he was very good at archery. One Halloween he promised to blow up her house, a threat that put the SWAT team up on the roof. Wherever she went, James advised her, she wouldn't be able to hide.

Not knowing when or where he would hit next or where she would end up, Sandy started feeling like a prisoner. Her father drove her to and from work. Once there, safety demanded that she not leave the premises for lunch or even for a quick run to the bank. At home, she couldn't even walk her new puppy down the street to the park. "I've spent more time in prison than he has," she said.

Despite the terror, Sandy did manage to move ahead with her life. Although the computer components company she worked for had been bought out several times, she rose from expediter to senior planner. James' pursuit cost her most of her old friends who were either afraid or forbidden to be around her, and limited her opportunities to make new ones. But eventually she met Ronol Potter, whom she married five years later.

Their marriage did not lessen the intensity of James' focus on Sandy, especially since he refused to accept its existence. "He'll tell you that I've never been married, that I shack up with Ron," said Sandy. The delusion doesn't bode well for Ron. "In James' mind, all he has to do is to get rid of my husband and he and I will get back together," Sandy explained.

James has threatened Ron's life on several occasions. An additional delusion—that Sandy is being kept from him against her will—prompted him to talk two ex-con bikers he had met in prison into going to her parents' house to "rescue" her. The scheme backfired. A short time before, James had turned his fists on Sandy again. When the bikers saw Sandy's two black eyes and the condition of the rest of her face, they went after James instead.

Despite Sandy's precautions, James' beatings had continued, becoming increasingly violent over the years. The physical harm, however, wasn't nearly as great as the emotional and psychological duress Sandy suffered. Especially when he would call her and detail everything she had done on certain occasions, describe the area, and comment on her outfits. If she had taken her two nieces—whom he assumed were her daughters—ice-skating or to the park, he would ask about them. "Do you know how scary that is? What if something happened to those kids?" asked Sandy, roughly wiping away the tears she couldn't control. "I can handle anything that happens to me. But don't go after my family."

THE STRESS FINALLY got to her. Although her life had revolved around outdoor sports like water skiing, roller-skating and bike riding, she shut herself away from the world. She was unable to eat and so depressed that she would cry for two hours straight, until she realized what that meant. "If I lock myself in the house and I stop doing what I enjoy, then he wins whether he knows it or not." That's when she pulled herself back together and emerged from hiding.

Although Sandy had filed charges against James every time he harassed her, assaulted her or vandalized property, little legal action resulted. Finally fed up with the lack of effective police intervention, her mother approached the district attorney. "Either you're gonna do something or this mother's buying a gun," she announced. "I'm gonna kill him and you're gonna have to put me in jail."

Ironically, Detective Mike Proctor—the stalking expert who finally put James in prison—was called in to investigate a charge against *Sandy*. James had called the Potters' insurance broker and claimed that Sandy was in the process of taking out an insurance policy on her husband and plotting his murder. Proctor called Ron asking about the state of his marriage. Aware that the call was really James' way of threatening Ron's life, Sandy panicked. That night, she met with the detective and his partner. It took two and a half hours to review her ten-year history of harassment.

"What she needs is separation from the threat of him," said Proctor, who quickly recognized the trauma and terror of the woman in front of him.

That separation has been all too brief.

After 13 months in jail, James was released and placed on probation. When he expressed a desire to go back to Alabama, the California probation department that supervised him put him on a bus without even processing an inter-state transfer. Officials in Alabama didn't know about him until James walked into the probation department there.

JAMES HAD RETURNED to his home state at least once before. Kaye—his first stalking victim—found out he was back in town as she was about to head off to her job at a finance company. Although 14 years had passed since she had heard from him, she froze at the sound of his voice. "I don't have anything to say to you," she said. "I don't want to talk to you, I don't want to see you. Don't come around."

When he called back, however, she talked to him. Had their sexual encounter impregnated her? Was her relationship with her husband sound? Was there any chance for reconciliation between Kaye and himself? Would there be if her husband was out of the way?

He called several times after that, at one point expressing his belief that he had actually fathered her son, now age eight. The fallacy alarmed Kaye. She continued to be concerned even after he returned to California—with good reason. After serving his prison time, James again made his way home. Though he didn't attempt to contact Kaye, the family's mail was coincidentally tampered with during his stay. A letter detailing her son's summer camp schedule had obviously been opened.

James remained in the state less than a month that time. On one occasion, Kaye and her husband found roofing tacks spread over their driveway. Later, a couple of tire sidewalls were punctured. Nothing else happened. No evidence directly tied James to the vandalism. Still, Kaye no longer rests well at night. Every little "bump and thump" awakens her. "I sleep with a .38 under my pillow. People should not have to live in fear."

JAMES CAME BACK to California. Shortly thereafter, he violated the conditions of his probation, which specified that he not come within ten *miles* of Sandy's work, her husband's work, their home, or her parents' home. (Most protective orders specify a distance of a few hundred yards at most.) James was arrested, but the news of his return frightened Sandy badly. It took 23 hours and a pep talk to regain her nerve. "Okay, fine," she told herself. "He's back. You know it. And you know where he's at again. So be a little cautious, get yourself together, and *deal* with it."

Dealing with it means calling the District Attorney, contacting the various neighborhood police offices, and meeting with the probation department. Dealing with it means making waves as often as possible. "The more people who know about me," she said, "the tougher it's going to be for them to read about me in the obituaries."

You Can't Bargain With the Devil

Never try to reason or bargain with your stalker. That only gives them insight into how much pressure—or how many phone calls, letters, or threats—it will take to make you cave in to his or her demands.

14

Maybe You Don't Want To Be Rich & Famous

DESPITE THE VAST NUMBERS OF ordinary citizens who find themselves the object of a fixation, the most visible and publicized obsessive love cases continue to involve people whom the stalker knows only through their fame. In an effort to enhance their own identities, these stalkers gravitate toward those larger-than-life figures who seem to have identity to spare.

Celebrity or prominence has always come with risk attached. Call it an occupational hazard. In our era, that risk has multiplied. In the 1970s, Charles Manson executed Sharon Tate along with several of her houseguests. David Bowie received multiple anonymous death threats while on tour. Frank Zappa was attacked on stage by the jealous husband of a woman who idolized him.

During the 1980s, John Lennon's death at the hands of Mark David Chapman, a fan who saw the ex-Beatle's murder as a way to prevent him from forsaking his ideals, seemed to set the tone for a decade of increasing jeopardy to public figures. Just five months later came the attempted assassination of President Reagan, John Hinckley Jr.'s bid to impress Jodie Foster. About the same time, actress Priscilla Presley frightened away intruders suspected of wanting to kidnap her daughter Lisa, then 13.

185

Linda Rondstat's Malibu home was ransacked, her sheets shredded. The note left on her pillow read: "You next time."

In 1982, Theresa Saldana, a promising 27-year-old actress, was the victim of an especially horrific assault. When her mother called to say that director Martin Scorsese's assistant had been trying to reach her and that she had provided him with Saldana's telephone number and address, the actress literally danced around the living room. The excitement lasted half an hour—when a second call from her manager told her that a "nut" was trying to locate her using a handful of fake identities, including that of assistant to Scorsese. Fear struck immediately. She called the Los Angeles Sheriff's Department. "Nothing happens in these cases 99 percent of the time," they told her. After several days, Saldana decided that she had overreacted.

A week later, as the actress unlocked her car, a man appeared and asked, "Are you Theresa Saldana?" One look and she knew. She tried to run, but the stranger caught her. Within seconds, he had plunged a large kitchen knife into her chest. "He's killing me! He's killing me!" she screamed, trying to fend off the thrusts. She was stabbed ten times before her cries finally brought help from Jeff Fenn, a deliveryman who wrested the knife away from Saldana's attacker and saved her life.

Arthur Richard Jackson, a Scottish drifter who believed he was "the benevolent angel of death" with the "divine mission" of killing Saldana so that he could whisk her off to heaven, almost accomplished his deranged objective. Saldana's heart actually stopped beating on the way to the hospital, and it took heart and lung surgery lasting four-and-a-half hours and over 1,000 stitches to save her.

Jackson was arrested and convicted of attempted murder. However, he continued to threaten Saldana. In letters mailed from prison, he referred to her as "assassination target Theresa Saldana" and indicated that executing him was the only way to ensure her permanent safety. "I am capable of alternating between sentiment and savagery," read one. He went on to say that neither police nor FBI protection nor bullet-proof vests would save Saldana.

She lived in fear of his eventual release and of what he might contrive from behind bars.

There's no waking up from the nightmare posed by this kind of threat. It extends day after day, night after night. "It's a very dangerous situation, not only for myself but for my family," said Saldana. "The way I deal with it emotionally is to compartmentalize it. I don't dwell upon it. If I did, I'm sure that my life would fall apart. It's too frightening and too real."

"SINCE 1968 THERE have been as many injurious attacks on public figures by mentally disordered people who gave some sort of warning as there were in the preceding 175 years," forensic psychiatrist Park Elliott Dietz, PhD, who has completed one of the most comprehensive studies to date on violence against public figures for the National Institute of Justice, told the *New York Times*.

In the age of modern technology, celebrity coverage has become so personal it's almost like having the stars in your living room. However for some 150,000 to 200,000 Americans, according to Dietz, these one-sided relationships seem not to be enough. They insist on attempting one-on-one contact. So, undesirable encounters between celebrities and their fanatic fans continue to escalate.

Why the sudden rise in these kinds of incidents? Experts, including Dietz, attribute the escalation in part to the intensified attention now paid to celebrities' lives. "In the media age, a famous person has a seemingly intimate relationship with millions, sometimes even hundreds of millions of people," said Los Angeles security adviser Gavin de Becker, the nation's foremost authority in the protection of prominent people. "You hope that the majority are influenced in a favorable way—to buy or enjoy your product, movie, song or whatever. But some are going to respond in unpredictable or inappropriate ways. Couple that with the increase in mental illness and the decrease in effective treatment for the mentally ill, and what we're ending up with is a situation that's ever worsening for media figures."

Most of us respond to some degree to the seductive appeal of television and movie stars and the power of sports figures. "But what is usually a mild drug, is a poison to some people," said de Becker. Especially if those obsessed fans are psychologically unstable.

- Ten years after John Lennon's murder, former Beatle George Harrison began receiving death threats reading "Time you went" and "Goodby [sic] George." He burned the first missive, but called in London police when five more materialized. The suspect was taken into custody soon after, and Harrison beefed up security around his palatial 34-acre estate. Ten-foot high walls, stadium lights, video monitoring and electronic gates, however, were not enough to keep a new stalker, Michael Abram, out. Convinced that the Beatles "are witches," the knife-wielding attacker broke into the singer's Gothic mansion and stabbed him in the chest. Despite a one-inch wound that just missed a main vein and a resulting collapsed lung, Harrison managed to fight off and subdue his assailant, who police then took into custody. Just one week prior, another alleged stalker, 27-year-old Crisin Kelecher was arrested inside Harrison's Maui, Hawaii, estate.
- In July 1994, Todd Lawrence jumped Madonna's eight-foot security fence before being arrested. According to court documents filed in support of the temporary restraining order Madonna obtained against him, Lawrence claimed to be her husband who was "coming home." Several years later, another intruder also

claimed to be married to Madonna. Robert Dewey Hoskins repeatedly visited her home before being arrested for stalking and sentenced to ten years. Then Stephen Stillabower crashed his truck through the gates of Madonna's home and ran toward her residence. In actuality, however, he was seeking the home's previous owner, actress and singer Olivia Newton-John. At the sight of Madonna's then-husband Sean Penn, he ran. Penn chased him and got his license plate number. Later that day, Penn and deputy sheriffs arrested Stillabower. In 2011, an obsessed fan who admitted to police that he had been stalking Madonna for months broke into her London townhouse by smashing a side window. Fortunately, the star was away.

- Gun-toting intruders have stalked both Tracey Ullman and Gene Hackman, the latter repeatedly.

- From 1990 to 1991, Olympic figure skater Katarina Witt received more than 50 pages of threatening and obscene letters, along with nude photographs and sex pamphlets, from a man who wrote that he considered her to be his wife from the moment he saw her.

- Scott Isley targeted singer Paula Abdul, whom he believed to be his lover. Other delusions included the notion that he and Abdul had attended the same first-grade class, that convicted mobster John Gotti had taken care of him when he was little, that President Bush had kidnapped him at the age of three, and that he was "the little boy of God." In May 1992, he hitchhiked from Maine to the home of Paula Abdul's mother. He has spent time in jail for trespassing and battery of a state officer.

- In March 1989, Joni Leigh Penn broke into the San Fernando Valley house that Sharon Gless—of 1980's TV series *Cagney & Lacey* fame—uses as an office, appar-

ently intending to sexually assault the actress and then
shoot herself with a rifle. Although Gless wasn't there,
Penn held police in a tense standoff for seven hours
before surrendering. The fan was booked for burglary
and denied bail. Penn, who used to visit the *Cagney &
Lacey* set several times a week, had tried unsuccessfully
to see Gless up close two years before. While a restraining order had kept her at a distance for a while, it hadn't
stopped a steady stream of more than 120 letters that
veered from romantic to hostile in nature. One included
a photo of Penn aiming a handgun into her mouth, another holding a gun to her temple, and a third featuring
a shrine to Gless of photographs and flowers—with an
attack rifle positioned at the center.

- Jail time doesn't seem to help. Howard Stern's stalker—
  43-year-old Michael Lance Cavin—had already spent six
  years in jail for harassing former President Gerald Ford.

- Stephen Spielberg attracted the attention of a 31-year-
  old sexually-obsessed felon named Jonathan F. Norman
  who, during the summer of 1997, visited the director's
  gated Pacific Palisades estate four separate times. When
  he was finally arrested, he was found to be armed with
  what prosecutors described as a rape kit, which included
  duct tape, a box cutter and handcuffs. "I really felt my
  life was in danger," Spielberg testified at his stalker's
  trial.

- After allegedly bombarding Debbie Gibson with letters,
  phone calls and more than 50 emails over a six month
  period, Michael Faulkner was arrested on May 24, 1998
  when he confronted the singer/actress as she left the
  theater following her performance of Belle in *Beauty and
  the Beast*. (Other actors who have been stalked during
  Broadway performances include Glenn Close, Brooke
  Shields, Jerry Lewis and Tommy Tune.) The stalker's

message in this case: If Gibson "didn't change her image, he would hold her accountable."

- Halle Berry drew the attention of 27-year-old Richard Franco, who was arrested at her Hollywood Hills home on July 11, 2011. His alleged campaign designed to terrorize the actress included scaling the back wall of her house.
- The Who's Who list of famous stalking victims goes on. Recent targets include Uma Thurman, Jennifer Aniston, Keira Knightley, Kim Kardashian, Miley Cyrus and even Facebook founder Mark Zuckerberg.

MENTALLY DERANGED PEOPLE who have not been able to relate to the real world often find more workable relationships in the fraudulent reality of the media, according to Gavin de Becker, whose clientele includes some of the biggest stars in show business. Some celebrity stalkers see public figures as being able to resolve some dilemma or grievance. Others incorporate public figures into delusions, believing them to be a spouse, associate, friend or enemy. "Most [stalkers] are after the goal of some union with the person they stalk," psychiatrist Dietz declared on ABC News' *20/20*. "But if they can't have a magical and perfect union, second best is this tortured relationship because it's better than no relationship at all."

Singers top the list of those likely to attract these kinds of problems. As country music stars have grown in popularity and visibility, for example, incidents of stalking have accelerated, with Reba McEntire and Tanya Tucker figuring among Nashville's celebrity stalking victims. Indeed, although de Becker won't name or discuss clients (some have been made public through court cases), framed notes from Tina Turner and Barry Manilow (the latter of which reads: "Thanks. I hope I never have to talk to you again. I mean that in the nicest way.") attest to their need for his services. "Songs go much more to visceral elements of our makeup than movies do," de Becker explained. "We've all had the experience of thinking, 'That song really said what I'm feeling now.' So songs are very powerful, which is why female singers will have more problems than any other kind of media figure."

Critics assert that sexually explicit entertainers like Madonna invite such problems. In reality, however, despite Madonna's troubles with stalkers, the "girl next door" types usually attract the most obsessive attention. "The nicer one appears to be and the more approachable, the more one will attract the serious and persistent and deluded subjects," Dietz stated in an interview for *Currents in Affective Illness*. "Their public personae foster an illusion of intimacy and receptivity and a willingness to come close in a nonthreatening manner to subjects who generally have difficulty with social relations."

Witness Olivia Newton-John, a de Becker client who has had her share of safety challenges. First came Michael Perry, a Louisiana escapee from a mental institution who became obsessed with the singer-actress after seeing her on HBO in the film *Xanadu*. After two twisted letters and five trips to California during which de Becker's personnel prevented him from gaining access to her property, Perry returned home. Within a matter of days, he shot his mother, father and three relatives in the face. He then fled with money and guns. Police found a handwritten death list which included family members—those killed and others—along with the names of Olivia Newton-John, her then-husband Matt Lattanzi, and Supreme Court Justice Sandra Day O'Connor, who reminded him of Newton-John. Fourteen days after the murders, Perry was arrested in Washington, D.C., just a few miles from the Supreme Court.

The Australian star also drew the attention of Ralph Nau, an unbalanced man who believed that Olivia Newton-John, Cher and Sheena Easton, a singer who once topped the charts, had all proclaimed their love for him through personal messages delivered during televised performances. In response to their supposed communication, Nau wrote hundreds of sexual fantasy letters to the stars (all sent in care of Newton-John) and traveled more than 20,000 miles in pursuit of them.

Aware of the significant danger that Nau posed to his clients, de Becker's office closely monitored him and even spoke with Nau's family several times. "He's another John Hinckley. We're all afraid of him," the stalker's father, Elmer Nau, told de Becker. They had reason to be. In 1984, Ralph Nau bludgeoned his 8-year-old stepbrother to death with an ax. The confessed murderer, however, was acquitted on a technicality. Remanded to an Illinois mental hospital, he was able to petition for release every six months.

Understandably, that prospect disturbed the entertainers, on whom Nau continued to focus. "We are concerned about the safety of our families and our own safety," they said in a joint statement. "While we have the highest concern for the fair and humane treatment of the mentally ill, when the situation involves persons who are violent, we must all first be concerned for their potential victims."

THERESA SALDANA KNEW all too well what it feels like to live with that kind of threat. Her attacker had repeatedly been scheduled for release, even though he had publicly announced his regret at botching Saldana's killing and his intention to try again.

Saldana and de Becker mounted a national publicity campaign designed to pressure officials into keeping him locked up. Although a bill passed by the California Senate provided for the continued hospitalization of those who still posed a hazard to others even after their prison terms expire, it did not apply to Jackson because of a timing quirk. "They're saying that it's unconstitutional to hold Jackson. I'm saying that it's unconstitutional to allow someone who plans to murder me to come out and try it again," the actress said. "If I were successfully murdered by Jackson when he comes out, I wonder if the same people who say there's nothing they can do will just shrug their shoulders and say, 'Gee, that's really a shame. We knew all along that this would happen.'"

The law may not have kept up with the phenomenon, but the handling of dangers posed to public figures *has* gotten more sophisticated. Gavin de Becker, Inc., has assessed tens of thousands of unwanted pursuit cases and keeps track of the movements, behavioral patterns or psychological states of thousands of people who may pose a hazard to clients. A computer-assisted threat assessment system designed by de Becker and known as MOSAIC—which was subsequently adopted by California law enforcement, the U.S. Supreme Court, the U.S. Capitol Police, the U.S. Marshals Service and the CIA—helps in evaluating which unfamiliar suspects are more likely to pursue a personal encounter with the object of their fixation. To monitor potentially dangerous fans, de Becker's team reviews any and all communications received—which range from letters, gifts of diamonds, and packages of dead animals or body parts, to blood and other body fluids—conducts investigations and surveillance and develops a network of police, mental health workers, family and other sources who will advise them of any relevant developments.

This kind of protection relies more on brainpower than manpower. And for good reason. "Never has a bodyguard been able to neutralize a firearms assault," said Jurg (Bill) Mattman, a former Secret Service agent who heads up The Mattman Company, a top Los Angeles security agency that specializes in guarding corporate heads and foreign dignitaries. "You just can't pull a gun fast enough to compete with a weapon that's already out."

Mattman also believes in solid advance planning, as opposed to traditional on-site protection alone. "Say your client is Lee Iacocca—with whom I have no affiliation—and say he's been invited to the American Film Institute's annual dinner," said Mattman. "One of the agents goes to the hotel several days before the event and contacts the head of security. Then he identifies alternate entrances so that the client doesn't have to enter through the front door. He also finds out where the nearest hospital is, what kind of medical services are available at the hotel, whether any demonstrations are planned, and what police response to an emergency would be. He'll even locate the bathroom so Iacocca won't have to wander around looking for it, endangering himself unnecessarily."

In the end, the process boils down to taking the best precautions possible and trying to make an informed judgment about someone's likely conduct. "Think of violence and violent inclinations as being like a ladder, with the bottom of the ladder being innocence, and the top being violence," said de Becker. "All of us are somewhere on that ladder. There are provocations for all of us that could move us right to the top of that ladder. What we are trying to observe is where in a person's life they are and what influences are affecting them, such as the loss of a job, the loss of a family connection, the loss of freedom. All these kinds of things tend to up the ante on someone's emotional state."

MOST INAPPROPRIATE COMMUNICATIONS or encounters are not overtly threatening. Only 5 percent of the letter writers, for example, announce themselves as enemies or "would-be assassins," according to Dietz's study. Most communications revolve, instead, around love (de Becker calls it "love sickness") and attraction. Danger, however, isn't contingent on which emotion generates the obsession.

Even hate mail can stem from what would usually be construed as positive feelings. Michael J. Fox, for example, received over 6,000 threatening letters in one year from 27-year-old Tina Marie Ledbetter, who considered herself to be the star's "number one fan." The correspondence, which began when he took up with his now-wife Tracy Pollan, increased in virulence proportionally with the growth of the couple's relationship. At first, the expletive-filled letters simply demanded that Fox dump his new girlfriend. After their marriage, however, anti-Semitic remarks about Pollan were compounded by death threats against the two actors and their unborn baby. Careful evaluation of two UPS packages of rabbit droppings eventually led to the apprehension of the California shipping clerk, who was sentenced to three years supervised probation.

While threatening or inappropriate letters can be disconcerting, encounters are the real problem. Dietz's research revealed that 10 percent to 15 percent of those who send inappropriate communications will attempt a physical encounter. Those who had called or had requested face-to-face meetings were most likely to approach. Surprisingly, obscene communications, hate mail and threats signaled less chance of an approach. In noncelebrity cases, it's the reverse.

THOUGH ENCOUNTERS AREN'T always violent, many are terrifying. After stalking Justine Bateman—then a highly visible TV actor on the series *Family Ties*, co-starring Fox—for five years, John Thomas Smetek, a 39-year-old Texan, tried to demonstrate how much he cared about her. He walked into the Berkeley (California) Repertory Theatre where she was rehearsing for a play and threatened to kill himself with the .22-caliber pistol he held in his hand. Smetek believed that he and Bateman had had an affair in Texas seven years before. It took police three hours to finally talk him into surrendering.

"The only crime he could be charged with was a weapons charge," Bateman told the Senate Judiciary Committee. "He was put on probation and ordered not to make any contact with me, but to this day he still maintains the delusion that we will meet and have a romantic relationship.

"I feel this man has violated me, and there is nothing I can do about it. I can't help but be concerned when I think of my future and what security measures must be taken to protect my future and children to ensure their safety. Why must I live in constant terror of this man's return?"

Even if John Smetek had succeeded in encountering Bateman, experts agree he wouldn't have known what to do with that relationship. "That's the way a lot of these people are. They plan up to the point of attaining the unobtainable, and then their planning ceases," said the FBI's Jim Wright, whose cases while in the FBI's behavioral sciences division included John Hinckley, Jodie Foster's overly ardent admirer.

"Hinckley had several alternate attention-getting plans. Rather than shooting the President, for example, he was going to hijack a plane in Washington. He had the hijack note. We found that, along with a toy gun that would have passed for a real gun. He was going to demand that the plane be flown to New Haven where Jodie would be brought to the plane and they would take off. What's wrong with that scenario? Even if she got on the plane, where are they going to go? What are they going to do? That's where the planning stops. Which is why you see a lot of very irrational behavior after stalkers have gotten their victim in their clutches. They have no idea about what happens next."

Some celebrity stalkers will admit as much. "If I did get to meet her, I would probably have a heart attack," reported one man after seven years of stalking and wanting to marry his famous target.

Whatever the intent, those who pursue celebrities often go to extraordinary lengths to achieve their objectives. One man spent $9,000 to hire a private investigator to track the object of his fixation. Another phoned in an order for flowers to be delivered to a public figure and then broke in to the florist's truck to obtain the address. Others have managed to get jobs with telephone or utility companies in order to find unlisted numbers and addresses. Some have even landed positions as security guards for the very stars on whom they're fixated.

ALTHOUGH THE PERSONALITY types of these fanatical fans don't lend themselves to categorizing, the themes behind their delusions do. The most common of these themes is that a special relationship exists between the stalker and his prey.

During a pre-show warm-up for the *Wheel of Fortune*, an audience member who believed he was going to marry Vanna White jumped up and started screaming that her boyfriend was a dangerous man associated with the mafia and that he would protect her.

Former legal secretary Billie Jean Jackson (no relation) was put behind bars for violating a court order to stay away from the late Michael Jackson's Encino home and stop representing herself as the singer's wife. Similarly, Michael Jackson's sister, Janet, was stalked by Frank Paul Jones, a 34-year-old who believed he was married to her, and who threatened the lives of her live-in boyfriend, her brothers Michael and Jermaine, and former President George Bush in an effort to gain her attention.

A David Letterman fan drove from Detroit to New York with her 3-year-old daughter and then refused to leave the theater until she married her idol. Letterman is all too familiar with this sort of situation. Starting in 1988, a woman who called herself Mrs. Letterman was arrested over and over for breaking into the late night talk show host's Connecticut home, once just three days after her release from jail, where she had served most of a nine-month sentence. Her stalking of Letterman finally ended a decade later when she committed suicide by kneeling in front of an oncoming train.

Another woman so believed she was married to a U.S. senator that she moved into his home and redecorated it while he was out of town. While this sort of deranged fan doesn't appear to wish any harm, there's no denying danger when one finds a stranger in the house at 2 A.M.—whether that person intends to offer flowers or inflict injury.

Other typical delusions include the idea that the celebrity owes the obsessive fan money, recognition, response, or a relationship, according to Gavin de Becker. "They wrote your songs or play, you stole their idea, you went into their brain," he explained. Many celebrity stalkers also believe they share a special communication with their targets. Ralph Nau was convinced that Newton-John, Cher and Easton sent him messages over the airwaves and through their songs. Then there are science fiction fantasies. Another of Olivia Newton-John's overly ardent admirers believed he had to save her by taking her to a different planet. Often stalkers believe they are messengers of God.

THEN THERE ARE those who take that extra, fatal step. Actress Rebecca Schaeffer, the young star of the television series *My Sister Sam*, had just broken through to the big screen in *Scenes from the Class Struggle in Beverly Hills*. Although hardly famous, her increased visibility had attracted a following of fans, including 19-year-old Robert John Bardo of Tucson, Arizona, to whom she had sent a personal note in response to his fan letter. Bardo's feelings surpassed mere admiration. He not only watched Schaeffer's sitcom religiously, he taped most of the shows in order to view them again and again. Once the series was canceled, he relied on his taped collection for most of his entertainment. For two years, the A-student-turned-high-school-dropout sent her a steady stream of letters telling her about himself and asking her questions about her life. Then a more ominous missive: "I'm obsessed with something I can't have," Bardo wrote his sister in reference to Schaeffer. "So I'm going to make it so that something doesn't exist anymore."

It didn't take long for Bardo to track Schaeffer down. For $250, he hired a private detective, convincing him that the object of his fixation was a long lost friend. Four weeks later, Schaeffer's address in hand, Bardo boarded a Greyhound bus headed for California.

The morning of his arrival in Los Angeles, he located Schaeffer's building and rang the buzzer to her apartment. Due to a broken intercom, she answered in person. As she walked to the door, a bullet ripped into her chest. Minutes later, she died. She was 21 years old.

Until 1989, there had been an even easier way for stalkers like Bardo to find their victims. For years, California's Department of Motor Vehicle records were accessible for a small fee. Bardo could have found Schaeffer's address there himself rather than spending money on a detective who would wind up doing just that.

Theresa Saldana's attacker also found out where she lived through the DMV. "I don't think it should be so easy to get in touch with someone. There are too many negative implications," said Saldana, who lobbied hard for the California bill limiting public access to personal information that was passed in 1989. Until 1997, few states—notably California and Virginia—prohibited the release of DMV records to everyone excepting legal, government and insurance agencies. These days, the national Driver's Privacy Protection Act prevents any state motor vehicle department from releasing personal information unless the individual in question has been given the opportunity to prohibit that disclosure.

Privacy laws will help, but they won't eliminate the problem. "We have to do something to protect the innocent individual," Pam Dawber, who starred with Schaeffer on *My Sister Sam*, told the California legislature when she testified about the need for such privacy laws as well as gun control following her friend's death. "You have no idea how many death threats there are in Hollywood," said Dawber, who had periodically been harassed by a fan.

Sharon Gless showed legislators a shopping bag full of deranged letters and photographs she had received prior to her stalker's break-in. "I would just like to be able to go home without being afraid," said the actress. "I would like to open my door without being afraid. I would like the people who come to my house to be the ones I invite there."

For the most part, these situations can be managed with some expert help. But that takes money, as well as a realistic appraisal of danger. The denial of the latter is perhaps the toughest to contend with. "Media figures are built to be liked," said de Becker. "That's what they're good at. Many don't understand or grasp the idea that anyone would want to harm them."

Whether you're rich and famous or not, an honest look at the cold, hard facts—no matter how disturbing—can make all the difference in the outcome.

Don't Go Asking for Obsessive Attention

Though she has had some trouble, strong women like Madonna don't get targeted as much as the nice girl-next-door types. Consider taking classes in self-defense and assertiveness training to shore up your own defenses against this—and other—crimes. Then line up any and all those around you who can possibly help you out should push come to shove.

15

Do the Right Thing

UNCONTROLLED IDOLIZATION OF PUBLIC personalities—or even of yourself—may look like adoration, especially when gifts and missives proclaim that exact sentiment. A closer examination, however, reveals just how wrong that is and how dangerous not taking the right precautions or not reacting appropriately can be.

"I loved her, and I still do," Robert Bardo, the man who stalked and murdered actress Rebecca Schaeffer, proclaimed while awaiting trial. That was his defense in court. A deluded courtship gone awry, a moment of insanity brought on by Schaeffer's off-putting reaction to him.

Yet consider what he brought with him that morning. Flowers? No. Chocolates? No. A ring? No. His shopping bag contained her address, a copy of *Catcher In the Rye* (which both Chapman and Hinckley had taken to their attacks), a gun and hollow-tipped bullets that would readily penetrate either glass or steel.

This was not the first time he had thought about harming Schaeffer. In search of her two years earlier, he had waited for her to exit from the soundstage where she had been taping her television show. He had armed himself with a knife. "I was even thinking of hurting her at that time because she sounded arrogant in *TV Guide*," he admitted during one interview. "If she was mean to me, I'd have done to her what Arthur Jackson did to Theresa Saldana."

Bardo had made a point of studying assassins. He particularly identified with Mark David Chapman, John Lennon's assassin, because he, too, felt like a loser. Although he saw himself as different from Theresa Saldana's assailant Arthur Jackson, he read up on him extensively and learned. In what can only be interpreted as a tribute to John Hinckley, Jr., Bardo actually emulated the man he had admired and identified with for years.

Early on, Bardo aspired to join the ranks of these notorious assassins. Even before he attached himself to Rebecca Schaeffer, he fantasized about killing. In high school, he felt a special affinity for one of his teachers. Yet when he thought she might think ill of him, he wrote about killing her. He shared these deadly compulsions with his counselor.

Samantha Smith, the young actress who as a girl had written to the Soviet president about world peace, was the first public personality to attract Bardo's attention. Her personal response to one of his letters cemented the lonely teenager's excessive interest. Convinced that they shared a unique bond, Bardo, then 13, stole $140 from his mother's purse and ran away to see Smith in her home state of Maine. Although his parents had consistently denied that their son had mental or emotional problems, his trip struck even them as inappropriate. Concerned for Samantha Smith's safety, they phoned Maine police.

Three years later, Bardo focused on Rebecca Schaeffer, who played a character by the name of Samantha on the television series *My Sister Sam*. "You're not like that guy John Hinckley. You're not going to try to do what that guy Hinckley did?" his father asked, when the then 16-year-old mentioned plans to visit Schaeffer in Los Angeles.

In 1987, Bardo tried to encounter the actress three times after reading a profile of her. "The way she talked, it sounded like she was available," he recalled. Yet he also made a point of attending appearances by Debbie Gibson and Tiffany, the latter of whose shows he always viewed from the front row. During one concert, Bardo was convinced that Tiffany had looked directly at him and then gestured to him while performing. He fantasized about a written correspondence between them that would lead to a courtship.

He never fully pursued his infatuation with Tiffany, perhaps in part because of the tight security surrounding her. In 1988, he did try to encounter Debbie Gibson, whom he actually followed to New York. His first stop was the Dakota, the apartment building where Chapman had gunned down John Lennon. Then he headed to Long Island, where he had read that Debbie lived. He spent the night at the high school he believed she had attended. Since one of her albums had specifically mentioned the school, his deduction seemed reasonable. His efforts to find her, however, proved fruitless because of the star's routine precautions. "I'm not an easy target," Gibson acknowledged. Bardo eventually abandoned the search, as well as that particular obsession. Although Bardo claims that his interest in her waned "because her nose and teeth are all messed up," his inability to meet her probably played a more active role in discouraging him.

"When a target proves inaccessible, everybody assumes that a fanatic fan will simply opt for another time and another place," said Gavin de Becker. "It's not so. If a public figure avoids an encounter once or twice, that's often the end of it for them. Their pursuer will likely focus on another target." Mark Chapman, for example, initially hung around New York's InterContinental Hotel intending to kill Johnny Carson. When that proved a problem, he shifted his attentions to John Lennon. Bardo was ultimately drawn to Schaeffer because he thought he could get close. "She seemed accessible," Bardo remembered. That meant that he would have a chance at realizing his lifelong dream of becoming a notorious assassin. When Schaeffer opened the door and he fired, he did just that.

Had Robert Bardo truly been in love with Rebecca Schaeffer, the death of his beloved (even at his hand) would have elicited a powerful reaction of sorrow or remorse. Instead, his response verged on the self-congratulatory. "I almost had a heart attack 'cause it occurred to me that I finally . . . killed somebody. Someone died 'cause of me." He didn't even refer to his victim as Schaeffer. She had been downgraded from an idol to a somebody.

Like most public figures, Rebecca Schaeffer might not have been able to accept that someone would want to hurt her. She might have felt that she was not enough of a star to worry about security problems. Or she might have reasoned that she wouldn't be able to afford more protection and dismissed the notion entirely. But Schaeffer was never advised of Bardo's attempts to reach her. Not by her producers, who knew. Not by studio security people, who knew. Not by her agents, who had received both letters and phone calls. So she never had the chance to make a decision at all.

That quite possibly cost the young actress her life. Because the way a case is handled can make the difference between whether the stalking becomes front-page news or just another case for the files.

TWO WEEKS AFTER Rebecca Schaeffer's murder, John Thomas Smetek approached the television actress of his dreams. Convinced that he and *Family Ties'* star Justine Bateman had shared a passionate love affair seven years earlier, during which she had repeatedly raped him, Smetek had managed to contact her three times on the Paramount sound stage where the show was taped. The first time he claimed that he wanted to give her a music cassette that Julian Lennon, John Lennon's oldest son, was about to release. On the next two visits, the 39-year-old Texas transient claimed to be a producer. Each time he was forcibly removed.

On this occasion, however, he followed Bateman to Berkeley, California, where she was performing in a repertory play. "I love you!" he shouted as the actress left rehearsal on the afternoon of September 1, 1989. Bateman didn't hesitate for a moment. Instead of ignoring the situation, she shot back into the theater and called Gavin de Becker, whose office had warned her about Smetek nearly a year earlier. Although Bateman was not a client, Michael J. Fox, her television co-star, was. De Becker had met with her as a courtesy.

A computer check confirmed Bateman's suspicions. The man who had hailed her was the same individual who had repeatedly accosted her at the studio, the same individual about whom de Becker's people had warned her the previous year.

De Becker's office advised the theater on how to handle any subsequent approaches and provided Bateman with half a dozen security procedures. Bateman followed all of them to the letter, including exiting from a side entrance into a waiting car after a lookout had provided the all-clear, and varying her travel routes.

The next day, Smetek dropped off two photographs for Bateman. On the back, he proposed that they meet at the Bob Hope concert "if you really are Bateman." That night, he returned to present an old business card to one of the theater's employees. On the back, an almost indecipherable note: "So you think I am bullshit. Don't [think] I will never talk to you again Justin [sic] . . . .You will never do a film again."

On September 6, Smetek went to collect his loaded .22-caliber pistol. He returned to the theater and demanded to see Bateman. Sitting in a light drizzle some 20 feet from the theater entrance, he pointed the large blue steel revolver to his chest. He had cocked the hammer. The gun was ready to fire.

During the three-hour stand-off with police, Smetek rambled about the relationship that he and Bateman had supposedly shared. According to him, they had met on the beach in Texas seven years ago, made love 18 times in a variety of positions both on the sand and in the water, and in a van. He stated that they had also exchanged vows of love and promises to marry seven years hence.

Smetek probably derived his fixation from a 1988 feature film in which Bateman played a high school graduate who spends the summer at a beachside resort and has an affair with an older man named Martin Falcon. Apparently, Smetek believed himself to be Martin Falcon, especially since he resembled Liam Neeson, the actor who had played Falcon in the movie. He blamed Bateman for not adhering to the story line, and for the suicide he had planned. But his death, he asserted, would ensure that the actress could never work again.

Authorities finally convinced Smetek to lay down his weapon. Five months later, he pleaded guilty to two felonies and a misdemeanor. "I just wanted to make sure [Bateman] knew how much I still cared about her," Smetek answered when questioned about his motivation.

Like Robert Bardo, Smetek refused to consider the possibility that the object of his obsession might have the right to refuse his attentions. Their relationship had been destined by God and could not be undone by anything or anyone, he wrote Bateman in a note police found in a maroon binder. Whatever Bateman said or did, he would love her always, he added regretfully.

And as with Robert Bardo, Smetek's armed advance was preceded by a number of warnings, including letters and personal approaches. However, Bateman's entourage—and indeed the actress herself—treated the situation as the lethal threat that it eventually became. Rebecca Schaeffer's people did not.

REBECCA SCHAEFFER DID not have to die. But ignoring the numerous episodes and signs that Bardo left in his wake almost ensured that she would, because her assailant was bent on achieving the recognition he had been deprived of his whole life.

Bardo had grown up feeling like the family cat that got fed but was otherwise neglected. His mother may have been schizophrenic. An older brother was abusive. Between them, they accounted for a great deal of his childhood suffering. "Help. This house is hell," read one note. "I'm going to run away again. I can't handle it anymore. Please help, fast. Living in my house is like living in hell."

By age 14, Bardo had threatened to kill himself and his two young nieces. He was committed to the Palo Verde Hospital in Tucson and diagnosed with a depressive disorder. Upon his release, his disheveled appearance—along with a severe case of acne, blistered lips and a speech impediment—almost guaranteed his continued social isolation. Increasingly, he took refuge in his fantasies about the entertainment world.

Bardo imagined himself as a famous actor, musician, or singer, although by all reports he lacked talent in those arenas. He wanted to be rich and famous. He wanted to be everything he was not.

Ironically, Bardo's dreams paralleled Rebecca Schaeffer's. He wanted to make his mark. As opposed to interpersonal stalkers who seek to manipulate relationships, or celebrity stalkers, whose psychosis is responsible for their delusions, Bardo hungered for identity and recognition. The stalking—and ultimately the death—of a Hollywood figure would provide both.

TODAY, FOR EVERY stalking incident that makes the papers, there are thousands more you never read about. But de Becker's research shows this wasn't always the case. Before the 1940s, fans admired celebrities from afar. They remained circumspect. They didn't wait for hours just for a glimpse of their heroes. They didn't write hundreds of letters or try to find out where they lived. If a fan had stood up on a chair and screamed through an entire concert, men dressed in white would have carted her away to a mental institution. By the mid-1940s, with the advent of commercial media that focused on stars as intimate love objects in order to exploit an emerging teenage market, that kind of behavior had become normal. The relationship between public figures and their fans had changed and would never be the same.

Both law enforcement and the media quickly reacted to this new phenomenon. But society still had lessons to learn. When 18-year-old Alexander Dorogokupetz stood up in a theater and launched an egg at Frank Sinatra's head, he stopped the show. And for that moment, he supplanted Sinatra as the star.

During that same period, a woman named Ruth Steinhagen focused in on a little-known baseball player named Eddie Waitkus. She devoted her life to collecting news clippings about him, writing him letters and attending his games. At meals, she would leave an empty chair at the table for him. At night, she slept with his picture under her pillow. When he was traded from the Chicago Cubs to the Philadelphia Phillies, she threatened to commit suicide because she felt she couldn't live without him.

In 1949, Ruth followed Eddie Waitkus to a hotel the team was staying in and sent him a note saying that she needed to see him. "We're not acquainted, but I have something of great importance to speak to you about," she wrote. Assuming that she was just another "Baseball Annie"—the players' term for a female fan with whom they could have sex—Eddie called. She persuaded him to come to her room. "For two years, you have been bothering me, and now you are going to die," Ruth announced as her idol settled into the armchair by the bed. Then she shot him in the chest with the .22 rifle she had just purchased from a pawn shop. The ball player would later say that his greatest thrill in baseball was being wounded by a deranged girl.

At the time, Ruth's actions—and her explanations of the episode—shocked the nation. "I liked him a great deal. I knew I could never have him. And if I couldn't have him, nobody could have him," she said. "Also, I wanted attention and publicity for once. All my dreams have come true." Today, those sentiments sound all too familiar. Like many assassins, de Becker points out, Ruth preferred to be wanted by the police than not to be wanted at all. She would become the first in a long line of public-figure attackers seeking the same recognition.

Ruth Steinhagen, like Robert Bardo, was obviously mentally unstable. But neither was crazy. Neither believed that a relationship between themselves and the object of their fixation had ever actually existed. Neither believed killing the object of their fixation to be some sort of divine mission. Yet both orchestrated events so the outcome would be assured regardless of the reactions of their victims.

Park Elliott Dietz's research reveals that 90 percent to 95 percent of those who stalk public figures suffer from some sort of mental disorder, ranging from borderline personality disorders to psychosis. Yet, these dangerous people continue to slip into the crevasse that separates mental health agencies and law enforcement. They've become the bastard children no one wants to acknowledge or deal with.

Heed the Warning Signs

Most stalking-related violence doesn't just happen out of the blue. Stalkers are looking for attention, so they drop plenty of hints about their intentions. Ignore these at your peril. Only by recognizing—or being made aware of—the danger can you take the necessary precautions to safeguard yourself.

16

Recognize When He's Mad For You

PSYCHIATRISTS WHO EVALUATED RUTH Steinhagen after she had threatened to commit suicide over an unexceptional ballplayer determined that there was nothing wrong with her. She simply needed to stop thinking about Eddie Waitkus. That's akin to telling alcoholics that all they have to do is just quit drinking.

Mental health practitioners have learned a lot since then. With appropriate treatment, the prognosis for improvement or even recovery of some mentally disordered stalkers—people like Ruth Steinhagen, Robert Bardo and John Thomas Smetek—has edged up to 75 percent.

But it's a different ballgame when dealing with psychotic pursuers like Ralph Nau and Michael Perry. Stalkers with borderline personality disorders or obsessive-compulsive disorders harbor obsessions, defined as recurrent senseless—but recognized—thoughts. Schizophrenics, however, nurse delusions they interpret as fact.

Michael Perry seemed like a normal kid at first. But he changed when his older brother was killed in an oilfield accident. Suddenly, he was convinced that everyone in his Louisiana hometown was watching him. "Everything got to be secret agent-type stuff," one local acquaintance remembered. Perry changed his name several times. When he tried to legally change it to God, the judge refused. His final choice: Eye.

Eyes played an important role for Perry. They were part of the reason he focused on Olivia Newton-John after watching *Xanadu* on HBO. Her role as a muse brought down to Earth also intrigued him. He began watching her televised movies and performances as often as possible. He listened to her recordings incessantly. He wrote her letters, and wrote her into his delusions. Her haunting photos, he told her, meant "either the dead bodies are rising or else there is a listening device under my mother and father's house. The voices I here [sic] tell me that you are locked up beneath this town of Lake Arthur and were really a muse who was granted ever-lasting life." He was especially taken with a scene where Newton-John's backup band featured two large eyeballs on the bass drums. When the singer turned around, Perry immediately marked her expression. "It was the same face that I saw on my mother in 1961," he later recalled when interviewed by Gavin de Becker.

He was also to tie that facial expression to Supreme Court Justice Sandra Day O'Connor, whose eyes, he claimed, reminded him of Newton-John's. "It's a face that's not . . . smooth. Of course, I'm not calling it a witch or anything, but it could be, you know, considering some of the witches I've seen in Disney movies and such."

Perry traveled to California five times. Twice he tried to gain access to Newton-John's residence. Security people, already aware that a computerized analysis of Perry's letters had rated him as the most dangerous kind of obsessed fan, turned him away both times. So for a while he set up camp in the mountains behind her Malibu home.

Shortly after he had returned from one of his California trips, the murdered bodies of Perry's parents, his 2 ½-year-old nephew and two cousins (one who apparently looked like Newton-John's then fiancé Matt Lattanzi) were discovered in their homes. All had been shot in the eyes.

Perry had warned a psychiatrist that he was going to kill his parents and others in groups of ten. Near the corpses, police found a list of ten names, including all the dead, two additional relatives and the names of Olivia Newton-John, Matt Lattanzi, and Justice Sandra Day O'Connor. They didn't find their suspect, Michael Perry.

The diagnosed paranoid-schizophrenic was finally arrested near the Supreme Court in Washington, D.C., after a full-blown manhunt that lasted close to two weeks. He had seven television sets in the hotel room where he had been staying. All were turned to static. All had eyes drawn on them.

Judged legally sane by the courts, Perry stood trial. The jury rendered a guilty verdict. He's currently on death row in his home state of Louisiana.

OFFICIALS AGREE THAT mental disturbance also plays a role with the romantically obsessed person drawn to a non-famous stranger or unable to let go of a relationship that's over. Severely disturbed stalkers show the same tenacity and similar levels of delusion, whether they're stalking celebrities or someone like you. They create a scenario for themselves and then act according to that rather than reality. When one 26-year-old was arrested after following his victim everywhere she went, violating the restraining order against him seven times and repeatedly threatening to kill her, he asked if he could go see her and then insisted on being allowed to call her when his first request was denied. "I love her maybe too much," he admitted in a moment of rare lucidity.

"None of the people who engage in stalking behavior are normal individuals. There's something wrong with each of them," Dr. Park Elliott Dietz told ABC's *20/20*. But crazy doesn't mean stupid.

Aliana Petrov, the Russian student who tutored Arthur Navarro just three times, tracked him like an undercover agent on assignment. When he moved to get away from her, she located his parents and sent him letters through them. When he got a restraining order to keep her away, she managed to see him anyway by dragging him into court with appeal after appeal.

She was arrested three times. Psychological counseling was mandated. Persistent follow-up calls from the arresting officers and the counseling center kept her attendance fairly regular. But the sessions did little to shake her obsession with Arthur. When her psychiatrist was unable to keep an appointment with her, for example, she made Xerox copies of some bullets and a knife she had with her and sent the copies—which she had annotated with threats—to Arthur.

Often in such cases, antipsychotic drugs comprise part of the therapy. But while potentially effective, these medications have their limitations, especially since there is no way to ensure that people actually take them once they've been prescribed. Mentally disturbed patients frequently discontinue their drug treatment because of negative side effects. Or, they stop because they're feeling so good that they cease to believe the drugs are necessary. Either way, their chances of getting effective, long-lasting care are slim.

The National Institute of Mental Health and the American Psychiatric Association have estimated that during any year, more than one-fourth of all Americans suffer from some kind of diagnosable mental disorder. Yet research indicates only one in five receives any kind of treatment. Even mandated psychiatric observation doesn't ensure that those at risk will get help. A three-year study of mentally ill subjects deemed dangerous by police and placed on a psychiatric hold revealed that over 65 percent had previously been committed for observation, 35 percent of them ten times or more. Yet, a full 84 percent received no mental health follow-up care whatsoever once the observation period had ended. "In other words, the mental health system did nothing about that person," said retired Detective Walt DeCuir, who co-authored a report entitled "Outcome for Psychiatric Emergency Patients Seen by an Outreach Police-Mental Health Team" and headed up the Los Angeles Police Department's Mental Evaluation Unit.

Clearly, the system is not responding to the needs of those it is intended to serve.

That's bad news for all concerned. It's especially bad news for those close to mentally disturbed pursuers. Ironically, the people at greatest risk usually aren't those being targeted, but rather the stalker's loved ones. Before launching his shooting spree at the Dana Point post office, Mark Hilbun stabbed his 63-year-old mother to death and then dispatched her dog, Golden. The two postal workers he shot, Charles T. Barbagallo and Peter Gates, were his two best friends on the job. Michael Perry killed five family members. Ralph Nau, another Olivia Newton-John stalker, smashed an ax handle through the skull of his 8-year-old stepbrother.

THE NUMBER OF mentally ill persons in America has risen in the last two decades. During that same time, mental health funding has decreased. The deinstitutionalization movement, which began in the mid-1950s, contributed in large measure to this escalating problem. The idea, of course, was to improve the treatment of the mentally ill by moving them from state hospitals where they had been largely warehoused to community mental-health centers where they would be monitored and regularly medicated. As a result, most were released. But the community-based treatment facilities never got funded and never got built.

"What we need to do is short circuit these kinds of cases with out-patient treatment programs within the community before they ever become really aggravated," said Lieutenant John Lane, who headed the Los Angeles Police Department's Threat Management Unit (TMU) for seven years.

Instead, we continue not to treat maladjusted Americans. They languish largely on the streets or in our jails.

To make matters worse, laws governing the involuntary hospitalization or treatment of people incapacitated by mental aberrations have become steadily more restrictive over the last 40 years. Even those who are violently inclined can't be committed against their will unless they pose an *immediate* threat to themselves or others. The usual response to a family's plea that a close relative be hospitalized because they fear his potential for brutality? "Call us once he does something illegal or violent."

Ironically, a mentally ill person who threatens to take his own life will get a quicker response from mental health services than one who threatens to take someone else's. If you pose a danger to yourself, treatment is almost guaranteed. "There are thousands of suicide prevention centers in this country," said de Becker. "Yet there isn't a single homicide prevention center." Part of the problem lies in the lack of credibility associated with threats, since so many are made for effect and not carried through. The same, however, could be said about suicide threats and attempts.

Laws have begun to rectify this imbalance to some degree. In California, for example, amendments to the civil commitment laws decree that people with a diagnosable psychiatric condition may be retained past their initial commitment period in the face of a "demonstrated danger of substantial physical harm." According to a 1992 U.S. Supreme Court ruling, however, dangerousness cannot be used as a rationale for continued confinement if the subject is no longer insane.

DESPITE THE OBVIOUS need for a close working relationship between mental health workers and authorities in these situations, communication about the release of patients who are potentially threatening to others remains sporadic at best. Confusion about issues like patients' rights and confidentiality compounds the problem. "Uniformed officers took one obsessed fan to the UCLA Medical Center and had her committed on an involuntary hold," Lieutenant Lane recalled. "But as soon as one of my officers in this unit called to find out whether or not they were actually going to hold this person and admit her, they would not even confirm that the person was in that facility because of their patients' rights perspective. Now that's absurd. We knew she was there because we brought her there. We didn't want to know any intimate details about what her problem was. We just wanted to know if they were going to hold her or if they were going to release her."

While the ethics behind the premise of patient confidentiality remain admirable, the lengths to which it has been taken can compromise treatment. In many states, for example, a patient can dictate whether or not a physician is allowed to contact family members. That limits the information that can be garnered and then used in treatment.

The issue becomes even murkier when another's life may be at stake. Prosenjit Poddar, a graduate student at the University of California, Berkeley, had discussed his intentions of killing Tatiana Tarasoff, the young woman with whom he had become infatuated, during counseling sessions with a university psychologist. Fearful about his patient's potential for violence, the therapist requested that campus police detain Prosenjit while he started proceedings to have him involuntarily committed. In strict compliance with his code of confidentiality, however, he shared no details about the nature of Prosenjit's obsession. So when Prosenjit promised that he would stay away from the college student, the campus police decided he posed no danger and released him.

Neither Tatiana—who was spending the summer in Brazil—nor her parents were warned about the concerns for her safety.

During the two months she was away, Prosenjit showed no evidence of violence. Shortly after her return, he stabbed and shot her to death.

Her parents sued the university, the psychologist who had treated Prosenjit, and the campus police for causing or contributing to the wrongful death of their daughter. The case was ultimately appealed to the California Supreme Court. A split court ruled that the police had made a discretionary decision, and could not be held accountable simply for being wrong. But the court also held that when a therapist knows—or should be able to determine—that a patient may pose a hazard of great bodily harm to an identified victim, he or she has a duty to inform either the victim (or significant others) or the police, or take whatever steps were necessary under the circumstances. "The protective privilege ends where public peril begins," concluded the opinion for the majority.

Since then, the Tarasoff ruling has become a national standard of practice. Even so, potential victims are all too often kept in the dark. In Hawaii, a patient told her psychiatrist she was going to set fire to the bar where her boyfriend worked, as well as to his home. The psychiatrist said nothing to law enforcement or to the boyfriend. The patient proceeded to carry out her plan unhindered.

PEOPLE SLIP THROUGH the system in other ways. In the fall of 1988, award-winning tennis coach Gary Wilensky was arrested after stalking two boys ages 11 and 12, and a young schoolgirl. The case never went to trial. Instead, the New York resident agreed to psychiatric treatment and the charges were dismissed. The therapy didn't help. In 1990, Gary became obsessed with and stalked a 13-year-old girl. When confronted, he abandoned his pursuit of her. Two years later, he began to coach 16-year-old Jennifer Rhodes, who would quickly become his next fixation.

By January 1991, her mother, Sonya, was so concerned about how the coach was reacting to her daughter that she dismissed Gary and suggested that he seek psychological help. He took her advice and began to see a therapist she had recommended.

The counseling didn't curb his obsession. Four months later, he tried to kidnap Jennifer, now 17, in order to take her to the remote cabin he had rented and filled with whips, chains, handcuffs and clamps. He bashed her head with a cattle prod three times and continued to club her when she crumpled to the ground screaming.

Jennifer's mother, Sonya, jumped Gary while managing to fling her daughter out of the way. "I'll kill you if you hurt my daughter," she shouted as Jennifer ran for help. Gary fled before police arrived, and mother and daughter were packed into an ambulance and rushed to emergency for a hundred stitches between them. When police spotted Gary's car an hour after the attack, he pointed a rifle into his own mouth and fired.

A MINORITY OF the mentally ill stalkers who are arrested are deemed to be incurable, either because of their condition or because of their refusal to take medication. Many present a real danger to those they've focused on. Yet mental institutions are often unwilling to accept mentally ill patients prone to violence.

When Lawrence Foker* was arrested for stalking, he was involuntarily committed to the Los Angeles county hospital for a 72-hour psychological evaluation, and then placed on a 14-day hold. Deemed manic-depressive, the articulate Yale graduate was remanded to a lock-down mental health facility for psychiatric treatment. Because the county hospital was experiencing an acute bed shortage, Lawrence was transferred to a private facility. Although they had a locked section, personnel at the second hospital refused to treat him once they realized he was assaultive. So he was transferred again.

"We tracked him through five separate institutions. All were part of the county system, and all had the facilities to care for him. And they chose not to because he was too much of a management problem," said Lieutenant Lane. "Yet who else in society is better prepared to handle a mentally disordered individual? Certainly not the jail system."

That's exactly where most mentally disordered people end up. The number of mentally ill people currently incarcerated in Los Angeles County's jail system makes it in effect the nation's largest mental institution. Most shouldn't be there. They should be receiving full-time treatment for the sickness that triggered a crime. Yet, because this nation doesn't obligate hospitals to take in the very cases that threaten us most, they're largely going untreated. One study showed that even when mentally ill prison inmates do receive medication to control symptoms like hearing voices, they're often coerced out of the drugs by other convicts, or they sell or trade their medication on the prison black market.

The lack of effective treatment means that these individuals are often more disturbed and more dangerous when they're released than when they began their sentences.

Chronic mental patients pose an additional dilemma, since the severe shortage of funds means that their care often comes at the expense of those personality-disordered types who, being more functional, are perceived as less of a threat. Consider the case of one delusional woman who believed that singer Johnny Mathis had impregnated her. Convinced that he was in love with her and that they would marry, she began to write him lengthy abusive letters when he didn't respond to requests that he send her money. She wound up tracking down his residence and banging on the door. After her second visit, Mathis called the police. They picked her up but then let her go. This time she didn't stop at letters and attempts to visit him. She printed up signs calling Mathis a "piece of shit" who hadn't given her money or married her, and paraded them up and down the street in front of his office. She disrupted his shows by yelling and screaming.

Her delusions weren't limited to the singer, however. She was finally arrested in Beverly Hills after passing a number of bad checks, which she had signed in the name of Joanna Carson, Johnny Carson's wife.

Since she understood the nature of the charges against her and could cooperate with her attorney regarding her defense, she was judged competent to stand trial and was never provided with psychological care.

THE CRITERIA BY which different jurisdictions judge a person's mental state may vary a little. Some gauge whether the accused knows the difference between right and wrong, others whether he can participate in his own defense. But in all U.S. courts, insanity is a legal definition that has little to do with a medical determination of mental illness.

In Kimberley Poland's case that has meant that her stalker of eight years has gone free. "This is my job," her pursuer told a sheriff when questioned about why he didn't find work and forget about the Polands, a family from Maine. By then, his constant telephone calls and letters had escalated into threats of kidnappings, mailings of bloody arrows to the house, and the belief that he was going to marry Kim.

The man had been drawn to Kim, then 16, after a photo of her appeared in the local paper when she won the Miss Oxford County Fair Pageant. Her stalker was eventually incarcerated in two different mental facilities. Personnel from these institutions, along with doctors, lawyers, and even his mother, certified that he was criminally insane. Yet despite an obvious deterioration of mental stability, despite an escalation in the danger he poses, and despite charges of assault on an officer, terrorizing, and criminal mischief, he remained free. "Because he was deemed incompetent, the charges were dismissed and Doe* was released," Kim's mother, Sandra, testified before the U.S. Senate Judiciary Committee. "Where is the logic that says a person who is not sane enough to stand trial is sane enough to walk the streets, to renew his obsession, to continue to harass, to assault, to threaten?"

MENTALLY ILL PEOPLE don't commit as many crimes as sane people do, according to forensic psychiatrist Kaushal Sharma, MD, assistant medical director at the University of Southern California Institute of Psychiatry, Law, and Behavioral Science. But the minority who do and who have a history of criminal behavior show a higher propensity to repeat that behavior again and again and are more dangerous than either the mentally disordered or the simple criminal. Ironically, by protecting those judged insane from unfair prosecution, our legal system almost assures that these menaces will be out on the street again. "Most of those who meet the requirements for involuntary hospitalization will get temporary treatment with anti-psychotic drugs," said de Becker. "This stabilizes them enough to say the 'right' things in hearings. Then they're routinely released back to the streets."

Unless, of course, they still have to stand trial for a crime they committed. Even that, however, is no guarantee that the violently inclined, mentally ill subject will be put away.

Although Ralph Nau confessed to the murder of his stepbrother, he was deemed unfit to stand trial. For five years, the Chester Mental Health Center in Illinois pumped him full of drugs until they finally rendered him legally competent. They did little in the way of rehabilitation to make him safer, according to Nau's public defender. Yet, because he had waived his Miranda rights during a period of insanity, his confession was deemed inadmissible and he was acquitted. Only a frantic plea from the prosecutor convinced the judge to order another psychiatric evaluation.

While Ralph Nau was being held at the Elgin Mental Health Center, his delusions seemed to intensify. He focused on a nurse he believed intended to divorce her husband for him. He was angry that the late Farrah Fawcett refused to acknowledge that he—rather than Ryan O'Neal—had fathered her child. He believed that he was engaged to Marie Osmond. Letters he sent to *Good Morning America* former co-host Joan Lunden began referring to her daughters. And yet, he petitioned to be released.

"People like him murder repeatedly and frequently. Some of the most highly dangerous people in our society are like that . . . . And we don't have any adequate treatment for them except institutionalization," Dr. Ronald Baron, a psychiatrist who examined Nau, told the *Chicago Tribune*. "He's going to get out. Maybe not now, maybe not this year. But he's going to get out. It's just a matter of when."

Step Back From the Brink

The potential for violence exists in each and every one of us. Provocation in an already volatile situation, especially when dealing with a mentally unstable individual, can escalate the probability of violence. When dealing with stalkers of any kind, be especially sure never to compromise their dignity, since that could push them over the edge.

17

Your Day in Court: This is Justice?

IF YOU'VE BEEN STALKED, YOU probably know all too well that, until recently, the problem of stalking was virtually overlooked. Even now, our criminal justice system fails to respond adequately to the problem or to the needs of crime victims who have often gone to great lengths to seek protection from the courts and still experience no reprieve from the intimidation and violence they suffer.

At a hearing before the U.S. Senate's Judiciary Committee on combating stalking and family violence, then NOW (National Organization for Women) Legal Defense and Education Fund staff attorney Ruth Jones recounted just how tragic the consequences of that failure can be. "In one of my cases as an assistant district attorney, a woman sought and was given an order of protection while the criminal case against her abuser proceeded. On several occasions, he violated that order of protection by phone calls and letters, but I was never able to make the courts understand the gravity of the situation. Ultimately, he failed to return to court and a bench warrant was issued . . . . Before he could be arrested on that warrant, however, he stabbed and killed this woman in front of her son and shocked onlookers at a grocery store. She trusted the system and the system failed her. The system failed her because the court couldn't discern that the letters and the phone calls were a precursor to violence."

The prevalence of that kind of attitude leaves victims with little recourse and even less hope. Just ask Susan Foster, executive director of molecular & cellular biology at Harvard University, who—along with her boyfriend—was almost beaten to death by her former husband. During the two years he stalked Susan, he violated numerous restraining orders and made numerous threats. Eventually, she concluded that no one was able or willing to do anything to assist her. Only the intervention of a private citizen saved Susan and her boyfriend when her former husband attacked them.

All too often, law enforcement is guilty of contributing to the problem instead of the solution. Maria Navarro's call for help to her local sheriff's office went unheeded despite a restraining order against her estranged husband and despite his threat to blow her away. Secretary Anna Alfaro, whose former boyfriend eventually kidnapped and murdered her, had repeatedly notified police about his assaults and threats during the four months prior to her death. Tracey Thurman successfully sued the city of Torrington, Connecticut, and its police department for non-responsiveness after her estranged husband repeatedly stabbed her in the chest, neck and throat. During the eight months preceding the attack, authorities had consistently ignored or rejected her attempts to file complaints regarding his repeated threats upon her life and the life of her son.

STALKING VICTIMS NATIONWIDE tell the same story. The punch line they hear from most law enforcement personnel sounds like a refrain. "Call us when he does something," the police say, without understanding that the stalker has done something simply by standing on a street corner, following behind in a car or leaving telltale matchbooks on the porch, when those actions are part of a larger campaign of intimidation. His pursuit may have already turned the target's life into a hell. Reacting to a crime that's been committed rather than trying to prevent one does little to help a frightened victim.

In September 1989, just three weeks after Rebecca Schaeffer's death, then Los Angeles Police Department Captain Bob Martin faced a group of personal managers of celebrities, along with an FBI agent, and admitted the law's inability to deal with such situations. "Essentially we both stood up and said there was not a damn thing we could do to help," he recalled.

By 1990, two landmark statutes in California provided law enforcement personnel of that state with the beginnings of a mechanism to deal with obsession cases. "We're at the threshold of defining a crime that should have been identified a long time ago," John Wilson, now retired deputy City Attorney of the City of Los Angeles, said at the time. All 50 states (plus Washington D.C. and the U.S. Territories) have since passed similar legislation.

This unprecedented nationwide response not only testifies to the pervasiveness of the problem, but to a growing awareness of the toll it's taking. But there's still a long way to go. Most statutes define stalking as the willful, malicious and repeated following and harassing of another person. But in addition to a pattern of conduct, many mandate that an imminent, credible threat of violence be made against the victim for the activity to be considered stalking. Some states also consider the stalker's intent to instill fear as illegal, while others define criminal stalking as any activity that would instill fear in a reasonable person.

Thankfully, with the publication of the Model Antistalking Code in 1994, law enforcement agencies have finally begun to realize that a threat doesn't require words. A hand that's pointed at you in the shape of a gun conveys a message that's loud and clear, especially if it follows ominous correspondence or telephone calls. A bouquet of black roses delivered to your door, a dead animal received in the mail, or a photograph with your image crossed out can also communicate the same sentiment. If a former mate tells you that you'd better follow orders "because you remember what happened to Rover," and Rover was hit by a car, his meaning won't seem the least bit vague.

THE INFLICTION OF terror doesn't even require threats, be they articulated or inferred. Despite court orders, Jim Martin's* gay ex-lover has stalked him for the past eight years. Robert Tyler*, a handsome 47-year-old college professor, has never once threatened Jim's life. Yet, Jim lives like a prisoner in his mother's house, afraid to move lest he further antagonize his pursuer. "It's making me crazy," he said.

Their common interest in plants brought them together. They shared an apartment for 11 years. But the relationship changed during the last 24 months, after Jim completed his graduate school education. "He thought he'd lost control of me," said Jim. "And he had. I had become more independent both financially and emotionally."

That's when the battering started. The lack of frequency was of little comfort, especially since the assaults always caught Jim off-guard. He would be standing in the kitchen or sitting in an easy chair, and suddenly Robert would grab him by the arm and start pushing or shaking him. It didn't matter that Jim was a foot taller. It didn't matter that Jim hit back or pushed him off. Every few months, Robert would attack, always by surprise. Not knowing if—or when—the abuse would hit was bad enough. That Robert seldom remembered his violent acts scared Jim more than the incidents themselves.

He finally left after Robert cut his leather pants, along with a leather vest and pair of boots, into one-inch squares. Not an easy task. "I figured it took him at least a whole afternoon," Jim said. The realization of how much time and effort Robert's destructive task had required brought on a second realization: Jim had to leave the man with whom he had been in love. "I didn't feel safe," he said.

Robert, however, refused to let go. Over the next three years, he followed Jim to all the various bars and clubs he previously professed to hate, and enlisted his friends' assistance when he couldn't handle the task personally. When Jim was granted a mutual stay-away order, Robert violated the injunction nine times in just two days. He continued to show up at Jim's house regularly, wanting to talk, and was suspected of vandalizing Jim's car numerous times, as well as the natural gas line to the water heater in the garage.

The time apart didn't diminish Robert's penchant for violence. Two years after the relationship had ended, he came to visit following a car accident in which Jim had been badly injured. Robert seemed so concerned that Jim's mother let him in the house. After 20 minutes, however, he got angry and threw a computer at his invalided ex-lover. Then he tried to beat him up.

The police just told Jim to ignore the abuse. They took the reports, but never investigated.

Robert then embarked on what Jim called "recreational litigation," slapping Jim with a subpoena on his next two birthdays. In court, he claimed mutual combativeness. Most of the time, the strategy worked, largely because judges understand the nature of gay domestic violence—and the fact that it occurs just as frequently as heterosexual spousal abuse—as little as they understand the nature of stalking.

The fact that the harassment has continued as long as it has frightens Jim more than anything else. "The first year I could handle it. 'This is going to end,' I thought. 'He'll find somebody else or something else to do.' But he hasn't. And that's what's scary."

In response, Jim carries a copy of the restraining order he was awarded against Robert, along with his cell phone and a camera, whenever he goes out. "But I'm tired of dealing with it," he said. "So I just stay home."

There are things he would like to do. He would love to attend the big gardening shows coming to town. "But I know Robert will probably be there, and something else would happen." So, in an attempt not to feed the problem, he has cut himself off from his entire life. "I feel totally alone," he said.

EVEN IF ROBERT Tyler's actions had made Jim fear for his life, at the time state law would probably not have been able to prosecute him. Although an amendment now allows for a more liberal interpretation of what constitutes a threat—defining it as a deliberate pattern of activity that provokes (or should provoke) fear in a reasonable person—similar activity in some states still would not be deemed a credible threat.

But limited understanding of what constitutes threatening or intimidating conduct is only part of the problem. A quandary remains. How do you arrest someone for something you think he or she ultimately might do?

Many of the answers the states have come up with have proved unworkable. Some of the laws on the books were simply too limited in scope. At one point, West Virginia, for example, required previous cohabitation or a prior intimate relationship in order to prosecute for stalking. Other laws have been so narrowly defined as to be virtually unenforceable.

The constitutionality of various antistalking laws has also become an issue. Those that are overly vague deny an individual the right to due process by not making clear exactly what behavior constitutes criminal conduct. Those that are too broad threaten to criminalize activities and speech protected under the First Amendment. Like standing on a street corner. Or writing someone a letter. Or picking up the phone.

WHAT DIFFERENTIATES INDEPENDENT activity or communication from stalking is a pattern of behavior and its cumulative effect. "It should be criminal to repeatedly follow and harass a victim, particularly when you combine this conduct with statements and actions that make it clear you might do them harm," said de Becker. "When you put your victim in fear for their life, regardless of whether you speak the threat or just make the threats clear by your actions, it should be a crime."

The recognition of this simple notion, however, along with the adoption of comprehensive, constitutional laws, would be only half the battle. The system is set up so that the patterns and histories of stalkers are obfuscated. As a result, all too often they continue to be dealt with ineffectively or never recognized at all. "Judges in family and civil courts . . . do not have access to the criminal histories of alleged stalkers, or even to the current arrest warrant information relating to those stalkers," U.S. Senator and future Vice President of the United States Joseph R. Biden, Jr., told the Committee on the Judiciary, which he chaired at the time. So stalking activity is frequently judged on the basis of individual episodes that sound inconsequential when taken alone, rather than as a sequence of harassment that has escalated over time.

The man who killed 21-year-old art student Kristin Lardner had a long criminal history that included assaulting ex-girl-friends. He was on probation for attacking a former lover with a pair of scissors when Kristin sought judicial assistance. She had dated him just two months before breaking up with him. That evening he followed her, beat her, and left her lying on the street unconscious. Four weeks later, Kristin went to the police. The officer she spoke with was concerned enough to fill out a one-day emergency protection order (which he got a night judge to sign), as well as paperwork asking that Michael Cartier be charged with assault and battery, larceny and violation of the domestic violence law. But the judge who heard her petition for a temporary restraining order the following day knew nothing about that. He didn't check Michael's record, and, as a result, didn't press for his immediate arrest.

The following week, Kristin applied for a permanent injunction. That judge, too, treated her request as routine and did not check for any criminal record. And since the police officer's original criminal complaint application was sitting in the clerk magistrate's in-box—along with a second one resulting from

Michael's violation of the temporary restraining order Kristin had filed against him—the judge never learned about either. So instead of sending the ex-con back to prison, he released him to the streets after a hearing that lasted five minutes. Eleven days later, in broad daylight, Michael shot Kristin to death in front of a sandwich shop.

In reaction to her death, the Massachusetts legislature passed a bill to set up a statewide registry of domestic violence offenses that will include the criminal histories of all perpetrators. Any judge handling a case involving restraining orders will be required to consult that information. Massachusetts, however, is the exception rather than the rule.

UNFORTUNATELY, MOST STATES lack the mandate—and the mechanisms—for such information sharing. That explains, in part, why the legal system usually treats these offenses so mildly. In the United States, most first-time stalkers are charged with misdemeanors that typically carry sentences of up to one year in jail and a $1,000 fine.

Initially, James Otis Sims served just 13 months for his 14-year-long stalking of ex-girlfriend Sandy Waite Potter, which included brutal beatings and thousands of dollars' worth of vandalism. This despite the court having access to the serial nature of his stalking, which extended over two states and victimized some ten people. Each time he violates the conditions of his probation, he is sentenced to a year in jail. He usually serves six to eight months of his sentence. As soon as he's released, he resumes his harassment.

Sandy, now 38, still fears that James will manage to take her life. She has every right to be frightened. "In my opinion, most of the state antistalking legislation is toothless," said Jim Wright. "The first time, a stalker's hand merely gets slapped. The next time, it gets slapped a little harder, and the time after that a little harder than that. Boy, if it happens a fourth time, that's a felony. Well, many times it would be a felony anyway because it's a homicide."

Federal legislation has attempted to deal with these shortcomings. But controlling stalkers through the law is not easy. Most stalkers are smart enough to push right up to the limit of the law without breaking it. When a restraining order mandates them to keep a distance of 100 yards from the victim, they'll set up a surveillance post exactly 101 yards away. Forbidden to follow or contact their target, they'll harass his or her family and friends instead. One man responded to a court order to stay away by enlisting his brother to carry on the harassment for him.

Nevertheless, the Model Antistalking Code, parts of which have been adopted by all 50 states, went a long way toward formulating a constitutional and enforceable legal framework for dealing with the problem. The law was developed by the National Criminal Justice Association, under the direction and oversight of the National Institute of Justice and in collaboration with groups ranging from the Police Executive Research Forum and the American Bar Association to the American Civil Liberties Union. The highlights:

- Rather than define exactly what acts constitute stalking (a list which some judges might rule to be exclusive) or the stalker's intent, the code prohibits a course of conduct that would cause a reasonable person fear. This includes any "threats implied by conduct."
- A stalker's threats to harm immediate family or anyone who has regularly resided in the household during the prior six months can be used as evidence of the stalking of his primary victim.
- For conduct to qualify as stalking, it must be purposeful. In addition, the defendant must—or should—know that the activity will cause fear.
- Serious, persistent, obsessive behavior that causes a victim to fear bodily injury or death should be prosecuted

as a felony. Penalties for stalking should be established which reflect and are commensurate with the seriousness of the crime. A continuum of charges would allow law enforcement officials to intervene in the early stages (during which a victim may be emotionally distressed as opposed to scared), and to prosecute for aggravated stalking in those recurring cases.

- Mechanisms must be put into place to protect victims once their stalkers are released from prison, whether that happens pretrial or once a sentence has been served. Victims must be allowed input about their safety needs during the process that determines any release conditions.

- No-contact orders should be considered as a condition of release for those stalkers on probation or parole, as well as the possibility of monitoring their activity electronically or through house arrest. Required psychological counseling should also be considered.

- For convicted stalkers with mental disorders, psychiatric evaluations should be required and counseling offered as part of any sentence.

- States should authorize the imposition of pretrial release conditions. These could include placing the accused in the custody of a person or organization agreeing to provide adequate supervision; restricting the accused's movements; prohibiting the accused's possession of weapons; prohibiting the accused's use or possession of drugs and alcohol; prohibiting contact or communication with the victim or those close to the victim either directly or through an intermediary; drug treatment and testing; mental health treatment and testing; a specified curfew; and restricting those activities—like following victims or going to or near their home, their workplace or their child's school—that a protective order would include.

- Reasonable efforts to supply victims with pretrial release orders, along with information about how and to whom to report violations, should be included as provisions in pretrial release or bail laws.

(To find out about your state's stalking laws, visit The National Center for Victims of Crime at www.ncvc.org/law/statestk.htm.)

THE FEDERAL MODEL Legislation also recommended education and training programs to combat the widespread lack of understanding among prosecutors and judges, which results in cases either never going to trial or perishing once they get to court. Boston's Teresa Bean slept with a loaded gun, a knife and dog repellent by her side because a judge released her estranged husband from jail after he had been arrested for violating the protective order she had against him. This despite prior assaults during which he fractured her skull and stabbed her left breast with a broken coat hanger.

The importance of enlightening prosecutors and judges can't be overstated. According to Park Elliott Dietz, arresting a stalker and then failing to imprison or prosecute inevitably makes the problem worse for the victim. "As a general rule, it's perceived by the mentally ill stalker as a confirmation of the relationship, and by the less seriously ill stalker as an angering challenge," he told *USA Today*.

But change won't happen overnight. In a legal system that's been proven to be traditionally biased and systematically discriminatory against women, the ingrained assumption that every stalking case is either a lover's spat or the product of an overactive imagination still runs deep. And as with rape, often the only witness to a stalking is the victim.

LAW ENFORCEMENT ALSO needs to learn more about the problem of stalking, the recourses they have to deal with it, the systems that would facilitate the tracking of stalker activity, and the proper way to inform, support, and assist its victims.

In addition to years of harassment, Sarah Jane Williams has had to deal with everything from police insensitivity and outright come-ons to interminable repetitions of her story after every new offense. "You're going through this nightmare and trying to get help," she said. "But the system continues to abuse you."

In response, police departments across the country have begun to revise training procedures and add social workers to their staffs. But they have yet to determine the safest and most effective course of action when it comes to stopping the stalker without jeopardizing the victim.

The prevailing disagreement revolves around the use of restraining or protective orders. Although several hundred thousand of such orders are issued every year in the United States, experts from Park Elliott Dietz to Gavin de Becker to FBI behavioral scientist Jim Wright are convinced that in most serious cases they don't work and only serve to worsen the situation. "If you look at every case where there was a long-term pursuit that ended in homicide, you'll always find intervention in its history—usually a restraining order," said de Becker. "That's not to say that some of these people wouldn't have killed them if they hadn't gotten restraining orders. But it is to say that the sooner you let the air out of the situation the better, and interventions do the opposite."

It makes sense if you think about it. For the person still capable of listening to reason, a restraining order will communicate with the force of a mallet the notion that his activity is unacceptable. That means there were probably other ways to get the message across. But a stalker whose obsession renders him incapable of heeding signs or information that would logically put an end to his pursuit is hardly going to be receptive to a court order. And he may see it as a provocation or offense.

Everyone agrees that cases require intervention once they pass a certain threshold. The difference comes in defining where that threshold lies. For most of the law enforcement agencies and victims' advocates across the country, telling a target to get a restraining order has become a knee-jerk reaction. Police tend not to suggest that you watch and wait because that's not what victims want to hear and that's not what police are trained to do. Cops want to put away the bad guy. So they set the stage, even though engaging the stalker in this manner will often enrage him and cause his behavior to escalate.

The use of restraining orders can be especially incendiary if their issuance humiliates the stalker. When a person's dignity has been compromised, so have the inhibitors that would ordinarily prevent him from acting out in a violent or harmful way. That's why so many stalking situations explode at this stage. How does Laura Black feel about the restraining order she was prompted to seek against Richard Farley? "That was the catalyst that pushed him over the edge," she told the court during his murder trial.

If restraining orders work so poorly and often so adversely, why do most authorities continue to recommend them? Because under the current laws, violations of restraining orders are one of the few legal hammers the police can wield when trying to incarcerate stalkers.

As we've seen, however, locking up perpetrators doesn't typically solve the underlying problem and often worsens it. "In most cases, neither jail nor mental hospitals are therapeutic environments," said de Becker. "They're places where you separate, where dignity gets taken away, and where many stalkers get angrier and angrier."

IN SOME CASES, incarceration doesn't even provide the victim with a reprieve. Gang members convicted of stalking, for example, will simply direct their homeboys to take over the intimidation while they're in jail. Some stalkers even manage to harass their victims personally from behind bars.

Herbert Bruce Lemont, Linda Pride's stalker, obtained her tax returns for the last five years from the IRS by sending forged papers granting him power of attorney. The returns provided him with her address. Then the convicted child molester/killer, who claims to be Linda's ex-husband and the father of her grown daughter, succeeded in getting her family's mail forwarded to him in prison by filing falsified change of address cards. When Linda (who had been responsible for Herbert's arrest ten years before) found out, she phoned the prison authorities. A secretary refused to put her through to the warden. Linda finally talked to the stalker's counselor. "Inmates do that all the time," she was told.

Imagine how effectively gang members acting in concert instead of alone could be, especially when not in prison.

BUT ORGANIZED GROUP stalking isn't confined to gang members. Many stalking victims find themselves the target of a group engaged in a campaign of harassment and defamation intended to intimidate and terrorize them. Sometimes individuals are targeted by organizations that believe in different things. Doctors performing abortions or people who work in labs that conduct testing on animals are prime candidates for this kind of organized "cause stalking" by groups of people opposed to what they're doing.

In contrast, "gang stalking," preferably referred to as "group stalking" since it doesn't always involve gangs, generally involves a stalker and his friends and family members who are seeking to discredit the victim and the victim's complaint.

Either way, this kind of joint stalking seems to be on the rise. According to a 2009 U.S. Department of Justice special report, 18 percent of stalking victims said they had been stalked by two people and 13 percent claiming to have been stalked by three or more people. Follow-up documents released by the U.S. Department of Justice clarified that of that 13 percent, 185,050 people (or 41 percent of those surveyed) indicated that the harassment "involved stalkers working together as a team or group."

So how do you prevent such relentless people—whether operating as a team or alone—from carrying out obtrusive, alarming or life-threatening acts when all past experience indicates that they will do it? Legislation and education are a start. But it will take comprehensive cooperation between law enforcement, private security firms, mental health professionals, prosecutors, parole and probation officials, and victims' support groups to make the kind of headway that is so desperately needed.

Protecting victims has to become the first priority. They must be introduced to safety measures that will help make them inaccessible. Units specifically trained in this area should investigate and, if charges are filed, prosecute the case. Procedural changes—like requiring the police (rather than the complainant) to swear out a warrant for the arrest of a stalker—would quite possibly lessen the stalker's animosity toward that individual.

Once the legal machine has swung into motion, protective measures are more important than ever. Defendants who pose a danger to their targets must be detained so they can't harm the victim during proceedings. Likewise, they must be given more than token prison sentences if convicted.

A realistic assessment of the potential danger confronting a stalking victim demands full disclosure, not just of the facts of a particular case but of the stalker's complete civil and criminal history from all the states. In 1993, Senator Barbara Boxer proposed legislation in the U.S. Senate Judiciary Committee mandating that judges have access to—and consider—all pertinent information when making what amounts to life-and-death decisions. "The Stalker and Family Violence Enforcement Act,

or the SAFVE Act, would for the first time give all judges in all
courts that deal with stalking and domestic violence access to
the Federal criminal history records now available only to state
criminal justice officials," explained then Senator Biden, who
presided over the committee at the time. Sadly, the bill never
made it to a vote.

Amplifying those federal criminal history records with complaint files would also help. Such files contain information
collected by police that may not have resulted in an arrest. In
addition, an automated system that would allow for interstate
access to all civil actions needs to be developed, so that any patterns of behavior that might be revealed by those infractions
could be considered as well.

MENTALLY ILL OFFENDERS shouldn't have to go through the
courts at all. "It costs $10,000 to $20,000 every time a person
comes through the court system," said John Wilson, formerly
of the Los Angeles city attorney's office. "That money can be
better spent in a psychiatric setting." Diversion to mental health
facilities could be aided by restructuring procedures during the
pre-filing stage to include mental health professionals. Deputies
would be trained to screen for those cases that indicated psychological disorder and pass them to these experts for analysis.
Those stalkers deemed mentally ill would be placed in a mental
hospital or community mental health program.

Of course, for any of the above to take place, you have to be
willing to enter a judicial process that is complex, intimidating,
and time-consuming. In addition, since civil proceedings are not
self-enforcing, you must return to court in order to have a stalker
held in contempt every time a protection order is violated. To
render court proceedings more user friendly, some courts have
assigned personnel to follow each victim through the duration
of his or her case.

Karen Ahrens's position as a victim assistance coordinator in Olympia, Washington, allowed her to focus on the needs of the victim even when charges weren't brought. In addition, because her office was located at the police station, she could scan every single police report. "A lot of supervisors screen the reports, but only for their areas," she said. "Yet a lot of these crimes cross boundaries and involve multiple jurisdictions."

Finally, the creation of a centralized reporting vehicle (such as a 1-800-STALKER hot line or a clearinghouse for information about violent individuals), as well as the exploration of stalker deterrence and rehabilitation programs need to be considered.

However, no law—or restructuring—will help unless an effective antistalking strategy is implemented. Only a multidisciplinary approach that includes police, prosecutors, judges, social service professionals, and other criminal justice officials will effectively combat this encroaching crime. And as you may have discovered, our national judicial system has a long way to go before such a coordinated response becomes the standard instead of the exception.

Opt for A Better Way

If you're being stalked, you probably want to see your perpetrator thrown in prison. But how long will that reprieve last and what happens when he's released, having spent his incarceration angry and focused on you? Insist on effective, interdepartmental programs and counseling geared toward changing your stalker's behavior instead of simply punishing him.

18

Policing the Threat

WHILE LAW ENFORCEMENT HAS JUST awakened to the problem of stalking, a few departments across the country recognized the challenge before the rest and implemented new policing procedures and programs to combat it. The earliest—and one of the most comprehensive—of those efforts has been in Los Angeles.

In 1990, following the death of Rebecca Schaeffer, the Los Angeles Police Department established a one-of-a-kind unit designed to deal with obsessive individuals before their activity turned criminal. Considering the locale, some might have expected the new threat management unit to concentrate on fans pursuing celebrities. From the beginning, however, it was apparent that at least half the complaint calls were coming from ordinary citizens who were the targets of stalkers.

Captain Bob Martin, who originated the Threat Management Unit (TMU), still remembers the pre-TMU days when he would go on radio calls and then have to say he could do nothing. "We needed a mechanism to help people where no crime had been committed yet," he said. "If a call comes in about a guy being everywhere the caller goes, a typical desk sergeant would say, 'Yeah, yeah, yeah.' Or he might ask whether the individual had actually threatened the caller. But it wouldn't go much beyond that. In this unit, we take that kind of thing real seriously."

Since its inception, Angelenos have become increasingly aware of the unit's existence. In addition to those who take the initiative to call, referrals come from other law enforcement details, from the mental health arena and from the entertainment community. As a result, the phone never stops ringing. "We're turning people away," Martin said in 1991. "I could probably sign 30 people and make a division out of this unit and we'd still have too much to handle."

In its first three years, the LAPD TMU's five detectives and one police officer handled 208 cases where "an individual demonstrates an abnormal fixation and generates a long-term pattern of harassment, threats, stalking, or unsolicited acts of visitation or telephonic or written communication in an annoying or threatening manner toward another person." Since then, the unit's increased staff has actively handled several thousand cases, engaging in everything from investigation to surveillance, from consultation to hand-holding.

ONCE A CASE has been assigned, the detective interviews the victim, explains the dynamics of stalking cases, and helps that person identify the pattern of obsessive behavior he or she has been subjected to. From the outset, victims are reminded not to blame themselves for what has occurred.

Next, a game plan is developed. Since the problem may be long-term, targets are presented with alternative modes of coping with the situation. Apart from whatever steps may be available on the law enforcement front, they're encouraged to take specific precautions to increase their safety and serenity. Options presented include changing their phone numbers (de Becker actually recommends adding an additional phone line and keeping your old number so your stalker doesn't go looking for the new one), screening calls with an answering machine, obtaining a private post office box for mail, and relocating. The feasibility of moving, switching jobs, altering social patterns—and, in severe cases, assuming a new identity—is discussed. Specific security measures (which will be covered in an upcoming section) are recommended. In addition, detectives present therapeutic options like support groups, which allow the victim to work out any fears and frustrations.

One message is made clear from the start: While the TMU will help, the victim must accept his or her role in the process and assume certain responsibilities. "We treat victims as clients," said Lieutenant John Lane, who oversaw the unit until 1997. "This is their problem. They will get help in managing their problem. But it's unrealistic to expect that life will improve just by filing a police report."

After the preliminaries have been completed, the detective handling the case determines the nature of the situation and assesses the dangerousness of the stalker. Factors considered include the suspect's degree of obsession, acuteness of focus, any past dangerous behavior, access to the victim, access to weapons, mobility, resources, substance abuse, and any prior psychological counseling or arrests.

If the suspect is a known stalker of public figures, the system is checked for any criminal history or warrants. Files from the LAPD's Mental Evaluation Unit, the Secret Service, de Becker's organization, along with the TMU's own database, are reviewed for any possible matches. Technology such as the MOSAIC-2 computer program, developed and donated by de Becker, helps to assess the probability of a violent encounter between stalkers and their targets.

Unless intervention seems likely to aggravate an already precarious situation, that's usually the next step. Although many feel that this flies in the face of the unit's original mandate to provide an alternative to standard police practice, the victim is almost always advised to obtain a restraining order so that suspects may be arrested and detained in the event of a violation of that order. (For more about the advisability of restraining orders, as well as other forms of intervention, please see pages 28, 42, 233–4, 238–9.)

Next, the detective will contact the suspect either by mail, by telephone or face to face (at home, at work, or at the police station), depending on which action is likely to have the most impact. Should an arrest occur, bail enhancements can frequently keep potentially violent stalkers behind bars.

Incarceration—in jail or a mental facility—doesn't signal the end of the TMU's involvement. Instead, the case is flagged, and the suspect's activities are once again tracked upon his release. Only when both the TMU and the victim are satisfied that the suspect has discontinued his pursuit does the TMU actually sign off. Should the activity start back up again, even years later, the TMU simply reopens its file.

THE PRIVATE SECTOR has more leeway for creativity when it comes to threat management. When dealing with potentially volatile stalkers in the workplace, for example, one agency deludes them into thinking that they've won a radio show contest. Then the airline tickets are sent out and the employee is escorted onto the plane. His time away calms him down while allowing his employer or supervisor to take appropriate action in his absence.

Sometimes more intrusive tactics are used, such as going undercover. One pair of Southern California investigators frequently gains access to a stalker's home by posing as pollsters, talent agents, or fan club representatives. Once they've been invited inside, they conduct an interview to find out as much as possible about who and what they're dealing with. They inquire about the stalker's interest in his target. They subtly ask about his health. They find out whether he has been taking medication.

Responses are analyzed for signs of anger, as well as paranoid or irrational thinking. Refusals to reply tell the investigators as much as answers do, since they reveal mistrust. "Obviously, the more trusting someone is, the lower the risk," said one of the investigators.

Actually, most of what they learn about someone comes from what they see rather than what they hear. Their eyes scan the stalker's residence the moment they walk through the door. They search for signs that the stalker owns weaponry such as guns, knives, or crossbows. They look for evidence of weapons experience: skeet- or trap-shooting awards, hunting heads or trophies, action or military photographs that show the stalker holding a gun. They notice anything out of the ordinary, such as indications of disguises, odd photographs, or extensive news clippings about a particular person or incident.

Finally, they scrutinize the person in front of them. Lack of hygiene can betray his mental state. Body language also discloses telltale clues. Does the stalker make eye contact? Do his actions indicate high levels of anxiety?

WHEN SITUATIONS INVOLVE mentally ill stalkers who may need to be involuntarily committed, private agencies in Los Angeles often team with community social services, as well as the LAPD's psychiatric division. Even so, those cases are trickier to handle, especially considering the historical antagonism between law enforcement and mental health agencies.

"Law enforcement is trained to deal with the criminal justice issues and mental health deals with mental health issues. And those two don't normally meet. In fact, they see one another sometimes as enemies. Especially when immediate goals of keeping the peace conflict with long-term goals of psychological wellness," said Walt DeCuir, former director of the LAPD's Mental Evaluation Unit. "It's not until you have units like this that deal specifically with the mental health system in concert with the criminal justice system that we see that the mental health system can complement the criminal justice system if we understand how to utilize various laws."

The Mental Evaluation Unit serves as a 24-hour mental health emergency command post. A staff of specially trained police officers tracks and profiles mentally disturbed people who come in contact with police, and provides assistance to fellow officers who are required to call in when dealing with mentally ill suspects. Unit officers screen for mental illness based on the on-scene officers' observations and check the person's mental health and criminal history. (Since 1985, the unit has documented every single contact involving the mentally ill in Los Angeles, whether those individuals are arrested, civilly committed, or referred to various agencies.) The unit officers note any patterns that might suggest mental deterioration, warn on-site officers about any danger the mentally deranged suspect might present, and recommend ways to calm down an agitated person and avoid antagonizing him. Then they refer those suspects determined to be in need of psychological assistance to the nearest psychiatric facility with space available.

When urgent situations require greater psychological expertise, a special Department of Mental Health hotline is available to unit officers 24 hours a day. Cases requiring hands-on assistance are handled by system-wide mental assessment response teams (SMART). These teams, comprised of unit officers and specially trained psychiatric nurses, pool mental health and criminal justice information about the suspect.

"Once they leave the office, the information the team receives is confidential. That way, mental health can divulge all the information they have on an individual with their law enforcement teammates. So the team has the clearest picture that we can possibly put together on what they're going out to see," said DeCuir. "What we're trying to do is professionalize our response by having as much information as we can on contact with the situation and then knowing how to use that information to keep the peace and, if possible, provide some kind of quality of life for that individual."

On the theory that prevention is the most efficient form of law enforcement, the specialized teams do a follow-up within 10 days of each contact, sooner if necessary. They follow-up again after six months—earlier and with greater frequency if indicators warrant. On the phone, they sound more like cheerleaders than the law. "Are you going to go see the therapist today?"

That bit of encouragement can make all the difference. "It sounds kind of weird that law enforcement is a part of this process," said DeCuir. "But it serves our purposes, because we're keeping the peace and preventing situations from occurring."

First and foremost, this method of networking diverts mentally ill individuals in need of psychological help away from the legal system and into treatment. Clients who have previously been in treatment, for example, are referred back to the facility that last cared for them. In addition, it saves both systems time and money, and reduces danger to all parties. Finally, since the Mental Evaluation Unit is linked to the TMU, it can handle any after-hours stalking-related calls, thereby insuring that victims receive the proper response and assistance.

Los Angeles' Central District has also streamlined the way it deals with stalking-related prosecution. Both misdemeanors and felonies are handled by specially designated individuals who understand the unusual nature of this crime. And instead of being reviewed by one attorney who files it and passes it along to a second attorney for the arraignment—who gives it to yet a third to actually try the case—a single City or District Attorney assumes responsibility for the case from beginning to end. Vertical prosecution makes a big difference. Detectives communicate directly with the District Attorneys, so the D.A.s have hands-on involvement even before the case is filed. They can interview the victim, as well as other witnesses. That enables them to analyze what types of crimes have been committed, how serious the situation is and how the case should be handled.

THIS KIND OF prosecution makes the process easier on victims, who no longer have to repeat the same story over and over again to each new attorney. Vertical prosecution is not only more victim-friendly, it's also more effective when it comes to getting convictions. Having a single judicial contact helps reinforce the notion that victims will be taken seriously and not just sloughed off as another anonymous case among thousands. Once that kind of trust has been established, victims frequently reveal information they haven't even told the police. So the D.A.s wind up understanding the dimensions of the problem more fully. That translates into a stronger case for the prosecution.

John Wilson became the special designee in the city attorney's office. Having him follow stalking cases through the system proved a time-intensive commitment, as well as a drain on the office. "But that's really what has to happen on these cases. You have to be right there," he said. "That's what threat management is all about."

An ardent advocate of finding alternative ways to deal with these cases, Wilson teamed with psychiatrists to determine whether treatment might help particular suspects and tried to abandon the traditional adversarial role that prosecutors normally share with public defenders. "These cases are not a contest that you win through the conviction of the suspect," said Wilson. "They're a problem to be solved."

In Los Angeles, that solution includes mandating counseling as a condition of probation or parole, and diverting some criminal cases to psychiatric treatment programs like the one John Key co-founded along with psychiatrist and former chief *psychiatrist for the* LA County Jail E. Eugene Kunzman, MD. The Center Against Abusive Behavior, an outpatient mental health clinic, combined a biological, psychological, and sociological approach to treating perpetrators of domestic violence and stalking. The nonprofit organization was staffed by treatment providers with expertise in the areas of physical, emotional, psychological and sexual abuse. Kunzman provided whatever psychiatric care or medications might be required based on a mental status examination and subsequent testing for any contributing biological factors.

Key based his therapy on a cognitive behavior model and focused on controlling each new client's abusive behavior as his initial priority. A movement contract required stalkers to call in as often as twice a day and to report their whereabouts and activities. To help keep track of them every moment, Key also demanded a daily itinerary. Spot-checks, he found, helped to keep stalkers honest.

After reviewing police and court records, Key had stalkers tell their side of the story from beginning to end. Then he confronted them with any discrepancies between the two versions. "Because somewhere between the two lies the truth," he said. A determination about what kind of counseling was required follows.

Whether the perpetrators wound up in individual or group therapy or both, the ultimate goal of such counseling sessions was to get them to acknowledge their actions, in part through monitoring their own behavior, and then to recognize the errors in their thinking that makes their actions seem logical to them. Call it a reality check. "These people indulge in fantasy and the suppression of thought. Everyone comes in here saying, 'I didn't do it. I just want to put this behind me and move on,'" said Dr. Key, whose background included working as a hostage negotiator, as a suicidologist, and as a master trainer for the management of assaultive behavior. "Until they take responsibility for some of what they did and see themselves not as the victim [who's been inappropriately hounded by the criminal justice system], they won't make any progress. They'll just step into the same river twice."

During this process of cognitive re-framing, patients were repeatedly asked to consider and talk about the mental process behind their actions. What prompted their decisions to stalk or act out violently? Psychological imbalances, seemingly unrelated traumatic experiences in their pasts, and social conditioning that contributed to the problem were explored. "My contention is that you can't move until you understand what has created the path of violence," said Key. "So my task is to bring it up in as many different ways as I can to get them to think about it."

His approach allowed perpetrators to deal with deep-seated issues that had provoked their conduct, and to challenge ingrained responses and behaviors that had become well-worn paths. Take the work he did with a dark-skinned Hispanic woman who became obsessed over—and ultimately stalked—her former Anglo boyfriend. During her first three months of counseling, she gradually grew aware of her self-esteem problems—many of which were tied to negative feelings about her dark skin. Eventually, she was able to recognize that her obsession with her blond boyfriend stemmed from her need for the affirmation she habitually denied herself. In short, by helping her navigate through her own cognitive and emotional problems and by monitoring her movements, Key was able to start her on a path to recovery that would include impulse control and techniques to redirect destructive feelings.

THE LOS ANGELES system, however, is not without its own glitches. While warehousing disturbed stalkers in overcrowded prisons is certainly not the answer, mental health facilities can't always help. Aliana Petrov, for example, mailed her target a bullet while she was in counseling, and fully resumed her stalking behavior once her parole (along with her court-mandated counseling) had come to an end. Even when psychiatric treatment does make a difference, there are no guarantees that those psychotic stalkers who have been biochemically stabilized will continue to take their medication once they're on their own, especially if the drugs either induce unpleasant side effects or make the individual feel so good that he deems the medication superfluous.

An ideal approach for those recalcitrant stalkers, according to Key, would be initially to work with perpetrators in a locked psychiatric facility. Once the stalker is ready for outpatient treatment, electronic monitoring would supplement restrictions on his movements for as long as necessary. Probation or parole would aggressively monitor the quality of treatment and the progress being made. Adjustments to the surveillance, the restrictions, and the counseling sessions would follow accordingly, until finally the rehabilitated stalker would be weaned off the counseling program altogether.

As previously indicated, procedural disagreements also exist on Los Angeles' law enforcement front. Although the TMU recommended that most of its victims obtain restraining—or protective—orders, a number of experts in the field strongly believe that these only worsen a case. Indeed, because the orders essentially constitute a response from the victim, they can actually encourage a stalker and reinforce his behavior.

"A restraining order can be a valuable tool if it's used very early on in a case. But later on, it can be the worst thing you can possibly do," asserted de Gavin Becker, who cites case after case where a restraining order provoked a stalker and led to homicide. Consider Laura Black, Kristin Lardner or Maria Navarro, along with so many others in this book.

An intervention can put an end to certain unwanted behaviors when the stalker never intended harm. But in cases that have escalated and carry the definite possibility of danger, interventions of any kind can aggravate the situation. "It amounts to a form of Russian Roulette," said de Becker. "Even though the odds are good, six to one in your favor, no reasonable person wants to play."

THE ALTERNATIVE? RADICAL non-intervention with a goal of safety rather than prosecution. "That doesn't mean you don't do anything," Park Elliott Dietz explained in a lecture about threat management. "It means that the subject is not aware of the actions you're taking."

With this approach, preventing encounters between the stalker and his target, rather than trying to control or discourage the pursuer's behavior, becomes the primary objective. "We need to change the only person we can change," said de Becker. "The stalker may be crazy. He's unreasonable. He's culturally ill. There's no button that can be pushed to reliably improve his mental state or control his conduct indefinitely. But the victim's behavior can change in ways that will put him or her out of reach. Eventually, the majority of stalkers transfer their attention to someone else."

The first step in this strategy involves having the victim cut off *all* response to what the stalker does (including asking police to warn him off), and then watching and waiting to see what happens next.

That means not even responding to a threat. "Threats are not guarantees of action. They're not a contract," said de Becker. "They're like promises." Indeed, whether those promises are kept depends largely on how the target reacts. It is that reaction that gives the threat its value, and gives the stalker his or her power. "Engage and enrage" is how de Becker describes the dynamic of many cases gone bad.

This doesn't mean that you do nothing. The key is to protect yourself by taking precautions that the stalker is often ignorant of and then trying to outlast him. A far-ranging plan can help you live with the situation for as long as it takes the stalker to go elsewhere, which the vast majority will do.

An important step at this stage is to avoid dealing with the stalker alone. Informing your neighbors—as well as your supervisors and co-workers—of the problem can facilitate that, especially if you enlist their assistance. Some victims have set up a pool of neighbors to meet them when they arrive home from work each day. Others summon help by sounding an alarm each time the stalker is sighted. By prearrangement, the neighbors respond at the sound of the siren or bell. These kinds of deterrents frequently discourage a stalker and persuade him to transfer his focus to someone more accessible.

You can always opt for direct intervention should your case escalate and become dangerous. The reverse, however, is not true. Once intervention has been attempted, you can never go back to a watch-and-wait policy. It's like opting to deal with a lesion on your kidney by surgically removing the entire organ. Once that decision has been acted upon, a less aggressive course of action is no longer possible.

Should intervention become necessary, a trespass arrest can bring the same results as a restraining order violation—but with less risk. The city, rather than you, becomes the prosecutor, which helps to depersonalize the situation. The stalker is convicted of a crime rather than just the violation of a civil order. And the conviction term is essentially the same.

LOS ANGELES HAS also drawn fire because of some of its legal tactics. The ACLU deemed the practice of bail enhancements (raising the bail to an amount the defendant can't pay in order to keep him in jail) an infringement on the Constitution's Eighth Amendment, as well as on state constitutional mandates which dictate that the court only consider the seriousness of the offense, the defendant's previous criminal record, and the probability of his or her appearing in court for trial when determining the amount of bail. (Whether the perpetrator poses a danger to his or her victim is often not a consideration.)

In 1993, Deputy City Attorney John Wilson was brought up on charges after he grew concerned over a particular case and ordered a psychiatric evaluation of a stalker. "The obligation of

a prosecutor who is specially trained is to prevent future dangerous conduct, even when it may have nothing to do with the
current case," said Wilson. So when the evaluation showed that
an alleged perpetrator presented a clear danger to others, he was
placed on a 72-hour psychiatric hold.

Wilson, however, neglected to consult the public defender
who had already been assigned the case. The public defender's
office erupted. By ordering these psychiatric exams, they argued, the City Attorney's office had attempted to deprive
people of their right to have counsel present (guaranteed by the
Constitution's Fifth and Sixth Amendments), and to force them
into involuntary mental health treatment. Further, they took issue with the reliability of the tests. "Psychological research has
shown that the least predictive way to gauge dangerousness is
through interviews," said Los Angeles criminal defense attorney
Neal Osherow. He pointed to studies showing that psychiatrists
trying to assess an individual's dangerousness failed more than
50 percent of the time.

The accurate prediction of physical violence is impossible,
agreed Kaushal Sharma, MD, forensic psychiatrist and assistant medical director at the University of Southern California
Institute of Psychiatry, Law, and Behavioral Science. Although
most people—including many in the field of psychiatry—incor-
rectly equate violence with dangerousness, there's no guarantee
that a dangerous person will act out or that a supposedly non-
dangerous one won't. "Nobody can predict the future. If we
could, we'd all be playing the stock market instead of working,"
he said. "But increased risk or the likelihood of violence can be
assessed."

Maureen Siegel, Los Angeles City Attorney Deputy Chief,
Criminal and Special Litigation saw nothing illegal, unethical or
immoral about her office's attempts to determine either a defendant's potential for violence or his mental health needs, and
then filing a case with the goal of diverting him into appropriate

treatment. To the contrary. "A lot of these defendants pose a danger to the victim and themselves, and are in desperate need of mental health care," she said, adding that drug addicts and batterers are routinely diverted into treatment. "But the role of the public defendant is not therapeutic in nature—it's to protect the defendant's criminal justice rights. By focusing solely on those rights, the defendant can often beat the judge home for lunch."

RETURNING THE MENTALLY ill defendant back to the streets doesn't help the target, the obsessed individual, or society. "There's nothing to be gained by recycling a defendant through the criminal justice system again and again when what they really need may be evaluation, treatment, medication and counseling," Siegel said. "Fines and incarceration for minor offenses won't accomplish anything along those lines."

The City Attorney's office had pursued a holistic approach, she argues. Filing a criminal case—however minor—protects the safety needs of the victim, while helping the mentally ill obtain sorely needed psychiatric treatment. The solution, she felt, benefitted both parties.

Obviously, not everyone agreed.

After the initial charges were filed against Wilson, the entire City Attorney's office was accused of discriminating against the mentally ill by pursuing borderline criminal cases they might otherwise not have prosecuted. All cases where a psychiatric exam was ordered before the case had been arraigned—and an attorney appointed—also came under legal scrutiny. As a result, "a lot of these people [got] released because at issue [was] not the suspect's condition and whether it [needed] treatment but what his rights [were]," said attorney and forensic psychiatrist Ronald Markman, who routinely worked within the Los Angeles judicial system.

These disputes dealt a severe blow—if not a death knell—to Wilson's vision of all parties working together for the welfare of the defendant. "The roles are too adversarial for criminal defense attorneys to reveal confidential psychiatric information about their clients to prosecutors without their client's consent," said Osherow. "The prosecutor—who can file and dismiss charges—and the judge—who has the right to sentence the suspect—constitute the power base. The defense attorney's only right is to advocate. We must have checks on the power that the prosecutor and the judge wield."

COMPROMISES THAT ADDRESS the psychiatric needs of the suspect while still respecting his Constitutional rights do exist. Markman, for example, proposed allowing an independent, objective psychiatric evaluation of the suspect (instead of the advocate style of evaluation where experts are hired by both the prosecution and the defense). Recommendations would be made, but neither they, nor any information garnered during the evaluation, would be admissible in a criminal trial. The court would, however, have the latitude to offer the suspect the opportunity for treatment and the subsequent cessation of proceedings based on that psychiatric assessment. Charges would later be dropped if the treatment proved successful and the suspect behaved himself.

But until such creative options are evaluated and adopted, stalkers—and their victims—will continue to be cheated. Even if a mentally disturbed suspect is convicted, the chances that adequate mental health counseling will be provided in jail are negligible. After his release, parole will be lax; due to a lack of funds, a single officer may handle more than 200 active cases. This is also true of probation officers handling cases that have been diverted from the legal system to the mental health arena. The selection of appropriate counseling programs presents yet another problem, since in most states convicted stalkers can choose which therapist they see or psychological program they attend. Treatment is unregulated and unsupervised.

MICHAEL PAYMAR, CO-FOUNDER of the Duluth Domestic Abuse Intervention Project and co-author of the *Domestic Violence Information Manual*, created a solution that helps the courts, the perpetrators and, ultimately, the victims.

At a time when counseling programs appropriate for these sorts of abusers were rare, Paymar brought together the five key players involved in domestic violence and stalking cases—judges, prosecutors, police, probation officers and advocates—along with four local mental health agencies under a single umbrella. The latter four agreed to provide specific psychological counseling services appropriate to stalkers and batterers, with the Domestic Abuse Intervention Project acting as the liaison between the participating agencies and the legal system. In addition, Paymar's organization assumed responsibility for supervising the perpetrator's psychological care, monitoring his attendance and progress, providing supplementary counseling when needed, and interfacing with the probation officer attached to the case or the court. In this manner, the stalker or batterer remained under strict supervision—in a program designed to address his exact problem—from the court trial through the completion of the program.

Paymar's approach constitutes one of the few comprehensive success stories around—a success that has been duplicated in multiple cities across the country, including Quincy, Massachusetts; Nashville, Tennessee; and San Diego, California. The difference? A number of independent agencies coordinated their efforts in order to effectively attack a common problem. In an era of accelerating problems and diminishing revenues, they recognized that networking was their only hope. (For more information about programs that help reduce domestic homicide rates for women, log onto http://www.silentwitness.net/index.htm.)

"In order to get a handle on this, law enforcement, the mental health system, probation, parole and all the other agencies

charged with providing resources and services have to understand that this is a partnership," said DeCuir. "We have to utilize
all the resources that are provided to this population, and pool
our resources so that one discipline isn't overburdened."

Thankfully, that's starting to happen in an increasing number
of communities. Established with little or no expense, these formal networks—comprised of all pertinent law enforcement and
social service agencies—benefit those involved by saving time,
reducing danger and diverting mentally ill suspects in need of
psychiatric care out of an over-burdened court system.

These networks even address the perpetrators' needs, which
are so often overlooked. "At the least, problem people benefit
by avoiding unnecessary involvement with the criminal justice
system," concluded the authors of a National Institute of Justice
Study titled "Police Response to Special Populations." "At best,
they receive assistance from human service providers to begin to
solve their problems." Which, of course, is the ultimate solution
for victims as well, and perhaps their only chance at regaining the
life they once knew.

AROUND THE COUNTRY, some other promising programs have
also taken shape. In Dover, New Hampshire, a $360,000
grant provided by the U.S. Department of Justice Office of
Community Oriented Policing led to the development of a
slightly different cooperative approach for all stalking cases. In
this case, the five-member team was comprised of the district
attorney, the two detectives who handled all the jurisdiction's
stalking cases right from the start, the victim's advocate and the
probation officer. The team met weekly in order to brainstorm
approaches on new cases and reviewed the status of old ones.
The resulting continuity, coupled with the detectives' concerted
efforts due to more comprehensive background checks on alleged perpetrators, allowed for better risk assessment. And that

analysis shaped how a case was handled, as well as allowing for higher bail requests. As additional security, satellite monitoring helped restrict alleged or convicted stalkers from coming within a three-mile range of their victims' home or office.

The Dover police department's antistalking unit, in conjunction with the U.S. Secret Service National Threat Assessment's Center, also produced three videos. The first was a ten-minute introduction to stalking and how victims can protect themselves. The other two videos focused on the perpetrators. Directed toward criminal justice professionals, a 30-minute training video called "Lessons from Domestic Violence Murders" featured three inmates who murdered their mates or former mates (some after stalking them). The video concentrated on what was going on with the men in the weeks prior to the murder, and how those murders might have been prevented.

From those interviews was culled a shorter 10-minute version called "On the Path to Murder: 'I Wish I Had Chosen to Get Help.'" This one focused on the remorse that the three inmates felt about losing control, the various factors that precipitated the violence, and the men's regrets that they didn't try to talk to someone in order to defuse the situation. The latter video was shown to anyone booked for stalking or domestic violence in the Dover jurisdiction. "Get help," advised one of the inmates. "If you go the way I went, there's no turning back." The video's objective? Scare a portion of individuals into getting the counseling they need by showing them what could happen if they don't.

THIS KIND OF forward-thinking approach is ultimately what will make a difference. But that's tough for law enforcement. "Most police officers are taught to be reactive," said Mark Wynn, for years a respected member of Nashville's top domestic violence unit, who went on to conduct coast-to-coast training programs to bring police, prosecutors, judges and victims' advocates up to speed on how to handle stalking and domestic violence cases. "But they have to be proactive if they're going to get ahead of the offender."

He also suggested that to get a handle on the problem, we have to involve the first line of defense that currently is all but ignored: those crisis line or shelter workers, emergency room nurses, police dispatchers, even ministers who come in contact with victims early on. "We need to broaden the victim's protective net. With the proper training, all those people could be tripwires to predicting future violence, and to protecting victims," said Wynn. "Instead, it seems that the bulk of the specialized training goes to the people in the inner governmental core, from police to prosecutors, who are by definition removed from the victims during the early stages where prevention might be possible."

Once a case does come to law enforcement's attention, Wynn proposes that the course of conduct—rather than the specific crime—needs to be the focus of concern. "I tell those I train, 'Here are the elements in 15 cases that ended up in murder. What are the commonalties?' Then when they see Mary Beth later on, they'll look at the progression of activity she's been subjected to as a ladder that the perpetrator is climbing—a potentially escalating course of conduct. And that will allow them to think ahead of the criminal."

WITH LUCK, THESE kinds of innovative programs will begin to make a difference. But there's only so much that can be done by law enforcement. "People think that all they have to do is call the police to make the problem go away," said Lieutenant Lane. "We can help them, but they're going to have to make some tough calls. In the end, people are 100 percent responsible for their own safety and lives."

Count On Yourself

Don't assume that the police will make it all better. While they may be able to help, they can't make your stalking situation disappear. And they can't protect you around the clock. *You* must take responsibility for keeping yourself and your loved ones safe and secure.

19

If It Happens To You:
A Safety Primer

EVEN ONCE THE LEGAL AND LAW enforcement systems have caught on and caught up, individuals will still be the ones best able to protect themselves. Which means that you'll need to know what to do should you or a loved one become the target of an obsessive individual. Remember, however, that nobody knows your situation better than you. Think carefully about any and all decisions before acting, and never hesitate to consult stalking experts, support groups, and other authorities about your particular case. Inform yourself before you act.

LET'S START AT the beginning.

If you don't want to pursue a relationship, say *no* quickly. Letting someone down "easy" doesn't soften the blow. It simply draws out the pain as well as the rejection process, and extends the other party's emotional investment. The earlier the message is delivered, the less likely your admirer will be encouraged to pursue you. As the Los Angeles County District Attorney's proactive antistalking website, located at www.lovemenot.org, states: "*No* is a complete sentence. Use it when necessary."

Be direct and clear, even if it doesn't feel comfortable. Since people see and hear what they want when emotions are at stake, if you're not explicit your message won't get through. Indeed, it'll be interpreted as encouragement.

Avoid circumstantial rejections or reasons when explaining that you don't want to get involved. Said Gavin de Becker: "The dictionary definition of 'no' doesn't include 'Not yet' (which the stalker hears as 'I'm changing my mind'), 'Give me time' (which tells the stalker to keep the pressure on), 'I'm not ready for a relationship' (which will be interpreted to mean that you really want him but just don't know it yet), 'I have a husband' or 'I have a boyfriend' (which indicates that your mate is what stands in the way), or 'Maybe' (which prompts the stalker to prove how much he loves you). If the pursuer doesn't hear—or heed—the words: *I'm absolutely not interested in a relationship with you*, then something is wrong."

Don't waver. If someone can sense that you're uncertain and comes to believe that persistence is the key, then it's too late.

Allow the individual to maintain his dignity. Your message should be firm but not patronizing, derisive or harsh. Give the impression that you expect a reasonable response.

Screen prospective mates and even people you meet more casually. Get them to talk about their family background in order to uncover issues they might be dealing with as well as any troubling interactions. Question them about who their best friends are. The answer will reveal whether they're loners who have trouble with relationships. Ask them to describe the best relationships they ever had and why they ended. Find out how they've handled rejection in the past. Discuss their views of men's and women's roles in a relationship. "Men who subscribe to rigid sex roles are more inclined to justify their use of violence against a partner who is struggling for equality," wrote Michael Paymar in his book *Violent No More*.

Listen to what's being said rather than what you want to hear. If someone says he loves you "too much," he's probably right.

Keep your internal radar tuned to pick up signals that something might be wrong. When a person you just met calls you the following day to say how much he or she has missed you, think twice before getting further involved. A girlfriend who waits several hours for you to pass by on your way out of town just so she can flash you a sign that reads "I LOVE YOU, HAVE A GOOD TIME" may merit a degree of concern. Other warning signs can include credit problems and/or debt (since uncontrolled spending can indicate an obsessive nature) or always wanting to be in charge.

Trust your instincts. If your gut says that a person is bad news, stay away. Don't give someone the benefit of the doubt even if he or she simply makes you uncomfortable. Listen to what your subconscious is telling you.

Take a close look at any of your own tendencies. We often get what we subliminally seek when choosing a partner. If you have a pattern of becoming involved in painful relationships or with obsessive mates, an unconscious desire to experience what you're familiar with may be dictating your selections. Knowing what your buttons are will help you to see the other person more clearly.

As SOON AS you see that someone is being overly persistent, you need to take the matter seriously. Although your pursuer may never resort to violence, the unwanted attention will most likely cause you discomfort and unpleasantness at the very least. So, whether you're dealing with a former lover, a colleague, or a stranger, you need to play it safe and protect yourself, your family, your home and your workplace. Ideally, of course, many of these protective measures should be in place *before* a problem arises.

Limiting your accessibility to unwanted pursuit should be your top priority. And remember that in the age of cyberstalking, where the only way to control information about you is to control information in the public domain, these precautions have really gotten critical. In these situations, Facebook is not your friend, especially if you're inclined to reveal a lot of personal information that would be better kept private.

If a potential stalker—either online or off—doesn't know where you live, make absolutely sure it stays that way. "The only way to keep your address from being available to people who might use trickery or guile to get it is to be certain that nobody at the places it might be sought has the information to start with," said de Becker.

THE FOLLOWING STRATEGIES can help you protect yourself:

- Utilize private post office Utilize private post office box services for all mail. If necessary, list your mailbox as Suite #123 or Apartment #123 instead of Box #123. File a change of address card with your local post office giving the box address as your new one. In addition, send that address to friends, as well as any businesses or organizations with whom you associate. Request that they remove the old one from their address books.
- Advise all utility and phone companies as well as creditors of the change. Request a copy of your credit report and see what it says. Then write a letter to the credit-reporting agencies to notify them of your "new address" so that they remove your home address (both past and present) from your credit history. (You might also want to sign up for the TRW Credentials Service, which will notify you the moment anyone runs your credit.)
- Notify any companies and catalogs of your new address and advise them that they cannot include your name on lists they rent or sell.
- Don't put your name on a list of tenants at the front of your apartment building.
- Register your driver's license and cars to an address other than your home. You'll need to file a change of address with the Department of Motor Vehicles and get a new driver's license with the new mailbox address on it.
- List real property in a trust rather than in your own name.

- Remove your home address from personal checks, letter-head, and business cards.
- Use a non-home mailing address for voter registration and credit card applications. (You can also file for confidential voter status.)
- Ask the three credit bureaus—Experian, Equifax and Trans Union—to flag your account in order to lessen opportunities for fraudulent access.
- Make sure your name doesn't appear on any service or delivery orders to your house.
- Rent an outside office if you're self-employed and your business requires personal visits from patrons or associates. Many therapists court disaster by seeing clients at home, said Lieutenant Lane. "That really buys into a lot of problems."

NEXT, TAKE PERSONAL and family precautions:
- Get an unlisted, unpublished phone number, and limit the number of people to whom you give it. Should you need to be more widely available by phone, opt for an off-premises answering service or voicemail. Indeed, you may want to consider using a common alias—i.e. John Smith—when you sign up for your phone service. Tell them that you're a first-time client and give them your alias instead of your real name. You'll probably have to provide a $200 deposit, but tracing you based on your former phone accounts will become impossible.
- Contrary to popular wisdom, Gavin de Becker advises you not to change your number should a stalker gain access to it. Instead, get a second one. (Again, consider using an alias when signing up for this new number.) Keep the old number hooked up to an answering machine. This will allow your stalker to vent his frustrations on tape instead of on you. Besides, every time he leaves a message, *he* gets the message that you can resist his ha-

rassment. In addition, those recorded messages can provide unparalleled insights into the caller's state of mind
and any patterns of escalation. And they're a perfect way
to document harassing calls.

- Make sure your address isn't listed in the phone book or
in the reverse directory, which lists addresses first, then
names.

- Call your local phone company to explore optional services such as call tracing and caller identification. If you
have Caller ID, order Complete Blocking (or Per Line
Blocking), so your phone number won't be disclosed
when you make calls from your home.

- Avoid calling 800, 888, 877 and 900 numbers, so that
your phone number isn't captured by a service called
Automatic Number Identification.

- Never verify your home address or any other personal
details over the phone.

- For maximum privacy, make sure the area where the
phone lines enter your home is inaccessible. And keep in
mind that cordless phones, baby monitors and hearing
aids allow for conversations to be picked up on scanners.

- Let appropriate people around you know what's going
on and enlist their help. Describe the threatening person
(along with any vehicles he or she drives and their license
numbers) to family members, friends, neighbors, co-
workers, school officials, secretaries, receptionists, door-
men, apartment managers, household staff, and police.
Photographs work even better.

- Carry an air horn or a whistle with you. Use it if the
stalker approaches.

- Know the whereabouts of family members at all times.

- Vary the routes you take, whether in a car or on foot, as
well as your routines and social habits. This may mean
finding new stores, health clubs, bars, or places of wor-
ship to frequent.

- Plan ahead. Know the locations of police stations, fire departments and busy shopping centers. Head there if you're followed and honk your horn to attract attention.
- Always park in well-lit areas. Opt for a secured garage if available. Avoid parking lots where car doors must be left unlocked and keys surrendered.
- Visually check the front and rear passenger compartments before entering the vehicle. Keep the doors locked when not in use.
- Equip your car's gas tank with a locking gas cap. The locking device should be controlled from inside the vehicle.
- Scanners can pick up conversations on cellular phones, so only use your cell phone when critical. Still, make sure you have one handy at all times so that you can call for assistance without leaving your car. You might even want to consider keeping it in your bedroom with you at night if you don't already.
- Don't stop to assist stranded motorists. Phone in a report instead.
- Ask a friend or family member to accompany you whenever possible. Never walk or jog alone at night.

IF YOU HAVE children, they need to know the score, what's at stake and what to do. So do those who care for them. You'll want to:
- Teach your children not to give out information to strangers. Tell them that you especially don't want them sharing your address or phone number with anyone.
- Accompany your children to school or bus stops. Always know their schedules and their whereabouts.
- Let the school and childcare center know about any restraining or protective orders.
- Have a third party drop off and pick up your children if your stalker has visitation rights.

- Keep an eye out for any adults in your child's life (such as teachers, coaches, or neighbors) who show signs of being overly invested in your son or daughter. Clues include hyper-control, obsession, speaking to a child as an object of affection or romance, personal notes, letters, and presents.

MAKE SURE YOU can be safe in your own home. Most police will supply a free home security check-up. In the meantime, consider the following suggestions, most of which were developed by the LAPD's Threat Management Unit:

- Positively identify visitors before opening doors. Install a wide-angle viewer in all primary doors.
- Install adequate outdoor lighting, including a porch light at a height that would discourage removal.
- Keep doors and windows locked to put off intruders.
- Install dead bolt locks in your residence, as well as an alarm system that's hooked into a police station or security organization. Don't hide an emergency key outside. If you've already got a dead bolt but can't account for all the keys, change your locks.
- Keep garage doors locked at all times. Use an electric garage door opener.
- Trim the shrubbery around your property. Install locks on all gate fences and invest in adequate outside lighting.
- Keep your home's fuse box locked. Have battery lanterns on hand in your residence.
- Install a loud exterior alarm bell that can be manually activated in more than one location.
- Maintain all-purpose fire extinguishers in your home and in the garage. Install a smoke detector system.
- Insist that salesmen or repairmen show proper identification before allowing them into your home.
- Never open an unusual package, box or device found on your property. Call the authorities and let them deal with it.

- When away for the evening, place lights and the radio or television on a timer. For extended absences, arrange to have deliveries suspended and let trusted neighbors know how long you'll be gone.
- Invest in a family dog—one of the least expensive but most effective alarm systems.
- Post emergency numbers by or on each telephone.
- Prepare an evacuation plan and brief household members on the procedures. Provide ladders or a rope if you live in a two-story residence. Know how to get to your local domestic violence shelter.

AT THE OFFICE, make sure all visitors and packages pass through central reception. If your name appears on any reserved parking areas, take it off. Inform any on-site security personnel of the situation and alert them to any suspicious people or packages. Have a secretary or co-worker screen all calls if necessary. Ask to be escorted to and from your car. And be aware of anyone who might be following you on your way home from work.

THE MOMENT THE situation starts to escalate, if you've already made clear that you have no interest, stop all contact on- or offline. This includes attempts at friendly persuasion, counter threats (an especially serious mistake), angry demands to be left alone, or efforts to negotiate. "If someone calls you 40 times and, in desperation, you finally call him back after the 41st message to try and entreat or reason with him, that simply teaches the caller that it takes that many attempts to get you on the line," said de Becker. "Besides, trying to talk sense into someone who has already departed from logical behavior is like trying to teach someone to row a boat when they've already jumped into the water."

Putting an end to all communication includes not responding—or reacting in a detectable way—to threats or intimidations, no matter how scared you are. As a precaution, consult your local police department or a threat-assessment professional. But remember to treat the threat like you would a promise: evaluate the issuer's character, motives, and the circumstances in order to judge how likely he is to carry out the threat.

"People think that if they don't respond to a threat, something bad will happen. But in many cases, it's better not to," said de Becker. "Threats are easy to speak and harder to honor. Often, they're just statements to try and convince you of something. But because they eventually lose their potency, threats beget more threats, which can ultimately beget violence. Letting the air out of a threat by not reacting to it can mean the difference between escalation and de-escalation. At a certain point, the person who doesn't get water from a well will go someplace else. Not contributing fuel to someone's obsessive conduct may up the ante for a while. But ultimately, most cases end in transference to another victim."

Needless to say, you want to avoid any personal contact. Treat any stalker as if he or she is extremely dangerous and stay away from that person whenever possible. Should the stalker confront you, however, try to curb any actions or words that might provoke an angry reaction. "Actions intended to intimidate or deter an unwanted pursuer fail to recognize that he often has little to lose," said de Becker. Keep unavoidable encounters brief and don't get drawn into discussions or negotiations. And be especially careful around holidays, since those seem to incite stalker activity.

RESTRICTING CONTACT AND communication doesn't mean that you tear up letters or erase messages left on your answering machine. You'll need proof of the harassment should arrest and prosecution become necessary. So start to gather evidence the moment someone's attentions begin to make you feel uncomfortable. To be extra safe, keep your original records in a safe deposit box, since stalkers have been known to break into a house in search of evidence that might prove incriminating.

Make written notes of any kind of identifying information about the person you might know, including address and phone number, license plate number(s) and make of car(s), any distinguishing marks on his person, and any features (such as his voice, speech, walk, etc.) that might set him apart.

Keep a log of any sightings or contacts. Include date, time, location, circumstances, and the names of any witnesses along with their statements. Descriptions of clothing and vehicles help as well.

Save all written messages, as well as the envelopes they came in. Should any unusual packages, boxes, or devices appear on the premises, leave them alone and call the police.

When possible, record any threatening or inappropriate phone calls. Note the date and time of the call. And don't erase messages left on your voicemail.

Chronicle activities such as property damage, vandalism, and personal injury with a camera or video recorder if you can do so safely.

If the conduct is criminal and the police are already involved, notify the authorities of each and every incident. Record the names of the responding officers, the report numbers, and the times you call. Obtain copies of any legal paperwork.

LAST, REALLY ANALYZE your situation and consider other options presented in this book before seeking a restraining order. As you already know, there are two distinct philosophies about how to handle stalking situations. Most law enforcement personnel favor the victim applying for a restraining order. This serves to set a legal boundary that, when violated, will provide just cause for arrest and prosecution of the perpetrator. It also proves that the victim is actually going to be willing to press charges. Yet case after case of women being shot down with restraining orders in their pockets indicate that these orders can be inflammatory and therefore downright dangerous, and that incarceration is a short-term and often ineffectual solution.

As this book has previously detailed, a safer, more effective course of action—and one advocated by Gavin de Becker, the foremost stalking expert in the country, as well as Bob Martin, the founder of the L.A.P.D.'s Threat Management Unit—is to cut off communication. Then protect yourself by eliminating (as much as possible) the stalker's access to you and see what happens. Your refusal to play his game by his rules might just entice him to find another victim who will. Otherwise, depersonalize your prosecution of him as much as possible, by having the city charge him with trespassing instead of you charging him with stalking. Your objective at all times must be to choose the path that will keep *you* as safe as possible.

Just Do It

The list of safety precautions may be long and sound like a lot of work, but this is not the time for shortcuts. Make sure you take all the precautions necessary to protect your privacy and keep yourself safe.

20

Getting Away

I N PARTICULARLY VIRULENT CASES, moving to a new location may become the only sure way to sidestep the danger your stalker poses. "Dangerousness requires a sinister intent by someone (or at least disregard for another's safety), the means to deliver harm, and access to the victim," said de Becker. "You can't usually stop someone from getting a gun. But you can make it so that he can't be in your environment."

This is not a decision to be taken lightly. But if circumstances point to its inevitability, make sure you do it right, because an ineffective move will betray you and leave you more vulnerable.

When Cathy Reilly realized that she had to leave her husband, Daniel, in order to protect herself and her baby, she planned every detail of her escape. Certain that Daniel would try to prevent her from going, she secretly rented an apartment and arranged for utilities and phone service to be hooked up. One morning after Daniel had left for work, Cathy's mother came to collect the baby. Two lookouts posted at each street corner made sure that her husband didn't return. Cathy already knew exactly what she would take and which suitcases to use. It took her just 40 minutes to pack two weeks worth of clothes, a few heirlooms, and all the baby's belongings. Then she left for good.

Should *you* decide to flee an abusive relationship, you need to do so in a manner that leaves *no* way for your pursuer or abuser to track you down. In addition to the safety precautions already suggested in the preceding chapter, you'll want to avoid using well-known moving firms—with names painted on the side of the truck—that might be remembered by neighbors. Otherwise, all your stalker has to do is chat with your neighbors to find out which company you used and then bribe or con an employee into revealing your new address. And remember to vary your habits and routines once you've moved. Don't pick up your mail at your former neighbor's apartment, for example, or visit favorite locations that your stalker would have been aware of. Moving doesn't help much if your activities still make you a target.

If you're a domestic violence victim in hiding, you may want to look into whether your state has an Address Confidentiality Program, which allows you to have your mail forwarded to the Secretary of State's office. (You can call your Secretary of State's office for more information. Check the government listings section of your phone book for the number.) If your state doesn't have such a program, consider putting pressure on your state legislators to set one up.

IF YOU'RE NOT ready to leave now but think you might be forced to at some point, develop a contingency plan that includes a list of safe places to stay, such as friends' homes or domestic violence shelters. You may want to keep a readily accessible packed suitcase, along with reserve funds. Have a list of contact numbers—for neighbors, family, attorneys, prosecutors, pet care—ready to use once you've resolved the immediate safety concerns. For more information or referrals to shelters and programs in your area, call the National Domestic Violence Hotline at 1-800-799-SAFE (or TTY 1-800-787-3224 for the hearing impaired). Their phones are manned by English and Spanish speakers 24 hours a day, seven days a week.

Educating yourself on the issues involved may well be your best protection. The National Coalition Against Domestic

Violence (http://www.ncadv.org/) offers a wealth of information. Domestic violence programs in your area can also provide you with local resources for help, information on local laws, and additional advice on how to protect yourself. They can even help you develop a safety plan that takes into account the risks and realities you face. Try calling your state's coalition against domestic violence for additional referrals and advice:

Alabama Coalition Against Domestic Violence
P.O. Box 4762
Montgomery, AL 36101
(334) 832-4842 Fax: (334) 832-4803
(800) 650-6522 Hotline
Website: www.acadv.org
Email: info@acadv.org

Alaska Network on Domestic and Sexual Violence
130 Seward Street, Room 209
Juneau, AK 99801
(907) 586-3650 Fax: (907) 463-4493
Website: www.andvsa.org
Email: info@andvsa.org

Arizona Coalition Against Domestic Violence
301 East Bethany Home Road, Suite C194
Phoenix, AZ 85012
(602) 279-2900 Fax: (602) 279-2980
(800) 782-6400 Nationwide
Website: www.azcadv.org
Email: acadv@azcadv.org

Arkansas Coalition Against Domestic Violence
1401 West Capitol Avenue, Suite 170
Little Rock, AR 72201

(501) 907-5612 Fax: (501) 907-5618
(800) 269-4668 Nationwide
Website: www.domesticpeace.com
Email: kbangert@domesticpeace.com

California Partnership to End Domestic Violence
P.O. Box 1798
Sacramento, CA 95812
(916) 444-7163 Fax: (916) 444-7165
(800) 524-4765 Nationwide
Website: www.cpedv.org
Email: info@cpedv.org

Colorado Coalition Against Domestic Violence
1120 Lincoln Street, Suite 900
Denver, CO 80203
(303) 831-9632 Fax: (303) 832-7067
(888) 778-7091
Website: www.ccadv.org

Connecticut Coalition Against Domestic Violence
90 Pitkin Street
East Hartford, CT 06108
(860) 282-7899 Fax: (860) 282-7892
(888) 774-2900 In State DV Hotline
Website: www.ctcadv.org
Email: info@ctcadv.org

Delaware Coalition Against Domestic Violence
100 West 10th Street, #703
Wilmington, DE 19801
(302) 658-2958 Fax: (302) 658-5049
(800) 701-0456 Statewide

Website: www.dcadv.org
Email: dcadvadmin@dcadv.org

DC Coalition Against Domestic Violence
5 Thomas Circle Northwest
Washington, DC 20005
(202) 299-1181 Fax: (202) 299-1193
Website: www.dccadv.org
Email: info@dccadv.org

Florida Coalition Against Domestic Violence
425 Office Plaza
Tallahassee, FL 32301
(850) 425-2749 Fax: (850) 425-3091
(850) 621-4202 TDD
(800) 500-1119 In State
Website: www.fcadv.org

Georgia Coalition Against Domestic Violence
114 New Street, Suite B
Decatur, GA 30030
(404) 209-0280 Fax: (404) 766-3800
(800) 334-2836 Crisis Line
Website: www.gcadv.org
Email: info@gcadv.org

Hawaii State Coalition Against Domestic Violence
810 Richards Street
Suite 960
Honolulu, HI 96813
(808) 832-9316 Fax: (808) 841-6028
Website: www.hscadv.org
Email: admin@hscadv.org

Idaho Coalition Against Sexual and Domestic Violence
300 Mallard Drive, Suite 130
Boise, ID 83706
(208) 384-0419 Fax: (208) 331-0687
(888) 293-6118 Nationwide
Website: www.idvsa.org
Email: thecoalition@idvsa.org

Illinois Coalition Against Domestic Violence
801 South 11th Street
Springfield, IL 62703
(217) 789-2830 Fax: (217) 789-1939
(217) 242-0376 TTY
Website: www.ilcadv.org
Email: ilcadv@ilcadv.org

Indiana Coalition Against Domestic Violence
1915 West 18th Street
Indianapolis, IN 46202
(317) 917-3685 Fax: (317) 917-3695
(800) 332-7385 In State
Website: www.violenceresource.org
Email: icadv@violenceresource.org

Iowa Coalition Against Domestic Violence
515 - 28th Street, Suite 104
Des Moines, IA 50312
(515) 244-8028 Fax: (515) 244-7417
(800) 942-0333 In State Hotline
Website: www.icadv.org
Email: admin@icadv.org

Kansas Coalition Against Sexual and Domestic Violence
634 Southwest Harrison Street

Topeka, KS 66603
(785) 232-9784 Fax: (785) 266-1874
Website: www.kcsdv.org
Email: coalition@kcsdv.org

Kentucky Domestic Violence Association
P.O. Box 356
Frankfort, KY 40602
(502) 695-5382 Phone/Fax
Website: www.kdva.org
Email:kdvasac@aol.com

Louisiana Coalition Against Domestic Violence
P.O. Box 77308
Baton Rouge, LA 70879
(225) 752-1296 Fax: (225) 751-8927
Website: www.lcadv.org
Email:sheila@lcadv.org

Maine Coalition To End Domestic Violence
104 Sewall St.
Augusta, ME 04330
(207) 430-8334 Fax: (207) 430-8348
Website: www.mcedv.org
Email: info@mcedv.org

Maryland Network Against Domestic Violence
6911 Laurel-Bowie Road, Suite 309
Bowie, MD 20715
(301) 352-4574 Fax: (301) 809-0422
(800) 634-3577 Nationwide
Website: www.mnadv.org
Email: info@mnadv.org

Jane Doe, Inc./Massachusetts Coalition Against Sexual
Assault and Domestic Violence
14 Beacon Street, Suite 507
Boston, MA 02108
(617) 248-0922 Fax: (617) 248-0902
(617) 263-2200 TTY/TDD
Website: www.janedoe.org
Email: info@janedoe.org

Michigan Coalition Against Domestic and Sexual Violence
3893 Okemos Road, Suite B-2
Okemos, MI 48864
(517) 347-7000 Phone/TTY Fax: (517) 248-0902
Website: www.mcadsv.org
Email: general@mcadsv.org

Minnesota Coalition For Battered Women
60 E. Plato Blvd., Suite 130
St. Paul, MN 55107
(651) 646-6177 Fax: (651) 646-1527
(651) 646-0994 Crisis Line
(800) 289-6177 Nationwide
Website: www.mcbw.org
Email: mcbw@mcbw.org

Mississippi Coalition Against Domestic Violence
P.O. Box 4703
Jackson, MS 39296
(601) 981-9196 Fax: (601) 981-2501
(800) 898-3234
Website: www.mcadv.org
Email: dvpolicy@mcadv.org

Missouri Coalition Against Domestic and Sexual Violence
718 East Capitol Avenue
Jefferson City, MO 65101
(573) 634-4161 Fax: (573) 636-3728
Website: www.mocadsv.org
Email: mocadsv@mocadsv.org

Montana Coalition Against Domestic & Sexual Violence
P.O. Box 818
Helena, MT 59624
(406) 443-7794 Fax: (406) 443-7818
(888) 404-7794 Nationwide
Website: www.mcadsv.com
Email: mcadsv@mt.net

Nebraska Domestic Violence Sexual Assault Coalition
1000 O Street, Suite 102
Lincoln, NE 68508
(402) 476-6256 Fax: (402) 476-6806
(800) 876-6238 In-State Hotline
(877) 215-0167 Spanish Hotline
Website: www.ndvsac.org
Email: help@ndvsac.org

Nevada Network Against Domestic Violence
220 South Rock Boulevard
Reno, NV 89502
(775) 828-1115 Fax: (775) 828-9911
(800) 500-1556 In-State Hotline
Website: www.nnadv.org
Email: nnadv@powernet.net

New Hampshire Coalition Against Domestic and Sexual
Violence
P.O. Box 353
Concord, NH 03302
(603) 224-8893 Fax: (603) 228-6096
(866) 644-3574 In State
Website: www.nhcadsv.org
Email: director@nhcadsv.org

New Jersey Coalition for Battered Women
1670 Whitehorse Hamilton Square
Trenton, NJ 08690
(609) 584-8107 Fax: (609) 584-9750
(800) 572-7233 In State
Website: www.njcbw.org
Email: info@njcbw.org

New Mexico Coalition Against Domestic Violence
201 Coal Avenue Southwest
Albuquerque, NM 87102
(505) 246-9240 Fax: (505) 246-9434
(800) 773-3645 In State
Website: www.nmcadv.org
Email: info@nmcadv.org

New York State Coalition Against Domestic Violence
350 New Scotland Avenue
Albany, NY 12054
(518) 482-5464 Fax: (518) 482-3807
(800) 942-6906 English In State
(800) 942-6908 Spanish In State
Website: www.nyscadv.org
Email: nyscadv@nyscadv.org

North Carolina Coalition Against Domestic Violence
123 West Main Street, Suite 700
Durham, NC 27701
(919) 956-9124 Fax: (919) 682-1449
(888) 232-9124 Nationwide
Website: www.nccadv.org

North Dakota Council on Abused Women's Services
418 East Rosser Avenue, Suite 320
Bismark, ND 58501
(701) 255-6240 Fax: (701) 255-1904
(888) 255-6240 Nationwide
Website: www.ndcaws.org
Email: ndcaws@ndcaws.org

Action Ohio Coalition For Battered Women
5900 Roche Drive, Suite 445
Columbus, OH 43229
(614) 825-0551 Fax: (614) 825-0673
(888) 622-9315 In State
Website: www.actionohio.org
Email: actionoh@sbcglobal.net

Ohio Domestic Violence Network
4807 Evanswood Drive, Suite 201
Columbus, OH 43229
(614) 781-9651 Fax: (614) 781-9652
(614) 781-9654 TTY
(800) 934-9840
Website: www.odvn.org
Email: info@odvn.org

Oklahoma Coalition Against Domestic Violence and
Sexual Assault
3815 North Sante Fe Avenue, Suite 124
Oklahoma City, OK 73118
(405) 524-0700 Fax: (405) 524-0711
Website: www.ocadvsa.org

Oregon Coalition Against Domestic and Sexual Violence
380 Southeast Spokane Street, Suite 100
Portland, OR 97202
(503) 230-1951 Fax: (503) 230-1973
(877) 230-1951
Website: www.ocadsv.com
Email: adminasst@ocadsv.com

Pennsylvania Coalition Against Domestic Violence
6400 Flank Drive, Suite 1300
Harrisburg, PA 17112
(717) 545-6400 Fax: (717) 545-9456
(800) 932-4632 Nationwide
Website: www.pcadv.org

The Office of Women Advocates
Box 11382
Fernandez Juancus Station
Santurce, PR 00910
(787) 721-7676 Fax: (787) 725-9248

Rhode Island Coalition Against Domestic Violence
422 Post Road, Suite 202
Warwick, RI 02888
(401) 467-9940 Fax: (401) 467-9943
(800) 494-8100 In State

Website: www.ricadv.org
Email: ricadv@ricadv.org

South Carolina Coalition Against Domestic Violence and
Sexual Assault
P.O. Box 7776
Columbia, SC 29202
(803) 256-2900 Fax: (803) 256-1030
(800) 260-9293 Nationwide
Website: www.sccadvasa.org

South Dakota Coalition Against Domestic Violence &
Sexual Assault
P.O. Box 141
Pierre, SD 57501
(605) 945-0869 Fax: (605) 945-0870
(800) 572-9196 Nationwide
Website: www.southdakotacoalition.org
Email: pierre@sdcadvsa.org

Tennessee Coalition Against Domestic and Sexual
Violence
2 International Plaza Drive, Suite 425
Nashville, TN 37217
(615) 386-9406 Fax: (615) 383-2967
(800) 289-9018 In State
Website: www.tcadsv.org
Email: tcadsv@tcadsv.org

Texas Council On Family Violence
P.O. Box 161810
Austin, TX 78716
(512) 794-1133 Fax: (512) 794-1199
Website: www.tcfv.org

Utah Domestic Violence Council
205 North 400 West
Salt Lake City, UT 84103
(801) 521-5544 Fax: (801) 521-5548
Website: www.udvac.org

Vermont Network Against Domestic Violence and Sexual
Assault
P.O. Box 405
Montpelier, VT 05601
(802) 223-1302 Fax: (802) 223-6943
(802) 223-1115 TTY
Website: www.vtnetwork.org
Email: info@vtnetwork.org

Women's Coalition of St. Croix
Box 2734
Christiansted
St. Croix, VI 00822
(340) 773-9272 Fax: (340) 773-9062
Website: www.wcstx.com
Email: wcsc@pennswoods.net

Virginians Against Domestic Violence
2850 Sandy Bay Road, Suite 101
Williamsburg, VA 23185
(757) 221-0990 Fax: (757) 229-1553
(800) 838-8238 Nationwide
Website: www.vadv.org
Email: vadv@tni.net

Washington State Coalition Against Domestic Violence
711 Capitol Way, Suite 702
Olympia, WA 98501

(360) 586-1022 Fax: (360) 586-1024
(360) 586-1029 TTY

1402 Third Avenue, Suite 406
Seattle, WA 98101
(206) 389-2515 Fax: (206) 389-2520
(800) 886-2880 In State
(206) 389-2900 TTY
Website: www.wscadv.org
Email: wscadv@wscadv.org

Washington State Native American Coalition Against
Domestic and Sexual Assault
P.O. Box 13260
Olympia, WA 98508
(360) 352-3120 Fax: (360) 357-3858
(888) 352-3120
Website: www.womenspiritcoalition.org

West Virginia Coalition Against Domestic Violence
5004 Elk River Road South
Elkview, WV 25071
(304) 965-3552 Fax: (304) 965-3572
Website: www.wvcadv.org

Wisconsin Coalition Against Domestic Violence
307 South Paterson Street, Suite 1
Madison, WI 53703
(608) 255-0539 Fax: (608) 255-3560
Website: www.wcadv.org
Email: wcadv@wcadv.org

Wyoming Coalition Against Domestic Violence and
Sexual Assault
P.O. Box 236
409 South Fourth Street
Laramie, WY 82073
(307) 755-5481 Fax: (307) 755-5482
(800) 990-3877 Nationwide
Website: www.wyomingdvsa.org
Email: info@mail.wyomingdvsa.org

SOME COURT SYSTEMS may have victims' advocates who can also
help you with critical guidance gleaned from years of dealing
with women who didn't plan their escape carefully enough. One
common mistake: Not setting up independent checking and
credit card accounts—or storing money in a secret place—before
leaving, thereby giving an abusive mate the power to retaliate
financially. Your local district attorney or prosecutor's office may
be able to direct you to a victims' advocate.

IF you're planning to leave, make sure to pack the following
important papers:
- Birth certificates
- Passports
- Food stamps
- Photo ID and/or driver's license
- Checkbooks
- Social Security cards
- Health insurance documents
- Immunization records for you and your children

WHETHER YOU'RE THE victim of domestic abuse or stalking,
you'll also need to protect yourself on the job. The Family
Violence Prevention Fund offers the following safety plan for
work:

- Talk with someone you trust at your workplace, such as your supervisor, human resources manager or employee counselor.
- Notify security of your safety concerns, if your company has security. Provide a picture of the batterer and a copy of protective orders to security, superiors, and reception area staff.
- Have your calls screened, transfer harassing calls to security, or remove your name and number from automated phone directories.
- Review the safety of your parking arrangements. Have security escort you to your car, and obtain a parking space near the building entrance.
- Ask co-workers to call police if your partner threatens you at work.
- Ask about flexible or alternate work hours.
- Ask to relocate your workspace to a more secure area.
- Review the safety of your childcare arrangements. Provide a picture of your batterer and a copy of your protective order, if you have one, to the day care provider. If necessary, consider selecting a new day care site.

YOU'LL ALSO FIND invaluable information for yourself and your local law enforcement in the Metro Nashville Police Department's *A Guide to Domestic Violence Risk Assessment, Risk Reduction and Safety Plan* at www.police.nashville.org/bureaus/investigative/domestic/stalking.asp. For support from other abuse survivors, check out the Stalking Victims' Sanctuary online chat board at www.stalkingvictims.com.

AS TOO MANY women know all too well, domestic violence victims often stay in their abusive marriages because they're simply too afraid to leave. They're sure that an escalation of violence will follow their departure. They're usually right—which is exactly what makes *all* the safety precautions previously mentioned, as well as the various stories that have been chronicled here, so important. Study them. Learn from the mistakes that other women—less fortunate and less informed than you—made in similar circumstances, so that you can get away safely and get on with your life.

Making a Clean Getaway

Make sure you have all your ducks in a row before you jump ship. Plan your move carefully, leaving no way for someone to track you. Take everything you'll need with you, line up allies who can help, and seek the advice and assistance of domestic violence professionals.

21

Keep Yourself Sane

WHATEVER OPTIONS YOU PURSUE to insure your physical safety, try not to neglect your emotional wellbeing. You may feel like you're alone in this nightmare, but there *are* places to turn for much needed support. While this may seem like yet another time-consuming task to add to your already strained nerves and schedule, self-healing can be the most effective defense against your stalker. "Though victims are often preoccupied with changing the intrusive behavior, controlling the impact of this behavior is sometimes more practical," wrote Gavin de Becker in his book *The Gift of Fear*. "Reducing one's vulnerability to unwanted approaches and encounters must be a part of any management plan."

Sharing your ordeal with other victims provides a way to inure yourself to the emotional impact of being stalked. Consider joining a support group to bolster you through the ordeal. A support group will give you a safe place to vent to people who truly understand what you're up against. It can provide an educational forum in which to learn more about the issue and how to better protect yourself. And group members can uphold each other at court hearings and help put pressure on recalcitrant legal or law enforcement entities.

To find a support group in your area, contact your local library's reference desk. Ask for the *Social Services Directory*,

297

which lists local support organizations, and look up headings such as "Stalking," "Domestic Violence," or "Adult Abuse." Even if you don't find resources specific to stalking, you will often find numbers for local domestic violence shelters and their walk-in centers. Walk-in centers are more likely to have information relating to support groups, so start there.

You can also call the National Domestic Violence Hotline at 1-800-799-SAFE. Though a national support group for stalking victims does not exist—except for the online chat room at the Stalking Victim's Sanctuary website (www.stalkingvictims. com)—many resources are available to stalking victims through domestic violence organizations.

Victims' organizations also will frequently provide information, advice, and referrals to other local support services. Try the National Organization for Victim Assistance (NOVA) at 1-800-879-6682. You can also try the iSafetyNet website, which provides a listing of community resources and services on the Web (http://www.isafetynet.org/).

Don't just give up, even if you find that the resources in your area don't meet your needs. Do what Jane McAllister did and start your own support group. "The impetus to start a support group came out of my own desperation and the question, "What can I do?"" said Jane. "I thought, 'The authorities can't help. And I am not willing to commit murder or suicide.' So I had to scratch those off the list and figure something else out."

When Jane was first interviewed about being a stalking victim, she made herself available to journalists on the condition that they would protect her anonymity, and include a paragraph about her interest in a support group. "Then I contacted the police's victim witness program and asked if they would allow me to use their phone number. They agreed. I originally met with six women in my living room, with a police cruiser one block down the street. We met every two weeks for a while. Then we started to meet in the recreation facility," recalled Jane. "At first we reviewed what had happened. Later we would focus on the week's worst case and try to troubleshoot. We started going to court with each other, and making phone calls, writing letters on each other's behalf. Eventually, we teamed up with another group, one of whose members was a therapist who worked with victims of stalking."

IF *YOU* HAVEN'T been able to find what you need in terms of emotional support, you're almost certainly not alone. As Jane's experience clearly shows, there are other victims out there who could benefit from a support group as much as you. So don't wait. Here are some basics to keep in mind when starting up.

Find one to five other people to join you as founding members of this group. After all, a support group is just that: a group. Begin the cooperative effort with its very founding and you will model the attitude that you want all your members to embrace. Search for core members by posting flyers in women's shelters, their walk-in clinics, and anywhere else that *you* thought to look when you wanted to join a support group.

When deciding on a suitable meeting place, consider that churches, libraries, and community centers usually offer low-cost or free use of their facilities. Although a member's house is also free, her privacy and safety might be jeopardized.

Publicize the first meeting in any of the places victims might seek support—probably the same places where you found your core team. Bring coffee and treats, and make sure your new members feel welcome.

Once you and your founders have done the legwork, follow these tips as you make your group a success:

- Meet consistently, such as every Thursday evening, or the first and third Monday of each month. Note that most people will be available on weekday evenings. The frequency of your meetings will be determined by how often members can attend, and what's deemed most beneficial.

- Allow every member an opportunity to speak at each meeting. You can go around the room and give each person a turn to share what's on his or her mind. Or, if you have a previously set agenda, you can set aside a block of time at the end of the meeting for open discussion.

- Educate yourselves. Poll members about which issues concern them the most, and learn about those together. Invite guest speakers—psychologists, police officers, or other experts. Or assign each person a small outside research project and compare notes at the next meeting. Empower yourselves with knowledge. Ideally, each meeting should have a theme, topic, and/or direction.

- Create a support network that exists between and outside of meetings. This will strengthen you as individuals and as a group.

- Welcome new members. As your group matures and older members begin the healing process, their wisdom and their triumph are invaluable to those who are just embarking on the road to recovery. Make your resources available to those in need.

BE AWARE THAT groups, like people, go through highs and lows. Let the energy of the others support you if your enthusiasm starts to wane, and be there for your co-members when they, in turn, need your dedication and enthusiasm to carry them through. Don't let the group coast on the efforts of one or two people—everyone should and must participate. And finally, always strive for an open and nonjudgmental atmosphere in your support group as you initiate your healing process. "Founding and chairing a group was real important because it gave my anger a channel that was very constructive, and allowed me to get my feet back under me emotionally speaking," said Jane McAllister. "It gave me my power back."

INDIVIDUAL THERAPY CAN also help you retain—or regain—your sense of self and sanity during and after a stalking. While support groups are based on the idea that peers—those who have shared similar experiences to yours—help each other, "therapy" involves the input of a mental health counselor. Therapists will meet with you one on one or as a group.

There are a few things to remember when choosing a therapist. The term "therapist" does not imply any license, degree, or professional training. Psychiatrists, physicians, psychologists, and occupational therapists are licensed professionals who all might be using the title "therapist." They are held to industry standards and to review by a disciplinary board. In contrast, non-licensed therapists are held to no standard or disciplinary sanctions. Both licensed and non-licensed therapists might apply any number of traditional or nontraditional therapies with their patients, so shop around until you find a combination of personality and therapeutic techniques that works best for you. Some of the traits patients often list when describing a good therapist include empathy, warmth, and genuineness.

Reputation is a good place to start when seeking a therapist. Ask women's shelters, friends, or your physician for recommendations. Shopping around is your prerogative, so don't be shy about asking questions and really getting to know what you're buying into. Your first phone call or initial meeting is the perfect time to ask:

- What is his or her training? Beware of therapists who don't welcome questions about their background.
- What are his or her therapeutic methods? Do they appeal to you? Do you want the kind of therapist who poses a lot of questions and interacts with you, or would you prefer a listener?
- Is he or she sympathetic and understanding when you describe your situation?

- How would he or she handle your case? Is his or her orientation directed toward problem-solving?
- Does he or she know how to treat Post-Traumatic Stress Disorder (PTSD), a condition from which many stalking victims suffer? Also ask about a breakthrough treatment technique called Eye Movement Desensitization Reprocessing (EMDR), which facilitates the access and reprocessing of repressed memories.
- Can you establish some short-term and long-term therapy goals together?

ONCE YOU HAVE your answers, check in with yourself. Do you trust him or her? What does your instinct tell you? Do not stay with a therapist who:

- Makes you uncomfortable.
- Is judgmental.
- Offers quick fixes or pushes you toward his or her conclusions.
- Behaves in ways that you feel are inappropriate.
- You don't like for any reason.

IF YOU HAVE children, remember that they're victims, too—and just as much in need of emotional support and perspective as you. Even if you've tried to shield your kids, they're bound to be affected, at the very least by your stress levels. Domestic violence groups can advise you about appropriate local counseling treatments geared toward juveniles.

Whether you opt for one-on-one or group counseling, avoid a woe-is-me focus that dwells on being a victim and winds up prolonging your misery. You'll definitely want a chance to explore what has happened, how it has affected you and the toll it has taken. You'll want to analyze safety concerns and options. You'll need to rage. At some point, however, the therapy must help you move on with your life. Because that's what it's all about.

PART OF WHAT you'll want to accomplish during any kind of therapy or support group sessions is a shoring up of your internal resources. There is little you can do to reason with—or change—a stalker, so focus your energy instead on nurturing the infinite resources and strength within yourself. Many women regain the self-confidence they lost, or never had, through self-defense classes. One such class is IMPACT, a full-contact self-defense course for women, available in most major American cities. These classes also teach verbal de-escalation skills and other ways to minimize the chances that you will be victimized. Go to their website at http://www.impactselfdefense.org/ for information and locations.

You'll be amazed at how much a self-defense class can help, even if you never have to use the knowledge you gain. Self-defense instructors often report dramatic changes in their students, even before they've finished the course. About halfway through, women start coming to class sporting a new haircut or overall look. They overhaul more than their appearance: some actually show up with a new boyfriend.

This internal evolution is perhaps the most vital byproduct of such self-esteem building activities. Students feel stronger within themselves, more comfortable in their surroundings, and better equipped to deal both physically and emotionally with their lives.

Therapy and self-defense classes can also teach you how to utilize an under-appreciated and powerful resource: your own intuition. You are the expert at understanding your personal situation—you have experienced every detail of it firsthand. This wealth of knowledge lies behind every gut feeling you have. You are the best judge of your situation and you always have your best interests at heart, so listen to yourself when you truly feel afraid, or when you feel safe, or when you think you need a change, because chances are you're right.

Making the transition from victim to survivor means empowering yourself both mentally and physically. You can do it. It's hard, but you can come out of this nightmare a much stronger person if you work at it. "Staying sane is a daily struggle," said Rebecca Watson. "You have to laugh through the pain. You don't just get well the moment your stalking is over. That just doesn't come. You have to make a conscious effort every day to make yourself be okay."

For some, the idea of ever being okay again is unimaginable. But recovery can, and does, happen. "I'm often asked whether I've gotten over it," said Jane McAllister. "I ask two questions in return. 'Have you ever been in a near-death plane crash? Do you still fly?' It's just like that. You get on with your life. It doesn't have to destroy you. It can. But it doesn't have to."

Help Yourself

Reaching out for help from friends, family, neighbors, co-workers, job supervisors, therapists, and other victims will help you get through the ordeal of being stalked. So don't be stubborn or shy. Ask for assistance and emotional support. You're going to need every ounce you can get.

Epilogue

What Now?

WHEN MY MOTHER WAS A JUNIOR in college in 1948, for a year an anonymous admirer showered her with gifts of flowers and even a string of pearls. "It seemed romantic," she recalled. "But now it would seem ominous."

The world has changed since then. In 1960, the homicide rate in the United States was 9,000 a year. These days, between 15,000 and 20,000 Americans are killed each year. Yet when it comes to stalking, too many people don't understand that the age of innocence has disappeared forever.

Two articles about stalking I wrote for *Cosmopolitan* introduced me to this nationwide problem. But it wasn't until I started researching and writing this book that I really understood its appalling dimensions. Every third time I mentioned what I was working on—whether to friends, to seat-mates on a plane, or to the office manager in my dentist's office—the listener had either been a victim of stalking or knew someone who had.

If you are or have been victimized by a stalker, you undoubtedly feel overloaded by how that has impacted your life. Still, it's essential to look beyond your own situation to the issue at large if we as a society are to get a handle on it, for obsessive love remains a largely unrecognized and misunderstood phenomenon. Police, prosecutors, judges, mental health workers, and the vast majority of the public still don't understand the

305

nature of the stalking phenomenon or its ramifications. This must be addressed through an awareness campaign that includes books, films, and training programs like the one developed by the National Institute of Justice. San Diego, California's solution was to form a stalking task force. "We in San Diego discovered in 1994 that although we had had a stalking law since 1990, we were not using it too much because of a lack of education," said retired detective sergeant Anne O'Dell, a 20-year veteran of the San Diego Police Department who has conducted training programs and given speeches on the issue of domestic violence around the country. "So we formed a task force (which people jumped to join simply because of the nature of the crime). From that we made many improvements."

We need to better protect victims, both by teaching them how to protect themselves and by being sensitive to their needs. Some efforts are already under way. A number of years ago, The National Victim Center in Arlington, Virginia, for example, began developing a training program for businesses and corporations to encourage just that kind of involvement with prospective—and past—victims of violent crimes under their employ. The stalking component explained the nature of the crime, as well as its impact on targets. The program also suggested how businesses could help their employees deal with resulting psychological and emotional problems that often diminish worker productivity. In addition, it addressed safety issues, like how best to protect those who work for them and how to respond appropriately to threatening situations.

Besides learning survival tactics, victims need to be made fully aware of how best to cope with their particular situation. Should a legal remedy become necessary, they need to know how to pursue every legal means currently available. And those legal recourses must be extended. Although critics charge that stalker laws may jeopardize people's civil rights, responsible legislation that takes this sort of violence seriously and allows police to intervene *before* it's too late must be adopted and upheld by each and every state.

Resources must be allocated. Law enforcement desperately needs more training, as well as sophisticated computer programs that can assist in the tracking and crosschecking of these obsessed individuals, so that patterns can be recognized in time. Institutional reforms, such as the establishment of a national clearinghouse, would also help. New mental health or rehabilitation systems must be set up across the country, and community care options extended. And all public and private agencies in the field need to network to extend the protection for victims that's so desperately needed.

But the efforts have to start well before the problem surfaces if we're ever going to beat this. "Society manufacturers these people," said Detective Mike Proctor, one of the nation's leading experts on stalking who has investigated several serial stalking cases, including Sandy Potter's ordeal.

And society is what has to change.

WE NEED TO cease tolerating abuse inflicted on dependent spouses and children and encouraging aggression as a typical—and acceptable—male response. We must insist on more early-intervention programs that challenge social preconceptions and established mind-sets that excuse criminal behavior and violence.

Ingrained notions about men and women must be challenged. A 1989 survey asked sixth-, seventh-, and eighth-graders whether a man who had taken a woman out for a ten-dollar dinner had the right to demand sex from her and force her if she refused. One-third of the boys and one-fourth of the girls said *yes*. With those attitudes, it cannot come as a huge surprise that so many protective orders are issued in this country every year.

Until we modify the ways we socialize girls and boys in this country, meaningful change will remain elusive. If you're interested in challenging those gender and power roles that boys and young men learn, you might want to check out an educational video developed for high school and college students called *Tough Guise*. The unabridged version is available from the Media Education Foundation at http://www.mediaed.org/cgi-bin/commerce.cgi?preadd=action&key=211.

INEVITABLY, HOWEVER, THESE concerns fall first and foremost to parents. No matter what other demands might conflict, parents must provide the proper foundation and example from which their children can build solid lives and solid relationships. Unfortunately, newborns don't come with manuals. But widespread relationship and parenting classes—not just for those parents who get into trouble, but for all prospective parents—could address these issues.

On the most elementary level, parents need to know when and how to stand firm to children's unreasonable demands if they are to raise them to be reasonable adults. "A significant number of people don't understand what *no* means because no one ever told them," asserted psychiatrist E. Eugene Kunzman. "A child throws a temper tantrum in a department store because he wants a toy he can't have, for example, and people start looking. So the parent gives in. The message the child gets is that if he harangues long enough, he'll change that *no* to *yes*."

Children also need to be taught a sense of ethics that extends past mere personal preference. Wrongness can no longer simply be viewed as a question of practicality that might not pay. Conflicts must be equated with moral issues rather than seen as technical problems to be solved.

Schools—in addition to parents—need to focus on how we socialize our youngsters. Until girls are raised to believe in themselves (along with their right and ability to be strong and independent), and until boys are brought up as fully emotional individuals instead of miniature tough guys, there's little hope of combating the issues of power and control that propel stalkers. Encouraging friendship between boys and girls (and later between men and women) through coed activities would help to redefine ingrained assumptions about gender roles.

Education also needs to address the kinds of communication issues evidenced in these situations. While children must be encouraged to verbalize thoughts and feelings, they must learn to hear what's being said, even when they don't like the message.

In Hawaii, for example, a mandatory two-week curriculum teaches students to examine their anger and violent behavior and then come up with ways to create harmony in the family.

In Bend, Oregon, Serendipity West, a local nonprofit organization founded by Carol Oxenrider (and located online at http://www.serendipitywest.org/), conducts day-long interactive workshops called Challenge Days in schools to help students and teachers confront issues of bullying, violence, and other forms of oppression.

Gavin de Becker proposes high school and college courses to teach women that it's all right to explicitly reject and to teach young men to heed those rejections.

FINALLY, THE MEDIA needs to assume responsibility for its contribution to the problem—from the attitudes about women and courtship it promotes, to the message that violence is the way real men solve problems. Entertainment at the expense of social and individual welfare is too high a price to pay.

Such wide-scale efforts may seem unrealistic in an era of diminished budgets and amplified challenges. Yet, they are paramount if we are to contend successfully with a nationwide problem that knows no bounds or boundaries, and costs us all.

Notes

Chapter One
Are *You* Being Stalked?

Page

1 Hey, somebody is watching . . . : Miles Corwin, "When the Law Can't Protect," Los Angeles Times, May 8, 1993.

3 Especially those aged . . . : Katrina Baum et al., "Stalking Victimization in the United States," Washington, DC: BJS, 2009.

4 Shortly after Sandra Henes . . . : Rachel L. Jones, "His Obsession, Her Terror," Detroit News & Free Press, August 23, 1992.

4 Regina Butkowski is kidnapped . . . : John Ward Anderson, "Virginia Targets Stalkers," The Washington Post, February 10, 1992.

5 Shirley Lowery waits . . . : "Woman Goes To Courthouse for Protection but Finds Death," Chicago Tribune, March 20, 1992.

5 Eleven days after Kristin Lardner . . . : George Lardner, Jr., "The Stalking Of Kristin; The Law Made It Easy For My Daughter's Killer," The Washington Post, November 22, 1992.

5 "If the courts had checked . . .": "Antistalking Proposals," The Committee On the Judiciary/United States Senate, Serial No. J-103-5, March 17, 1993, p. 30.

5 This may sound . . . : "The Use of Technology to Stalk," Discussion Guide, Stalking Resource Center, 2011.

6 In fact, 90 percent . . . : Kenneth L. Woodward, "Murderous Obsession," Newsweek, July 13, 1992, p. 61.

7 In his book . . . : Jeffrey Rothfeder, Privacy For Sale: How Computerization Has Made Everyone's Life an Open Secret (New York: Simon & Schuster, 1992).

10 "What does he have to do . . .": Kenneth L. Woodward, "Murderous Obsession," Newsweek, July 13, 1992, p. 61.

311

Chapter Two
You Never Know

13 Laura Black sat at her desk . . . : "The People of the State of California v. Richard Wade Farley," Superior Court of the State of California, Ar. No. 123146, July 8, 1991.

Chapter Three
Work It Out

29 Amazingly, murder is the leading . . . : http://www.cdc.gov/niosh/topics/violence/

29 With workplace violence on the rise . . . : http://www.cdc.gov/niosh/topics/violence/

29 Larry Voss, a Cheyenne substance . . . : "Officer Said Stalking Law Might Have Saved a Life," Denver Post, July 28, 1992.

30 In Houston, a 26-year-old secretary . . . : Jolie Solomon and Patricia King, "Waging war In the Workplace," Newsweek, July 19, 1993, p. 30.

30 Another 26-year-old secretary . . . : Diana Jean Schemo, "Woman, Stalked For a Year, Is Slain By Ex-Companion, Who Also Kills Himself," New York Times, May 27, 1993.

43 Some 20 years later . . . : Claudia Puig, "Accused Killer Found Mentally Incompetent," Los Angeles Times, February 17, 1989.

43 In order to better its bleak record . . . : Jolie Solomon and Patricia King, "Waging War In the Workplace," Newsweek, July 19, 1993, p. 31.

44 Upon discovering that a receptionist's . . . : Jolie Solomon and Patricia King, "Waging War In the Workplace," Newsweek, July 19, 1993, p. 34.

45 For over a year, Kim . . . : Marla Cone and Jodi Wilgoren, "Obsessed Dana Point Suspect Stalked Former Co-Worker," Los Angeles Times, May 7, 1993.

45 As Mark's threats increased . . . : Dan Weikel and Marla Cone, "Postal Workers Wonder If Attack Could Have Been Prevented," Los Angeles Times, May 8, 1993.

Chapter Four
Why? Understanding the Incomprehensible

47 Physiological studies . . . : Anastasia Toufexis, "The Right Chemistry," Time, February 15, 1993, p. 50.

48 Two thirds of . . . : Kris Mohandi et al., "The RECON Typology of Stalking: Reliability and Validity Based upon a Large Sample of North American Stalkers," *Journal of Forensic Sciences*, 51, no. 1, 2006.

48 Almost one out of . . . : Ibid.

51 "If there is something . . .": Dr. Stanton E. Samenow, Inside the Criminal Mind (New York: Times Books, 1984), p. 162.

54 Most men share . . . : Dr. Peter Rutter, Sex In the Forbidden Zone: When Men in Power—Therapists, Doctors, Clergy, Teachers And Others—Betray Women's Trust (New York: Ballantine Books, 1989), p. 76.

57 Which one in seven . . . : Katrina Baum et al., "Stalking Victimization in the United States," Washington DC: BJS, 2009.

59 After extensive therapy . . . : "When Passion Holds You Prisoner," The Oprah Winfrey Show, May 29, 1991.

60 In a paper titled . . . : Dr. J. Reid Meloy, "Unrequited Love And the Wish To Kill: Diagnosis And Treatment of Borderline Erotomania," Bulletin of The Menninger Clinics 53 (November 1989) : 477.

60 George Martin-Trigona's . . . : "Love Stalkers Would Rather See Ex Dead Than With Someone Else," Donahue, November 25, 1992.

61 In the 1981 . . . : Shere Hite, The Hite Report On Male Sexuality: How Men Feel About Love, Sex, and Relationships (New York, Ballantine Books, 1981), pp. 66-67.

Chapter Six
Limit the Obsessive Interaction

84 "Much—even most— . . .": Deborah Tannen, PhD, You Just Don't Understand: Women and Men In Conversation (New York: Ballantine Books, 1990) p. 37.

89 "The rejecter usually feels . . .": Daniel Goleman, "Poets Know How Spurred Suitors Suffer; Science Finds Pain On The Other Side, Too," New York Times, February 9, 1993.

91 In normal cases . . . : Daniel Goleman, "Poets Know How Spurred Suitors Suffer; Science Finds Pain On The Other Side, Too," New York Times, February 9, 1993.

Chapter Eight
I'll Be Watching You

109 This delusion . . . : Marie Brenner, "Erotomania," Vanity Fair, September 1991, p. 188.

113 For Jessica Weiss . . . : "Obsession: Her Obsession Was To Capture Underwear Thief" and "'He Picked Wrong Woman' To Be Victim," Press Telegram, July 4, 1993.

Chapter Nine
Know Your 'Net Worth

127 You may have . . . : "Topline Findings from Omnibuzz Research," Teen Research Unlimited, October 2005.

127 An equal number . . . : "Topline Findings from Omnibuzz Research," Teen Research Unlimited, October 2005.

127 And, according to . . . : "Protecting Teens Online," Pew Internet and American Life Project, March 17, 2005.

Chapter Ten
Even Your Kids Are at Risk

131 Caty Thayer, a . . . : "Antistalking Legislation," The Committee On The Judiciary/United States Senate, Serial No. J-102-86, September 29, 1992, p. 17.

132 Whether or not child . . . : Constance L. Hays, "If That Man Is Following Her, Connecticut Is Going To Follow Him," New York Times, June 5, 1992.

132 Eight-year-old . . . : "He's Stalking My Girl," The Maury Povich Show, February 28, 1992.

133 Laurisa Anello, now 19, . . . : "Women Winning Legal Help Against Stalkers," Chicago Tribune, April 16, 1992.

133 "This is the way . . .": Michael Goodwin, "Stalked!", Woman's Day, March 16, 1993, p. 49.

Chapter Eleven
SIDESTEP THE LONG ARM OF ABUSE

143 "If you leave me . . .": Judy Rakowsky, "Nightmare Ends In Death, As Husband Had Threatened," The Boston Globe, December 17, 1992.

144 The appalling fact is . . . : Joseph Kirby, "Stalking Law Sends a New Signal," Chicago Tribune, August 13, 1992.

146 When Karen Winn broke off . . . : Michael Grunwald, "Milton Patrolman Is Charged With Stalking Woman," The Boston Globe, March 31, 1993.

146 In Los Angeles, 18-year-old . . . : Jesse Katz, "Student Tells Of Dead Suspect's Obsession With Ex-Girlfriend," Los Angeles Times, May 17, 1991.

146 After Jennifer Kibbe broke off . . . : Patricia Nealon, "Terrors Of Stalking Relived," The Boston Globe, June 7, 1992.

147 Consider Betsy Murray's . . . : Judy Rakowsky, "Nightmare Ends In Death, As Husband Had Threatened," The Boston Globe, December 17, 1992.

151 Sarah Miller . . . : Linda Mae Carlstone, "The Stalkers," Chicago Tribune, Tempo Lake Edition, September 13, 1992, p. 3.

152 Judge Sol Wachtler had everything . . . : Pam Lambert and Maria Eftimiades, "Judge Or Be Judged," People, November 23, 1992, p. 74.

153 "And then I would again . . .": "Over The Edge," ABC News 20/20, September 17, 1993.

154 Six months later . . . : Michael Connelly, "Woman's Calls Buried By 'So Many Cases,'" Los Angeles Times, January 1, 1990.

155 She was finally granted . . . : Terry Wilson and Allan Johnson, "Living In Fear: When Women Are Stalked," Chicago Tribune, March 22, 1992.

155 "I couldn't live . . .": Allan Johnson, "Diary Of a Stalker: How I Killed My Wife," Chicago Tribune, June 26, 1992.

155 "The detective . . .": Jennifer Lenhart, "Cops Beginning To Get A Handle On Stalking Law," Chicago Tribune, November 30, 1992.

155 "I called so many times . . .": "Women Winning Legal Help Against Stalkers," Chicago Tribune, April 16, 1992.

156 The day he was released . . . : Miguel Bustillo, "Deputies Search For Man Stalking Ex-Wife, Family," Los Angeles Times, August 5, 1993.

156 In Chicago, . . . : Gera-Lind Kolarik, "Stalking Laws Proliferate," A.B.A. Journal, November 1992, p. 35.

157 "The day his sentence ends . . .": Niles Corwin, "When The Law Can't Protect," Los Angeles Times, May 8, 1993.

Chapter Twelve
Watch for the Signs

159 "They tell me . . .": John Ward Anderson, "Virginia Targets Stalker," The Washington Post, February 10, 1992.

Chapter Thirteen
This Can't Be Love

173 When the fear . . .": Joe Warner, "Stalking Victims Talk About Laws At Meeting," Charlotte Shopping Guide and Eaton County News.

174 Mark David Bleakley . . .": "I Know He's Out There," ABC News 20/20, January 10, 1992.

174 The very first chance . . .": James Quinn, "'Stalking' Law Violator Jailed a Second Time," Los Angeles Times, March 18, 1992.

Chapter Fourteen
Maybe You Don't Want To Be Rich & Famous

185 David Bowie received multiple . . . : "Many Stars Have Feared Their Fans," People Weekly, April 20, 1981, p. 37.

185 Just five months later . . . : Timothy Gollin, "Yale Rallies Around Freshman Jodie Foster As Her Anguish Deepens," People Weekly, April 20, 1981.

185 About the same time . . . : William Scobie, "Shooting For The Stars," MacCleans Cleans, August 10, 1981.

186 In 1982, Theresa Saldana . . . : Theresa Saldana, "He's Killing Me!" Redbook, October 1986, p. 96.

187 "Since 1968 there have been . . .": Daniel Goleman, "Dangerous Delusions: When Fans Are a Threat," New York Times, October 31, 1989.

189 From 1990 to 1991, Olympic . . . : Matt Lait, "Skater
Confronts Her Alleged Tormentor," Los Angeles Times,
March 12, 1992.

189 In March 1989, Joni Leigh Penn . . . : Jeannie Park, Lois
Armstrong, Doris Bacon, and Eleanor Hoover, "A Fan's Long
Suicidal Obsession With Actress Sharon Gless Leads To a
Tense Police Standoff," People Weekly, April 16, 1990, p. 62.

191 "Most [stalkers] are after the goal . . .": "I Know He's Out
There," ABC News 20/20, January 10, 1992.

192 "The nicer one appears to be . . .": "Psychiatric And
Sociological Aspects Of Criminal Violence: An Interview With
Park Elliott Dietz, MD, PhD, Part II," Currents in Affective
Illnesses XI (May 1992).

192 First came Michael Perry . . . : Stuart Goldman, "TV Addict's
Grim Legend On The Bayou," Los Angeles Times, September
8, 1985.

192 The Australian star also drew . . . : "Star-Crossed: Confessed
Murderer Ralph Nau Was Unfit To Stand Trial. Is He Fit To
Walk The Streets?" Chicago Tribune, August 20, 1989.

193 "We are concerned about the safety . . .": Pete Nenni,
"Celebrities Seek Tough Laws to Hold Violent Mentally Ill,"
Paddock Publications, December 13, 1989.

193 Her attacker had repeatedly . . . : Dianne Klein, "A Crime
without End," Los Angeles Times, June 2, 1989.

195 Only 5 percent of the letter writers . . . : Park Elliott Dietz,
MD, MPH, PhD; Daryl B. Matthews, MD, PhD; Cindy Van
Duyne, MA; Daniel Allen Martell, PhD; Charles D.H. Parry,
PhD; Tracy M. Stewart, MA; Janet Warren, DSW; J. Douglas
Crowder, MD, "Threatening and Otherwise Inappropriate
Letters To Hollywood Celebrities," Journal of Forensic
Sciences (March 1991) : 185.

195 Michael J. Fox, for example . . . : "Woman Gets Probation
For Threatening Actor," Los Angeles Times, December 16,
1989.

196 Dietz's research revealed . . . : Anastasia Toufexis, "A Fatal
Obsession With The Stars," Time, July 31, 1989.

196 "The only crime he could be charged with . . .": "Antistalking
Legislation," The Committee On The Judiciary/United States
Senate, Serial No. J-102-86, September 29, 1992, p. 91.

197 One man spent $9,000 . . . : Hilary Abramson, "Fan Love," The Sacramento Bee Magazine, July 12, 1988.

198 During a pre-show warm-up . . . : Susan Schindehette and Doris Bacon, "Vanna White and Teri Garr Ask The Courts To Protect Them From Fans Who Have Gone Too Far," People Weekly, July 16, 1990, p. 41.

198 Former legal secretary Billie Jean Jackson . . . : Richard N. Ostling, "A Fatal Obsession With The Stars," Time, July 31, 1989, p. 43.

198 Michael Jackson's sister, Janet . . . : "Obsessed Fan Gets Two Years For Threats To Pop Singer," Los Angeles Times, July 13, 1993.

198 A David Letterman fan drove . . . : "More Fan Trouble," Los Angeles Times, October 7, 1993.

198 Starting in 1988, a woman who called herself Mrs. Letterman . . . : Richard N. Ostling, "A Fatal Obsession With The Stars," Time, July 31, 1989, p. 43.

199 Actress Rebecca Schaeffer . . . : "The People of the State Of California v. Robert John Bardo," Superior Court of the State of California, Ar. No. BA001043, October 7, 1991.

Chapter Fifteen
Do the Right Thing

208 "I just wanted to make sure [Bateman] . . .": Bill Hewitt, "Justine Bateman Becomes The Latest Celebrity To Be Menaced By an Obsessive Fan," People, September 25, 1989, p. 112.

209 "Help. This house is hell . . .": Mike Thorpe, "In The Mind Of a Stalker," US News and World Report, February 17, 1992.

211 Park Elliott Dietz's research reveals . . . : Daniel Goleman, "Dangerous Delusions: When Fans Are a Threat," New York Times, October 31, 1989.

Chapter Sixteen
Recognize When He's Mad For You

213 Michael Perry seemed like a normal . . . : Stuart Goldman, "TV Addict's Grim Legend On The Bayou," Los Angeles Times, September 8, 1985.

215 "None of the people who engage . . .": "I Know He's Out There," ABC News 20/20, January 10, 1992.

216 The National Institute of Mental Health . . . : Richard E. Vatz and Lee S. Weinberg, "Sort Out Mentally Ill From 'Worried Well,'" Los Angeles Times, December 13, 1993.

216 Yet research indicates only one in five . . . : Janice Castro, "What Price Mental Health," Time, May 31, 1993, p. 59.

217 Ironically, the people at greatest risk . . . : Park Elliott Dietz, MD, MPH, PhD, and Daniel Allen Martell, PhD, "Mentally Disordered Offenders In Pursuit Of Celebrities And Politicians," National Institute of Justice, October 15, 1989.

217 The two postal workers he shot . . . : Marla Cone and Jodi Wilgoren, "Obsessed Dana Point Suspect Stalked Former Co-Worker," Los Angeles Times, May 7, 1993.

218 According to a 1992 U.S. Supreme Court ruling . . . : Linda Greenhouse, "New Protection For Insane," San Francisco Chronicle, May 19, 1992.

219 Prosenjit Poddar, a graduate . . . : Walter E. Barton, MD and Charlotte J. Sanborn, BA, ART, ed., Law and the Mental Health Professions, (New York: International Universities Press, Inc.) 1978, p. 156.

220 In the fall of 1988, award-winning tennis coach . . . : Michael Stone, "Break Point: A Tennis Coach's Fatal Obsession," New York Magazine, May 17, 1993, p. 63.

222 The number of mentally ill people currently incarcerated . . . : Hector Tobar, "Steps Urged To Keep Mentally Ill Out Of Jail," Los Angeles Times, May 19, 1993.

222 One study showed that even when . . . : John Hurst, "Handling Of Mentally Ill In Prisons Assailed," Los Angeles Times, May 12, 1993.

223 In Kimberley Poland's case . . . : "Antistalking Legislation," The Committee On The Judiciary/United States Senate, Serial No. J-102-86, September 29, 1992, p. 35.

225 While Ralph Nau was being held . . . : "Star-Crossed: Confessed Murderer Ralph Nau Was Unfit To Stand Trial. Is He Fit To Walk The Streets?" Chicago Tribune, August 20, 1989.

225 "People like him murder . . .": "Star-Crossed: Confessed Murderer Ralph Nau Was Unfit To Stand Trial. Is He Fit To Walk The Streets?" Chicago Tribune, August 20, 1989.

Chapter Seventeen
This is Justice?

227 At a hearing before the U.S . . . .: "Antistalking Proposals," The Committee On The Judiciary/United States Senate, Serial No. J-103-5, March 17, 1993, p. 44.

228 Just ask Susan Foster . . . : "Antistalking Proposals," The Committee On The Judiciary/United States Senate, Serial No. J-103-5, March 17, 1993, p. 14.

228 Secretary Anna Alfaro, whose . . . : Michael Connelly, "Woman's Calls Buried By So Many Cases," Los Angeles Times, January 1, 1990.

228 Tracey Thurman successfully sued . . . : "Tracey Thurman, et al v. City of Torrington, et al," United States District Court, Ar. No. 14-84-120, October 23, 1984.

233 "Judges in family and . . .": "Antistalking Proposals," The Committee On The Judiciary/United States Senate, Serial No. J-103-5, March 17, 1993, p. 2.

233 The man who killed 21 . . . : George Lardner, Jr., "The Stalking Of Kristin: The Law Made It Easy For My Daughter's Killer," The Washington Post, November 22, 1992.

234 In reaction to her death . . . : George Lardner, Jr., "After The Murder, Massachusetts Gets A Common Sense Law; 'If They're Behind Bars And Disarmed, That Stops Them,'" The Washington Post, November 22, 1992.

235 One man responded to a court order . . . : Teresa Wittz, "Women Tell Of Their Living Hell," Chicago Tribune, October 13, 1992.

237 Boston's Teresa Bean slept . . . : Colman McCarthy, "Better Protection For Women In Danger," The Washington Post, June 13, 1992.

237 In a legal system that's been proven to be traditionally biased . . . : Allan R. Gold, "Sex Bias Is Found Pervading Courts," New York Times, July 2, 1989.

238 In response, police departments . . . : Joseph Kirby, "Stalking Law Sends a New Signal," Chicago Tribune, August 13, 1992.

238 Although several hundred thousand such orders . . . : "Antistalking Proposals," The Committee On The Judiciary/ United States Senate, Serial No. J-103-5, March 17, 1993, p. 1.

240 Herbert Bruce Lemont, Linda Pride's . . . : Ken Hoover, "Prisoner's Long Distance Victim," San Francisco Chronicle, July 1, 1993.

241 "The Stalker and Family Violence Enforcement Act . . .": "Antistalking Proposals," The Committee On The Judiciary/ United States Senate, Serial No. J-103-5, March 17, 1993, p. 2.

Chapter Eighteen

POLICING THE THREAT

262 "At the least, problem people . . .": Peter Finn and Monique Sullivan, "Police Response to Special Populations," National Institute of Justice, October 1987.

Epilogue

What Now?

307 A 1989 survey asked sixth-, . . . : "Antistalking Proposals," The Committee On The Judiciary/United States Senate, Serial No. J-103-5, March 17, 1993, p. 81.

307 With those attitudes . . . : "Antistalking Proposals," The Committee On The Judiciary/United States Senate, Serial No. J-103-5, March 17, 1993, p. 1.

4418587R00187

Printed in Great Britain
by Amazon.co.uk, Ltd.,
Marston Gate.